V I I

V II

SEVEN PAGES MISSING

VOLUME II: PREVIOUSLY UNCOLLECTED TEXTS

1968–2000

Steve McCaffery

Coach House Books

first edition

Published with the assistance of the Canada Council for the Arts and the Ontario Arts Council

NATIONAL LIBRARY OF CANADA CATALOGUING IN PUBLICATION

McCaffery, Steve
Seven pages missing / Steve McCaffery.

Poems.
Includes bibliographical references.
Contents: v. 1. Selected texts, 1969–1999 – v. 2. Previously uncollected texts, 1968–2000.

ISBN 1-55245-049-X (v. 1). – ISBN 1-55245-051-1 (v. 2)

I. Title.

PS8575.C33S48 2000 C811'.54 C00-932533-6
PR9199.3.M29S48 2000

To Karen Mac Cormack and Marjorie Perloff

and

in memoriam
Dick Higgins and Nicholas Zurbrugg

Contents

Introduction 11

K as in Sleep 13

Visual and Concrete Poems 15

Oceanside: a lipogram 16
from *Epsilon Series* 20
Capture: Two Versions 22
A Short History of Literature 23
First Fenollosa Meditation 24
First Typestract: 'Solid Layer and Tissue' 26
Bilingual Typestract 27
Typestract: 'Babel' 28
Tissue Text: 'OXO' 29
Tissue Text: Random 'C' Field 30
Triple Random Field 31
Typestract: 'Once upon a been stork' 32
A Number Poem: 'as of ten' 33
Abandoned Section from *Carnival* 34
Homage to e.e. cummings 36
from *Epsilon Series* 37
from *Two Simultaneous Texts* 38
Three Grid Texts 42
Cartesian Vowel Glyph 45
Two States of Ur-Alpha 46
Semiotic Cartoon Glyph 48
from *Alpha: Discrete Series 4* 49
from *Alpha: Discrete Series 3* 51
from *Alpha: Discrete Series 5* 53
The Letter 'a' According to Chomsky 54
H: A History 55
Punctuation Poem 56
Punctuation Poem 'X' 57
Punctuation Poem 58
Kafka's Umbrella 59
The Structure of Sonnet 60
Panelogic 61

Two Signalist Texts 62
from *Demiplosive Suite* 64
Suprematist Alphabet 65
William Tell: A Novel 66
Two Poems on a Theme by Eugen Gomringer 67
A Puff of Magritte 68
Maps: a different landscape 69
Narrative: The Obsolete Absolute 73

Sound Texts and Musical Scores 87

Studies for Two Unperformed Four Horsemen Pieces 88
Concerto for Two Adverbs 90
SIZERZ 91
Cappuccino: A Suffix Structure 92
Love Song 94
Dilemma of the Meno 96

Longer Poems 99

from *The Abstract Ruin* 100
from *The New Work* 127
On the Red in General 149

Translations 157

A Portrait 158
Autumn 159
Psalm 49 160
Shakespeare's Sonnet 105 161
Shakespeare'sSonnet 1 162
Sidney's Sonnet XXXI 163
Marvell's To his Coy Mistress 164
Traité du blanc et des teintures 165
The Kommunist Manifesto 171
Poem for Sixteen Sequential Voices 181
Bergbo's Sonnet 92 183
Four Poems from the Chinese Versions 185
from *8×8: Experiment in Translation* 189
The Presbyterian Basho 192
The Baker Transformation 193

Miscellaneous Texts 197

Three Pieces for Audience 198
Aproprioprapus 199
Mrta 214
The Murder of Agatha Christie 215
Kemsher 220
Three Stanzas 222
Novel 7 223
song i and ii 224
Eruca Labra 225
Eros-ion 232
The Property: Comma 235
August Sixteen 1977 244
Muiopotmos 247
The Cetacea: Four Tides 248
A Book Resembling Hair 249
The Syllogistic Cinema 250
Poem "Murder": A Scenario 252
The Occupant 254
Words: Meditation Nine 256
Latin Lines 257
Novel Eighteen 258
Summary 259
Projects for *Procedures* 260
Fish Also Rise 263
The Perseus Project 265
A Sirius Series 275
from *What Else Should a Rubber Stamp Say?* 283
from *Divers Manière* 291
Deliberate Follicles 298
The Cabinet 303
The Swimmer 304
Peras: An Extract from a Page 307
from *Some Versions of Pastoral* 322
Logic of Six 325
On Paper 329
Etymology of Displeasure 330
No Title Please I'm Not Well 333
Prior to Meaning 334

Crystal Carrington 335
To Never Leave the Feeding Hand Unbitten 336
Sin Having Settled 338
Attritions 340
Monsieur X 342
Zero is Not Equivalent to Zeno 344
Eventual Research 345
A Theory of the Lyric© 351

Poetics and Notes 353

from 'The Unposted Correspondence' 354
A Note on Concept 357
Poetics: A Statement 359
Performed Paragrammatism 361
Notes 363

Introduction

The material in this second volume of *Seven Pages Missing* is grouped into more or less discrete sections: Visual and Concrete, Sound Texts and Musical Scores, Longer Poems, Translations, a general section of miscellaneous poems and prose, and a final short section of Poetics. The sections from *Maps*, *Two Simultaneous Texts*, and two sections from *The Abstract Ruin* are, strictly speaking, interlopers in this volume and should have appeared in Volume One; owing to the size of that book it was thought prudent to hold them over for this shorter second volume. I've restrained from publishing photo-documentation of performance works and of collaborative work. A comprehensive bibliography can be found in the terminal notes; the first date refers to time (sometimes approximate) of composition, the second gives the date of publication. Where a single date appears the text was written in the same year as publication. In gathering together this material I've taken the opportunity to correct typos and other errors that entered into their first printing and, on the odd occasion, to stylistically and substantively modify the text. My sincere thanks go to all at Coach House Books who have worked on, and believed in, this project, and to all the editors of the magazines, journals and anthologies in which this material first appeared. Special thanks to Alana Wilcox for her diligent copy editing, to Karen Mac Cormack for her patience, support and constantly wise counsel, and to Stephen Cain for his invaluable practical assistance with the manuscript when it needed it most.

Steve McCaffery
Toronto
April 10, 2002

K as in Sleep

Should find it hard
to relocate between these losses,
veils,
which isn't history.

The primary bigamist and pointing
to canonical attributes
where a body comes undone
conflictual in the mirror's dispossessed
aggressions.

Can't understand
as immobility
the sign
which is
or the hair amongst others
which authorizes
definition.

To turn aphasiac.
To frequent language
only when it troubles us.

One is never sure here
of the voice of passion
the televised desire to stay
the child in duty
as a recollection ordered, since
hatred agonized is different
to a scene possessed
then rearranged.

VISUAL AND CONCRETE POEMS

Oceanside: a lipogram

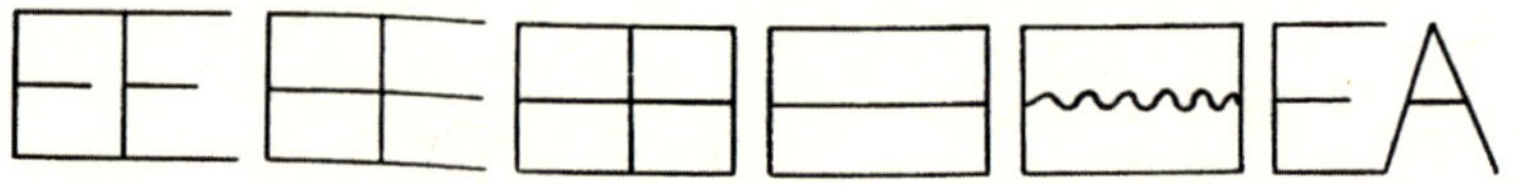

pullllllllllllllllllllllllll

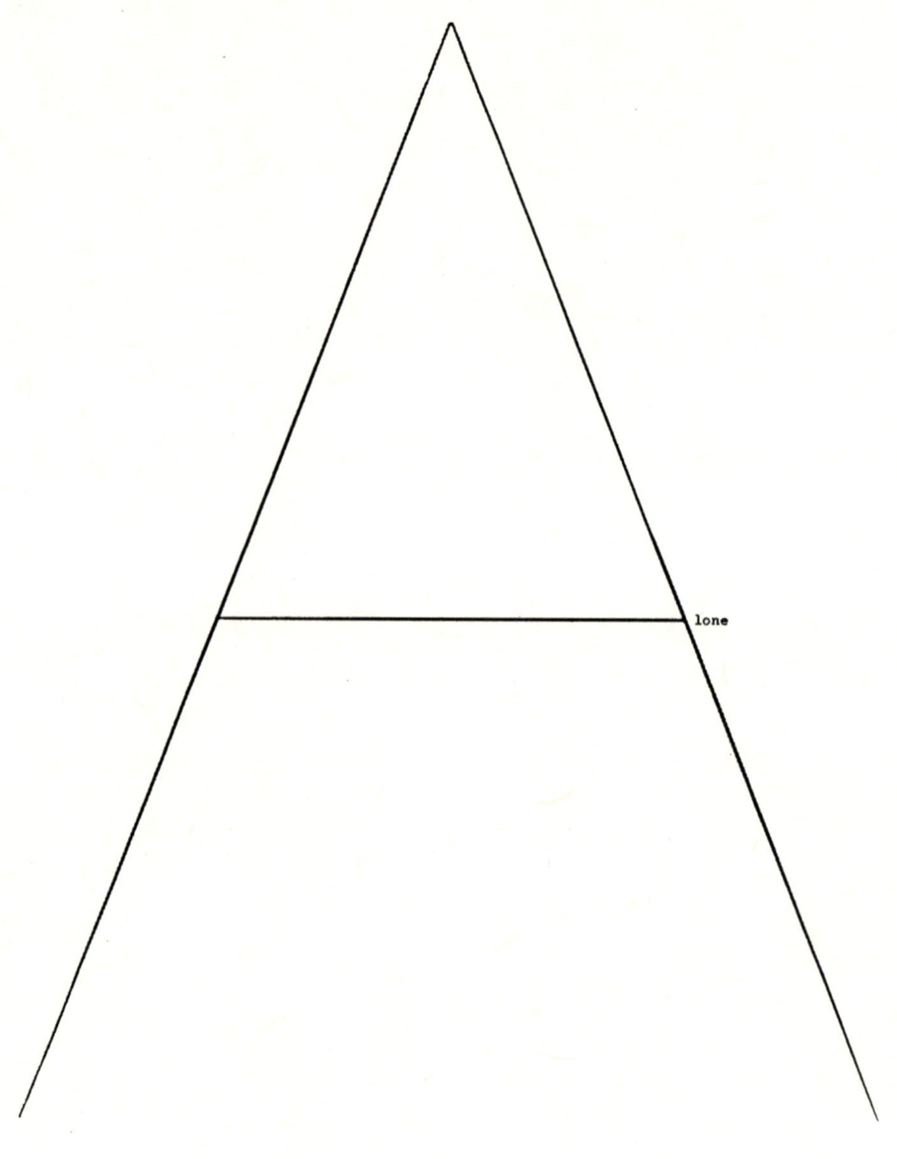
lone

c c
c c
c c
c c c
c
c c c
c c sea c
c c c
c c c c c
c c
c c c c
c c c c
c c
c c
c

from *Epsilon Series*

see ——— sea

seize

Capture: Two Versions

captur e

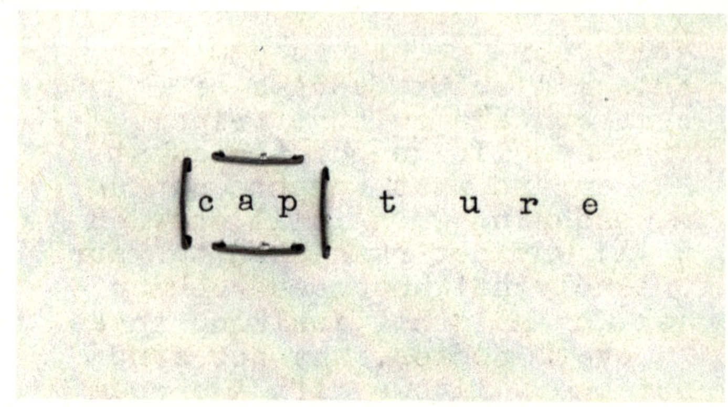

A Short History of Literature

OVID
VOID
OVID

First Fenollosa Meditation

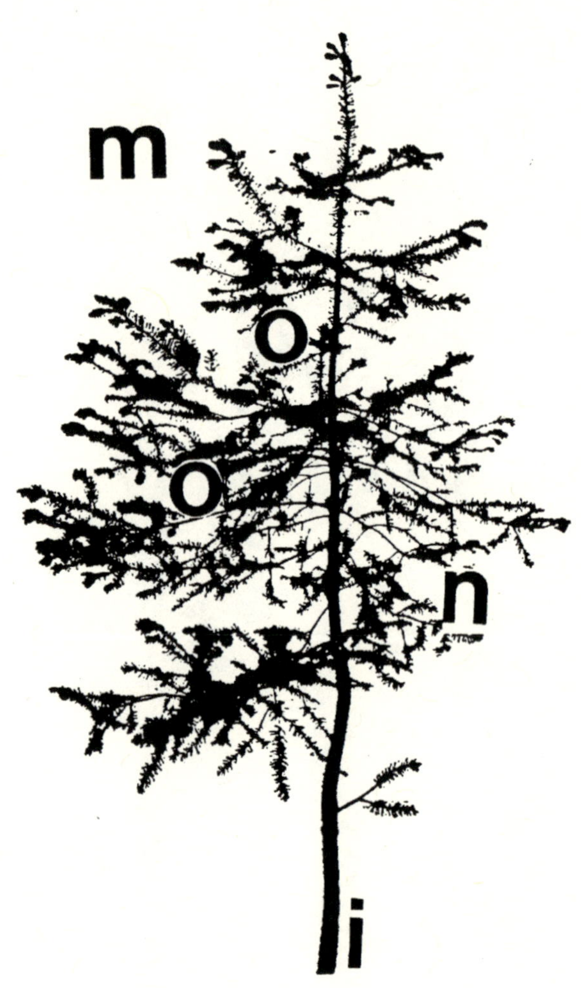

TUNNEL

First Typestract: 'Solid Layer and Tissue'

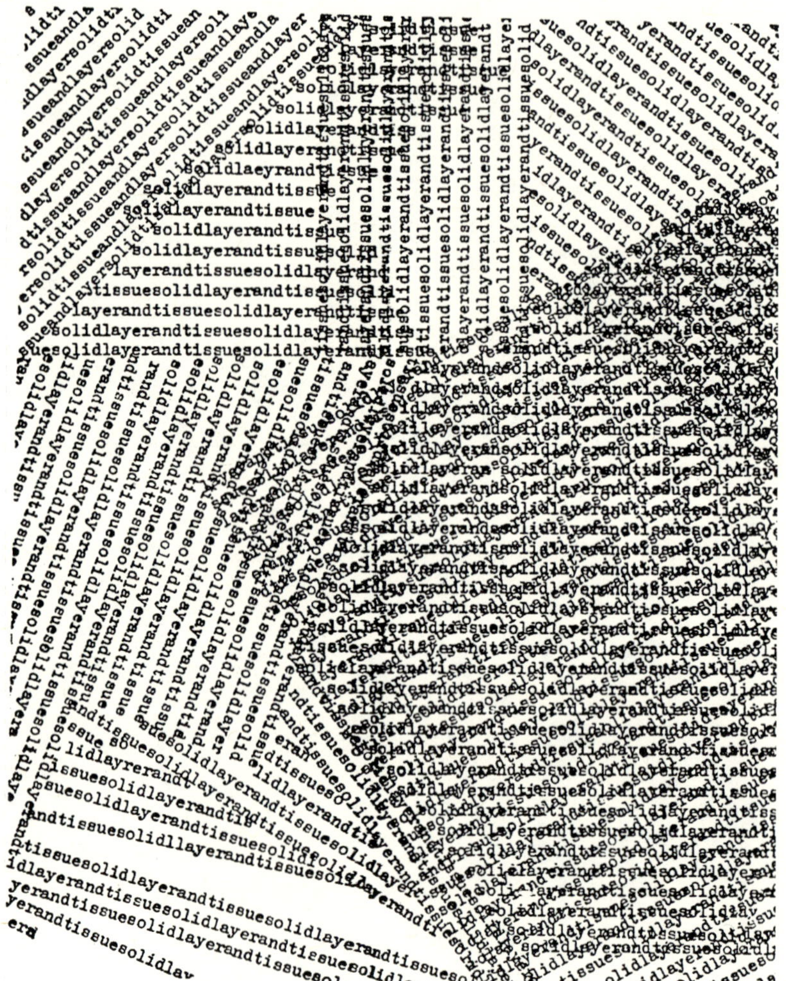

Bilingual Typestract

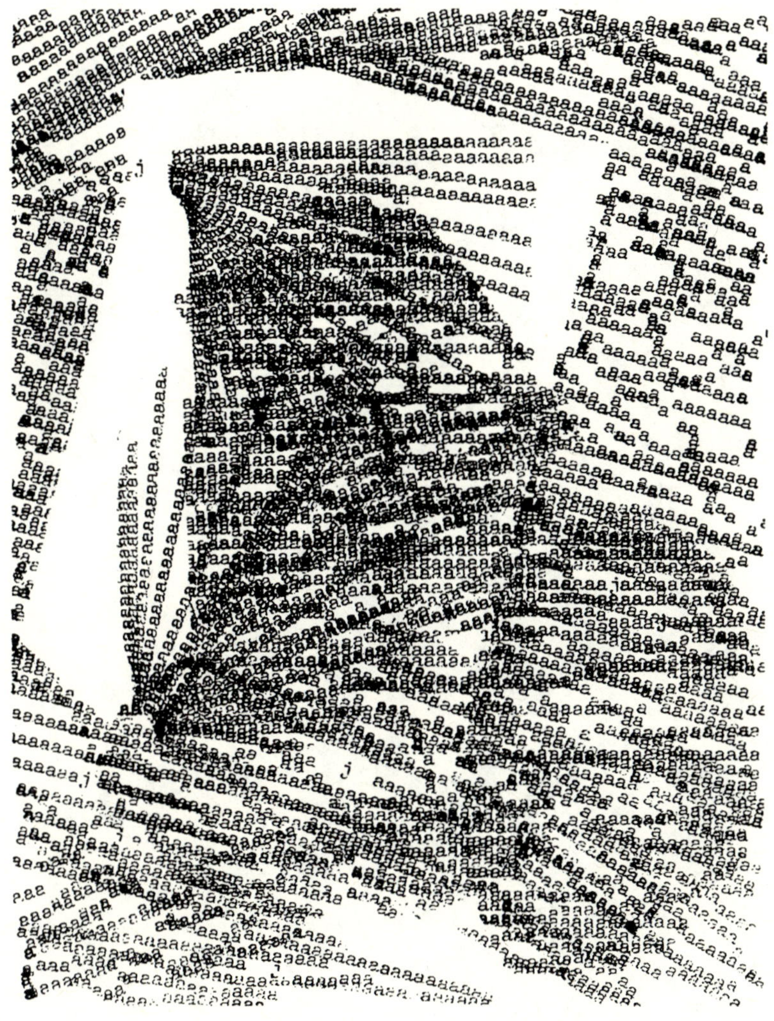

Typestract: 'Babel'

Tissue Text: 'OXO'

Tissue Text: Random 'C' Field

Triple Random Field

Typestract: 'Once upon a been stork'

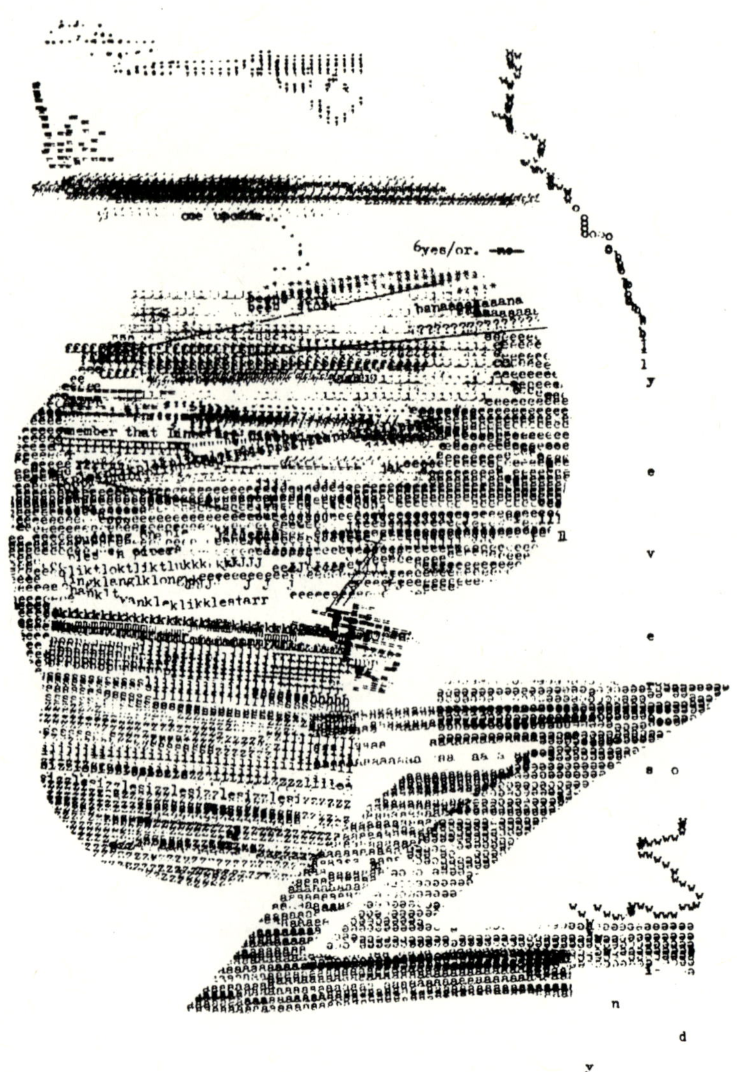

A Number Poem: 'as of ten'

(discarded section of *Carnival: The First Panel*)

Abandoned Section from Carnival

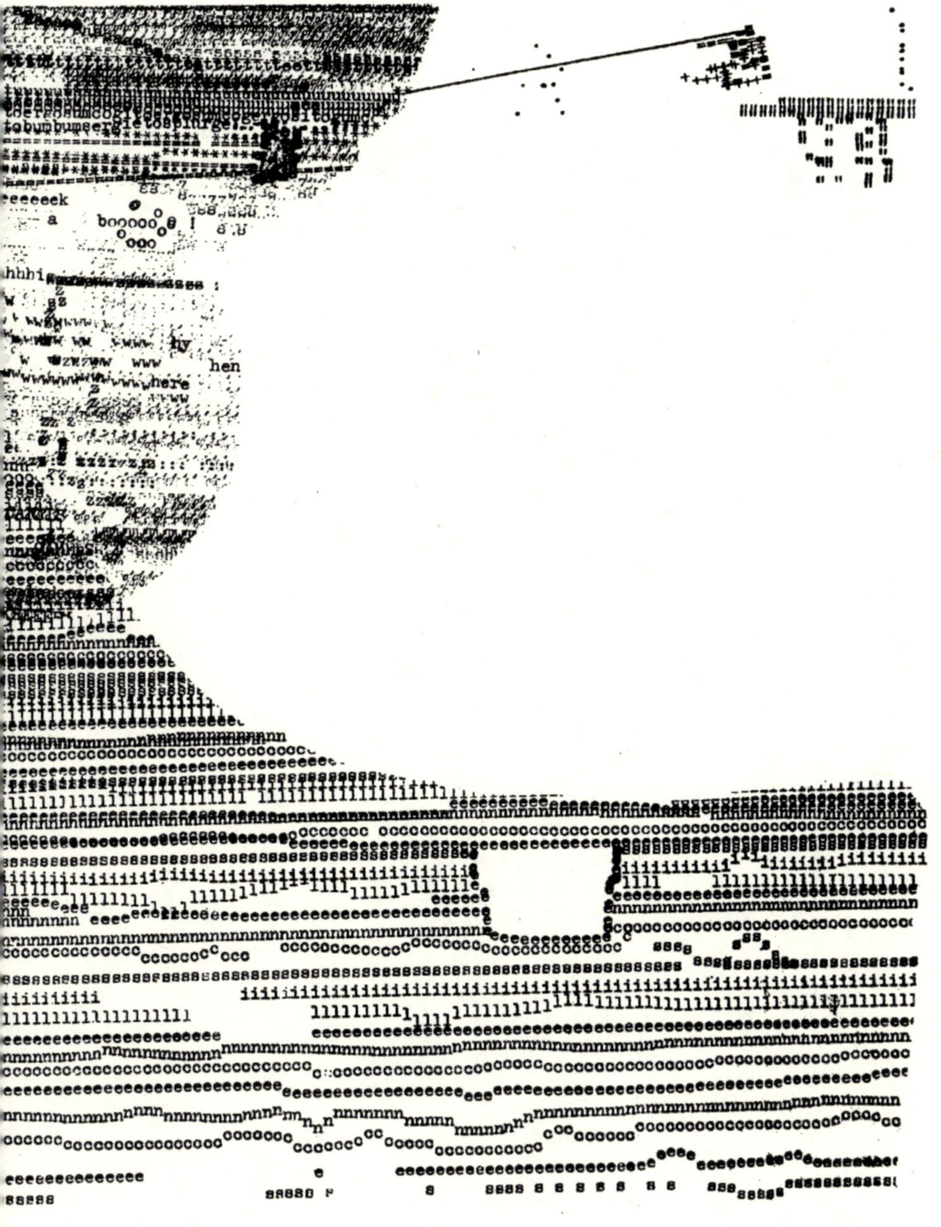

Homage to e.e. cummings

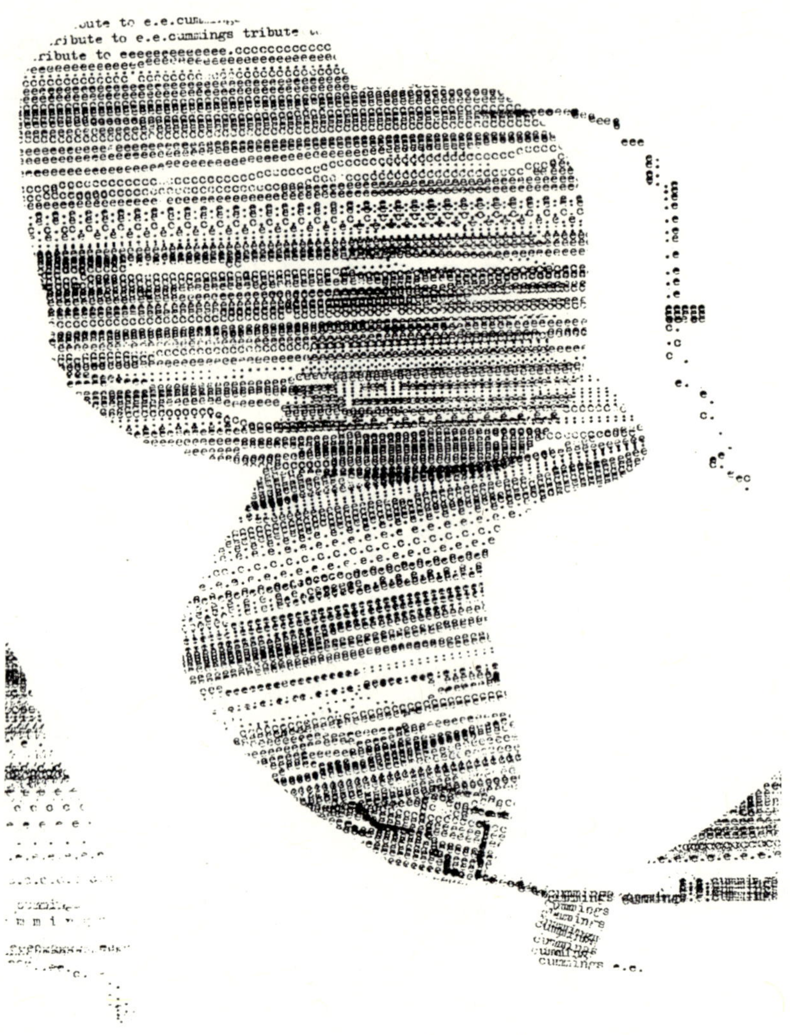

from *Epsilon Series*

from *Two Simultaneous Texts*

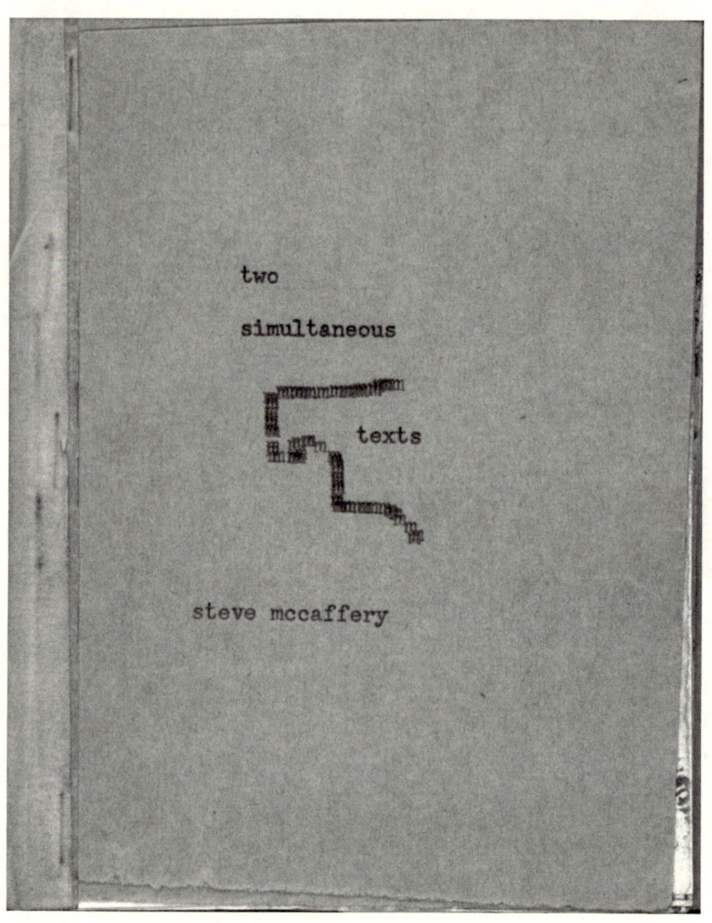

woman mother aided
Mrs. Beaudoin said the
woman told her she was se-
parated from her husb
and that her
children
been
by the
n's Aid Society.
The
to
Yesterday,
afternoon and awoke
p.m. to find Lisa and
woman gone.
police until 1
knee socks
shoes. She is
tall, has brown
and eyes and a light
complexion.
The young woman wore a
light-blue cotton dress and a
MRS. RHEA BEAUDOIN
$3.23 hourly and letter car-
riers $2.75 to $2.99. This re-
presents a weekly wage of
between $102 and $129.
taking second look
k market
develop-
cited
It illustrates
today.
ployment.

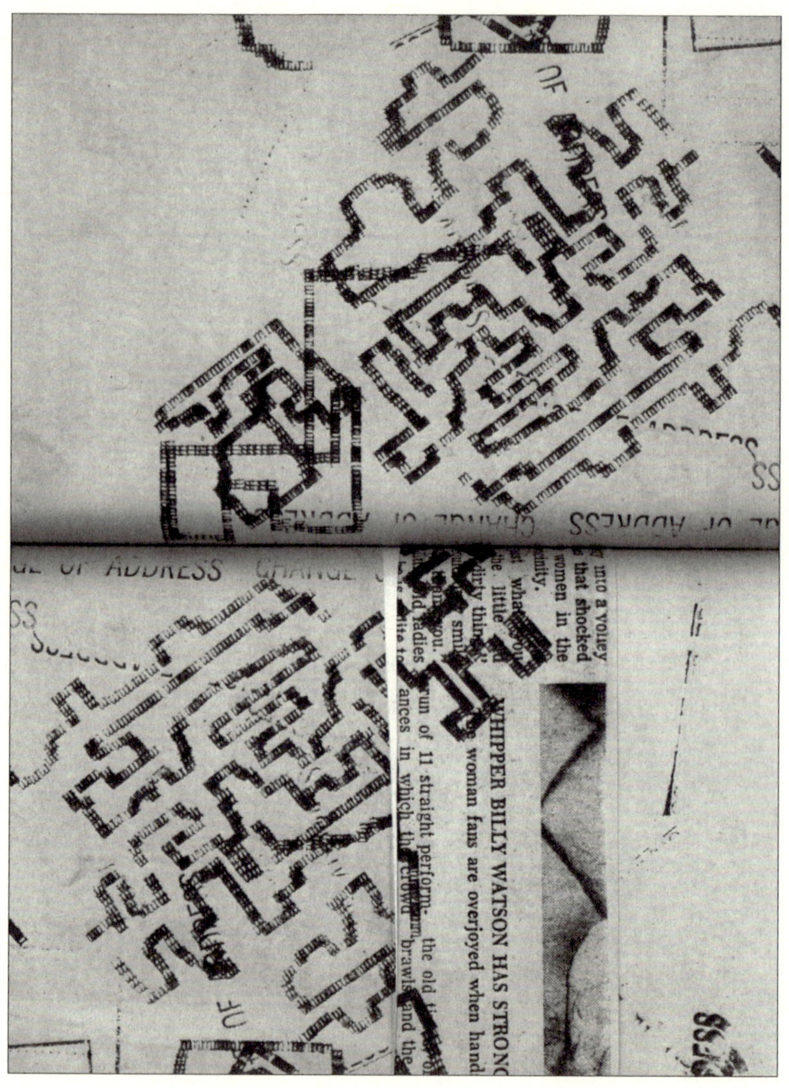

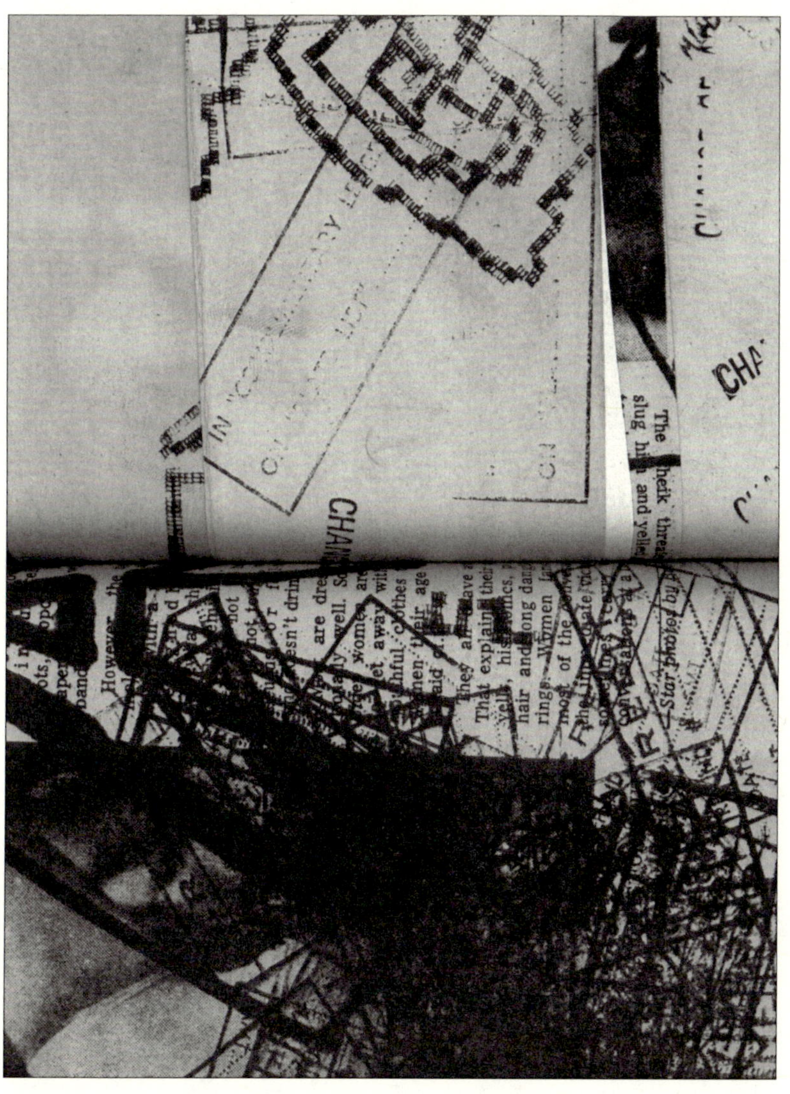

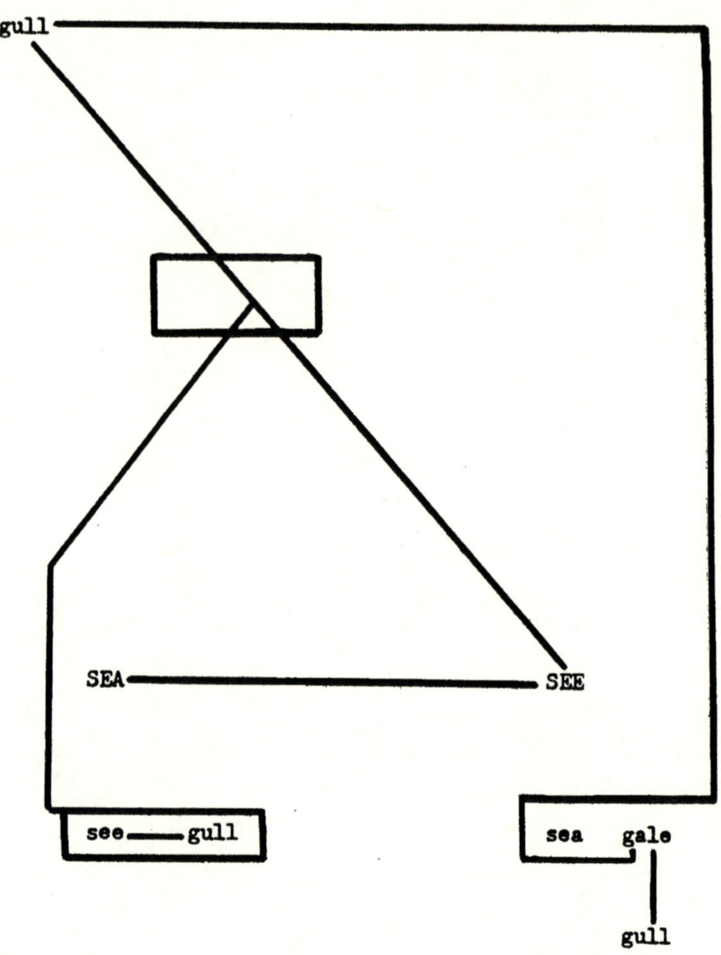
gull
SEA
SEE
see gull
sea gale
gull

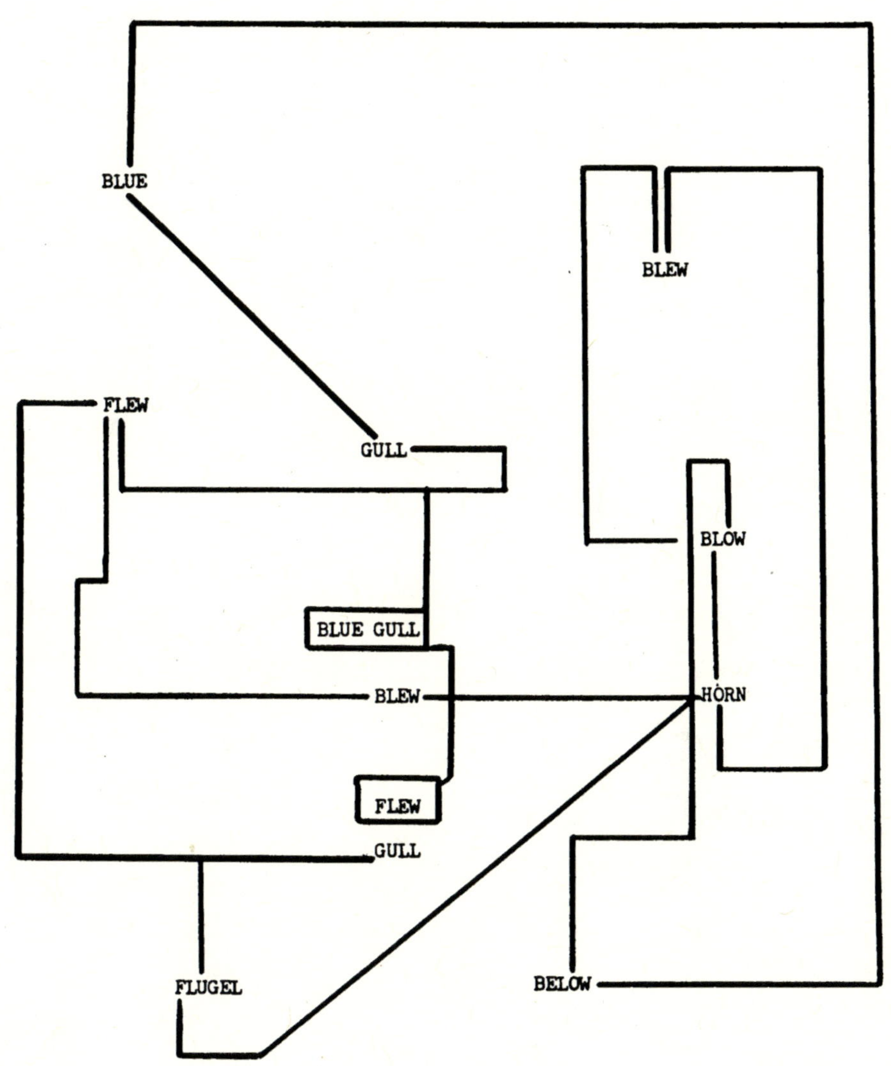
BLUE
BLEW
FLEW
GULL
BLOW
BLUE GULL
BLEW
HÖRN
FLEW
GULL
FLUGEL
BELOW

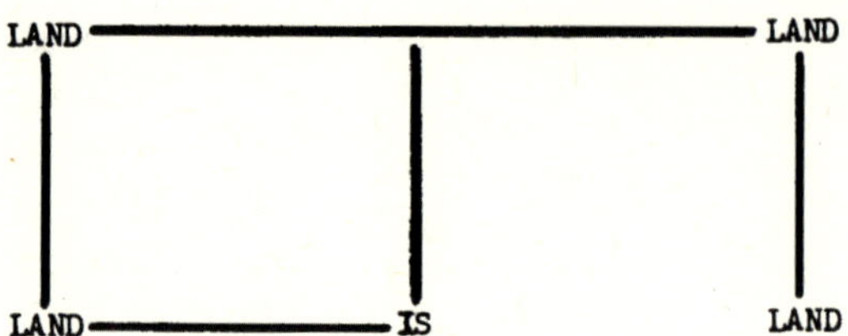
LAND
LAND
LAND
IS
LAND

IS
LAND

Cartesian Vowel Glyph

Two States of Ur-Alpha

Semiotic Cartoon Glyph

from *Alpha: Discrete Series 4*

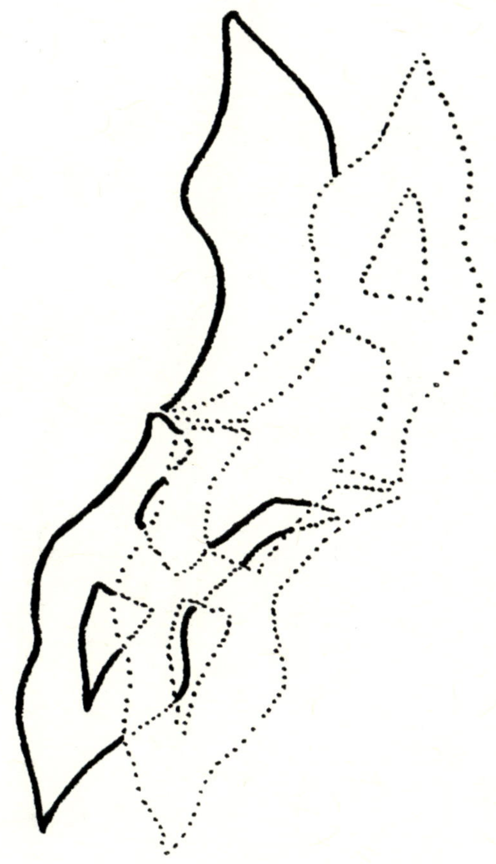

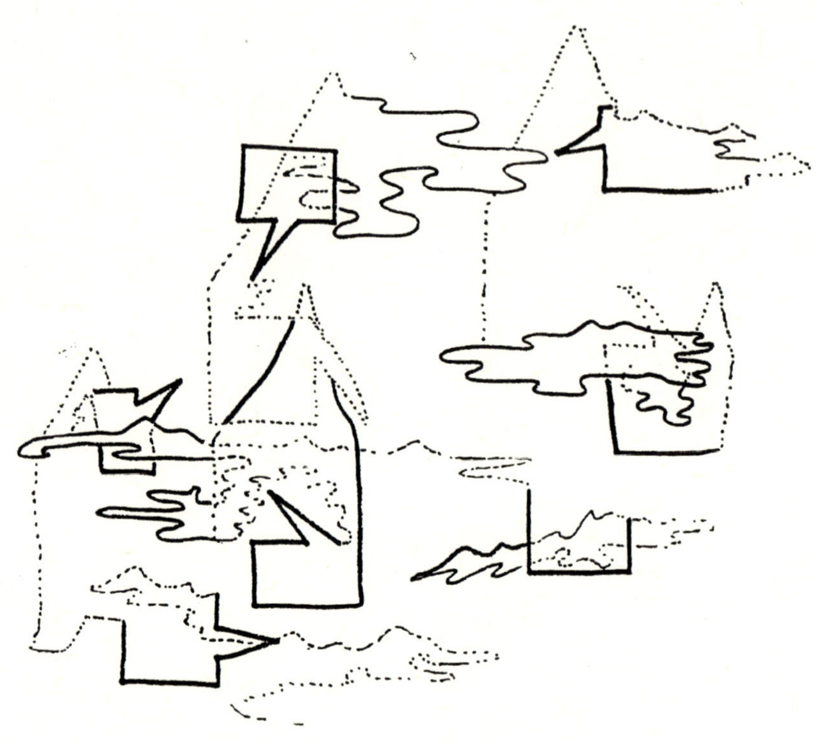

from *Alpha: Discrete Series 3*

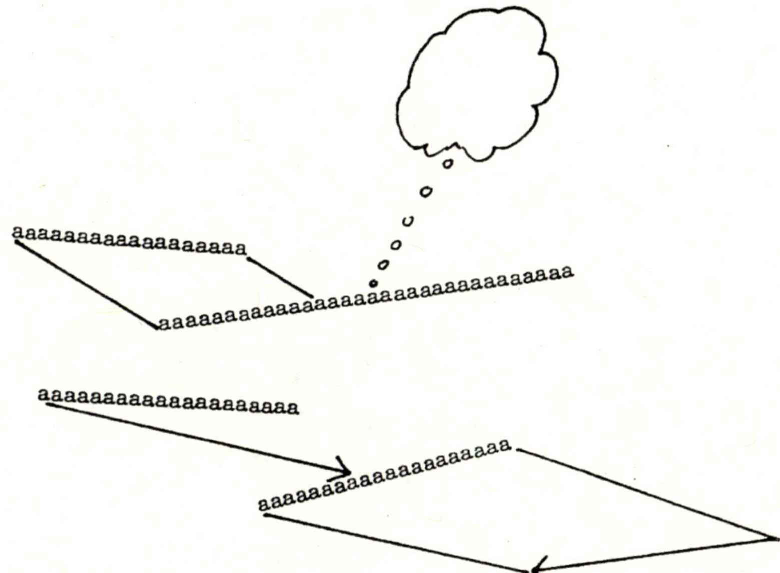

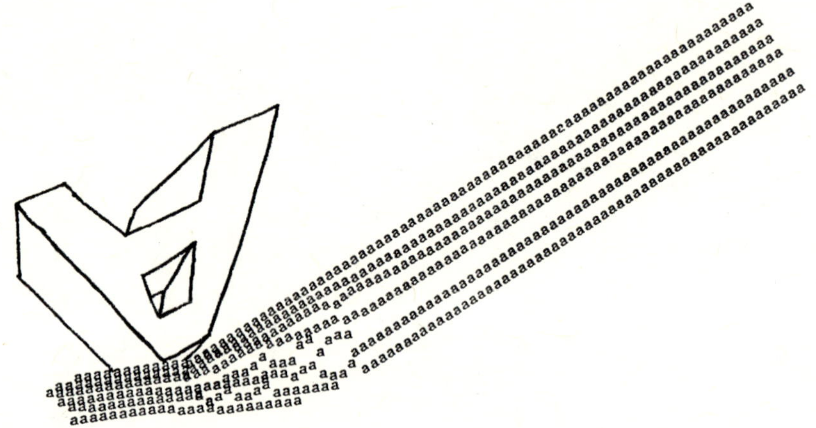

from *Alpha: Discrete Series 5*

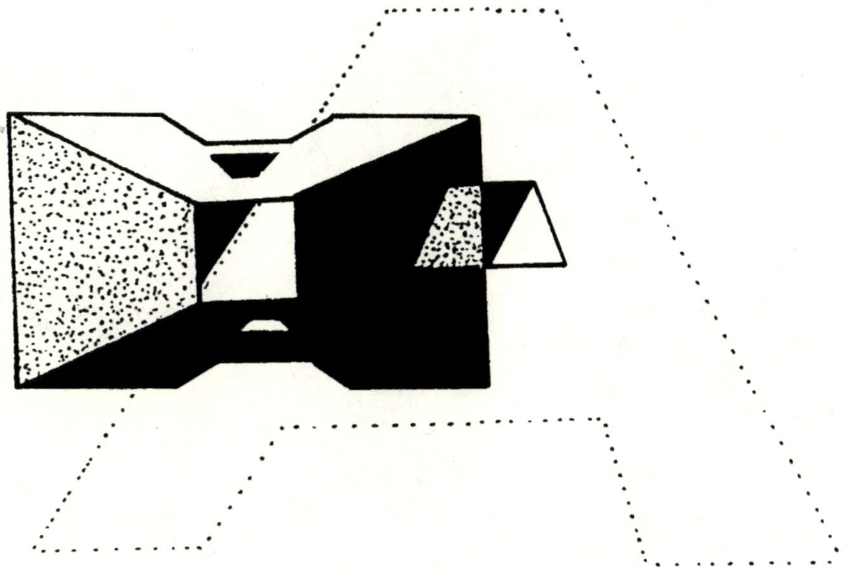

The Letter 'a' According to Chomsky

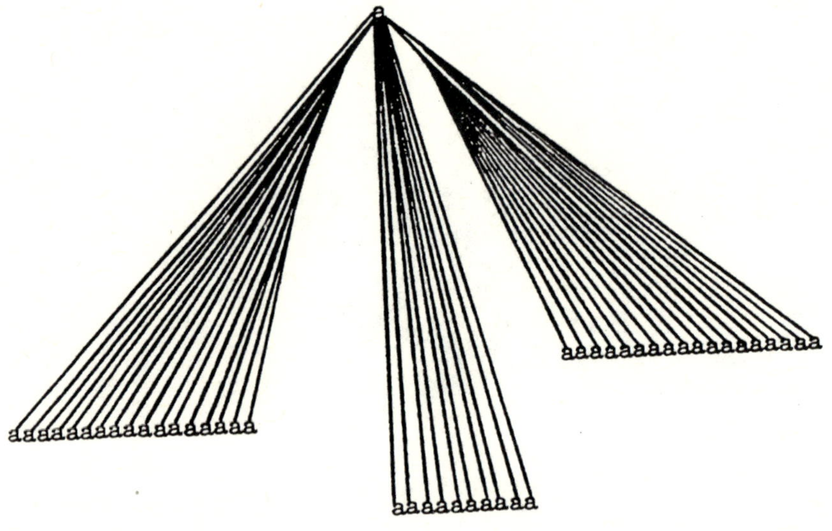

H: A History

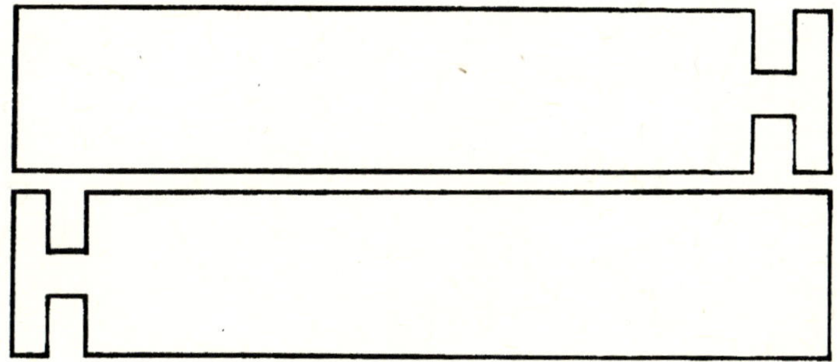

Punctuation Poem

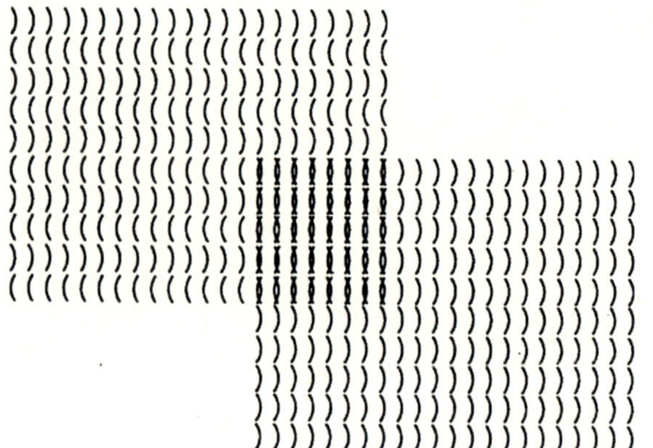

Punctuation Poem 'X'

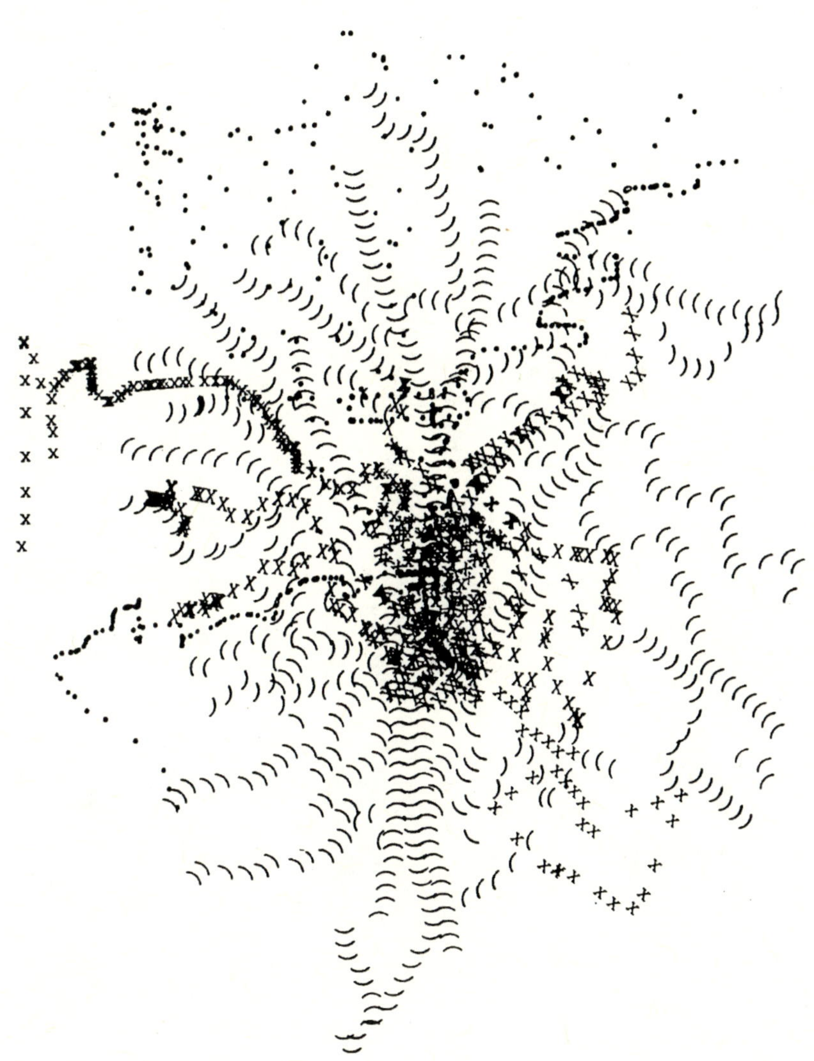

Punctuation Poem

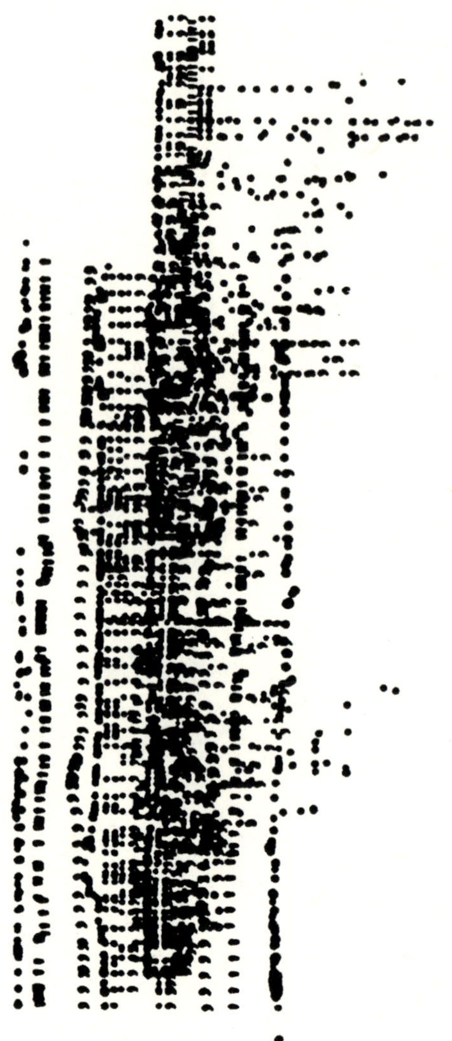

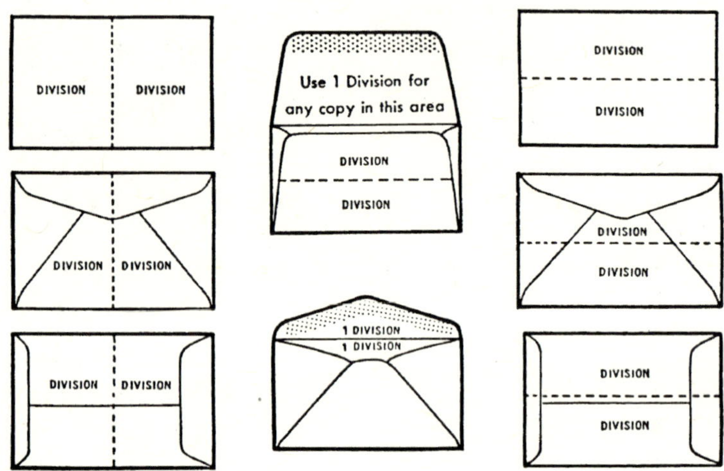
DIVISION
DIVISION
DIVISION
DIVISION
DIVISION
DIVISION
Use 1 Division for
any copy in this area
DIVISION
DIVISION
1 DIVISION
1 DIVISION
DIVISION
DIVISION
DIVISION
DIVISION
DIVISION
DIVISION

Panelogic

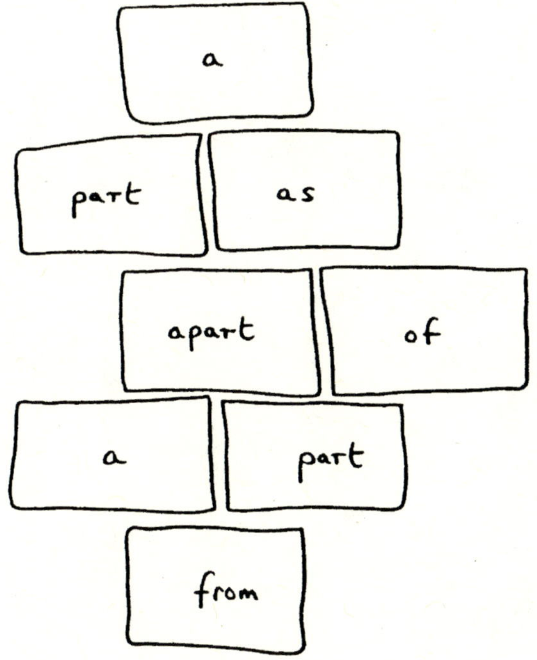

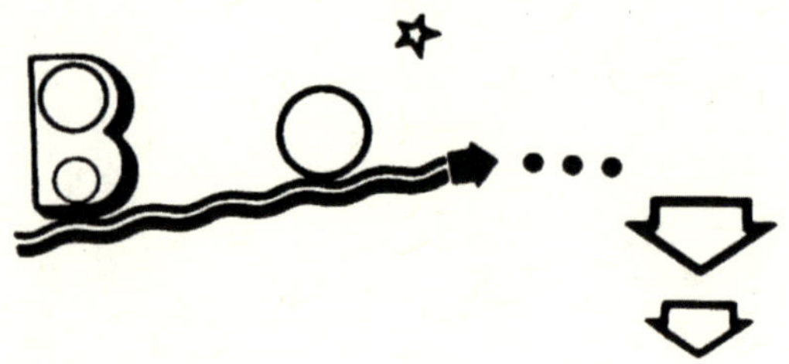

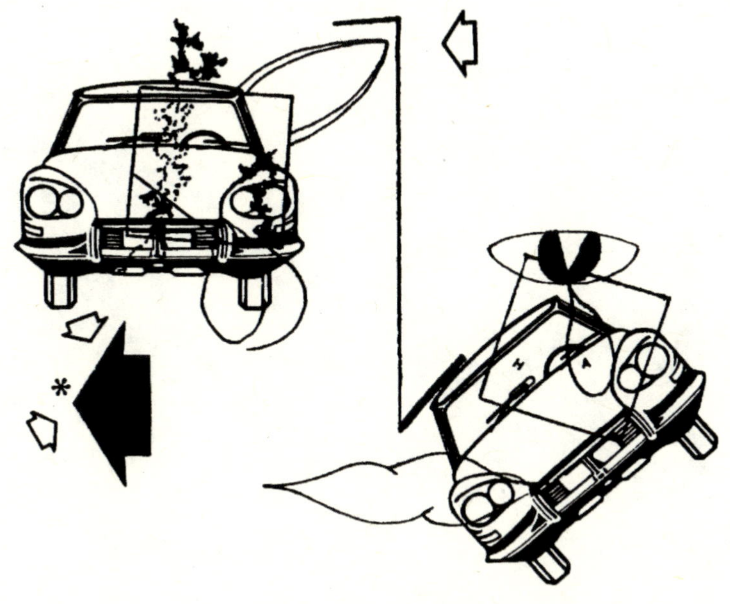

from *Demiplosive Suite*

Suprematist Alphabet

aaaaaaaaaaaaaaaaaaaa

William Tell: A Novel

Two Poems on a Theme by Eugen Gomringer

SOUND	**SOUND**	**SOUND**
SOUND		**SOUND**
SOUND	**SOUND**	**SOUND**

SILENCE	**SILENCE**	**SILENCE**
SILENCE	ping	**SILENCE**
SILENCE	**SILENCE**	**SILENCE**

A Puff of Magritte

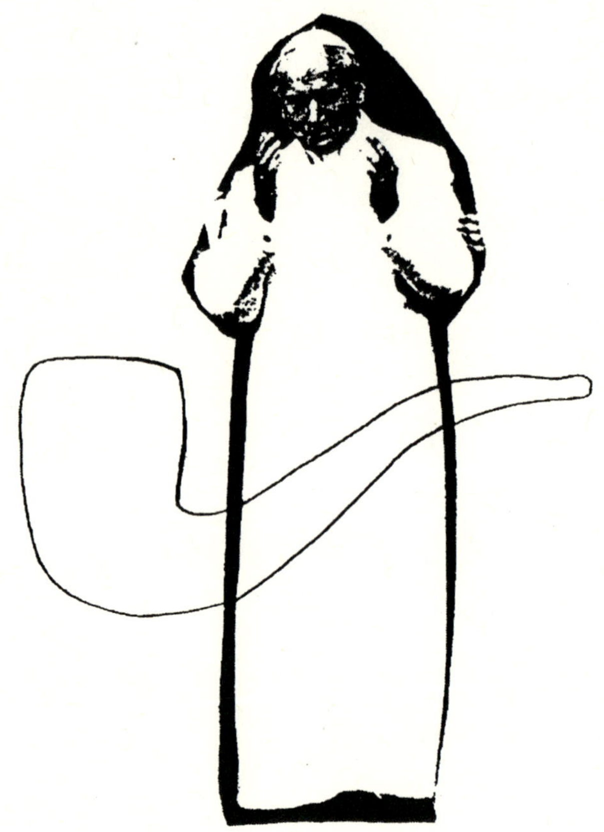

ceci n'est pas un pape

Maps: a different landscape

the line of words which is not the length that it pretends to be

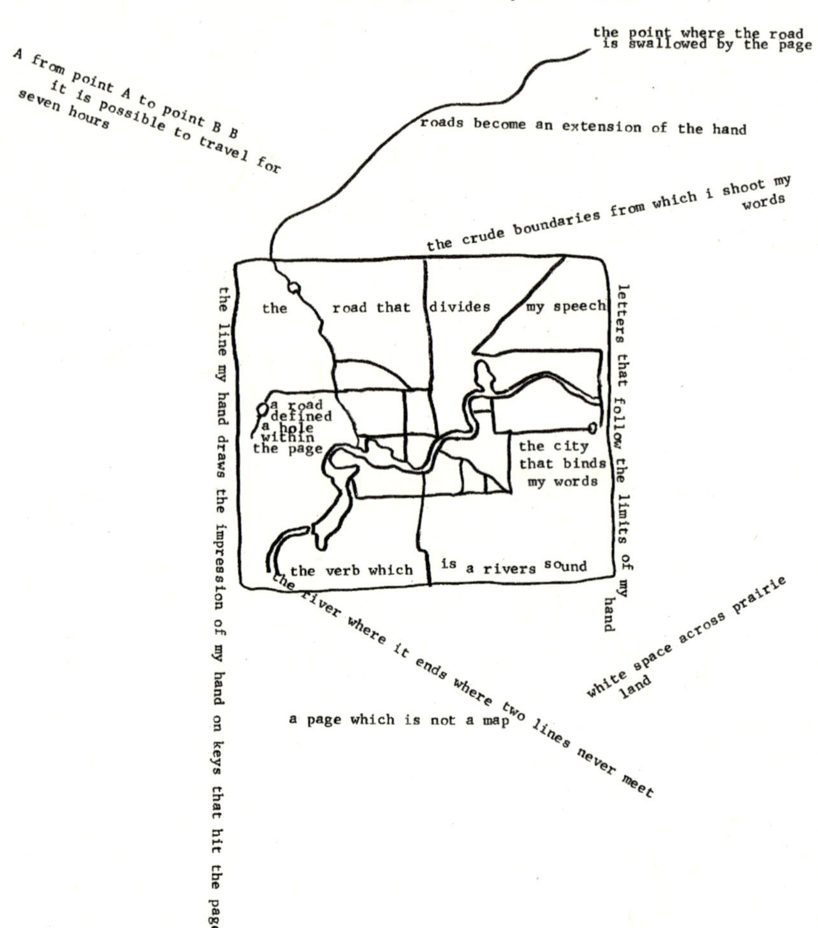

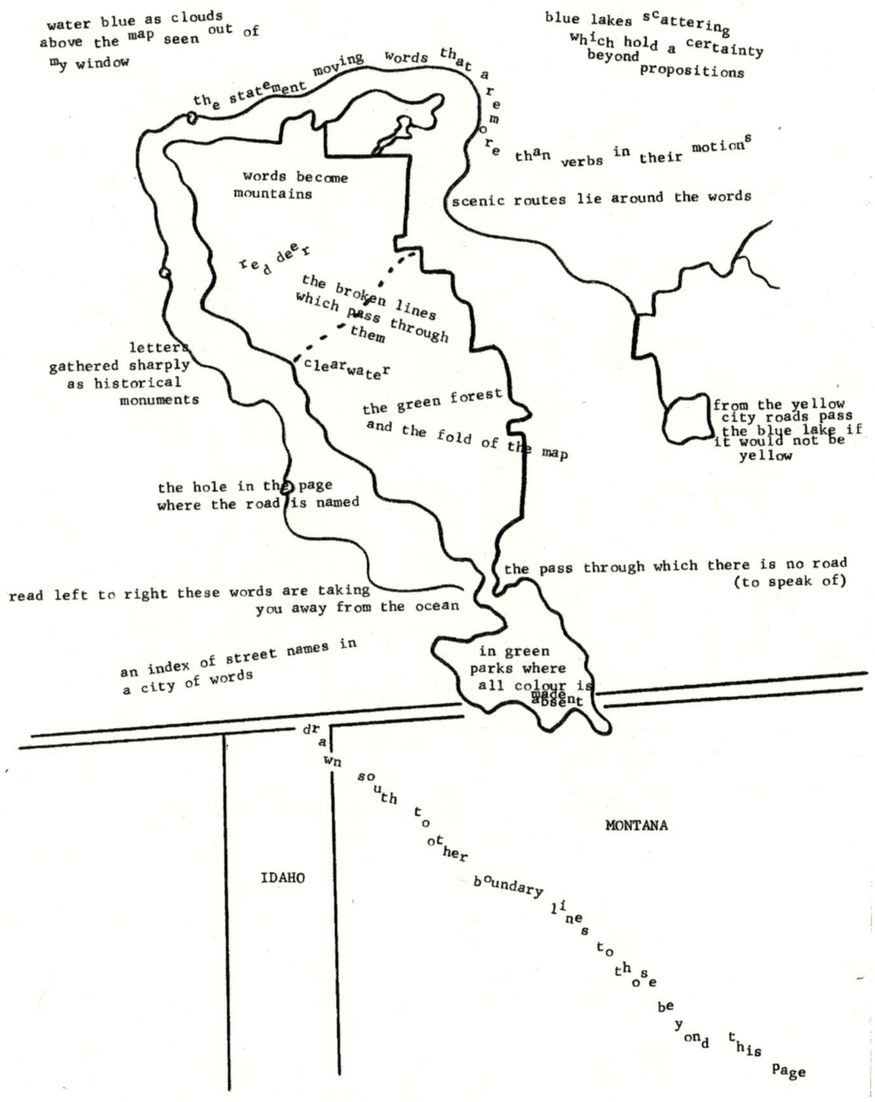

water blue as clouds
above the map seen out of
my window
blue lakes scattering
which hold a certainty
beyond
propositions
the statement moving words that are more than verbs in their motions
words become
mountains
scenic routes lie around the words
red deer
the broken lines
which pass through
them
letters
gathered sharply
as historical
monuments
clearwater
the green forest
and the fold of the map
from the yellow
city roads pass
the blue lake if
it would not be
yellow
the hole in the page
where the road is named
the pass through which there is no road
(to speak of)
read left to right these words are taking
you away from the ocean
an index of street names in
a city of words
in green
parks where
all colour is
made
absent
drawn south to other boundary lines to those beyond this Page
MONTANA
IDAHO

page as a part of land

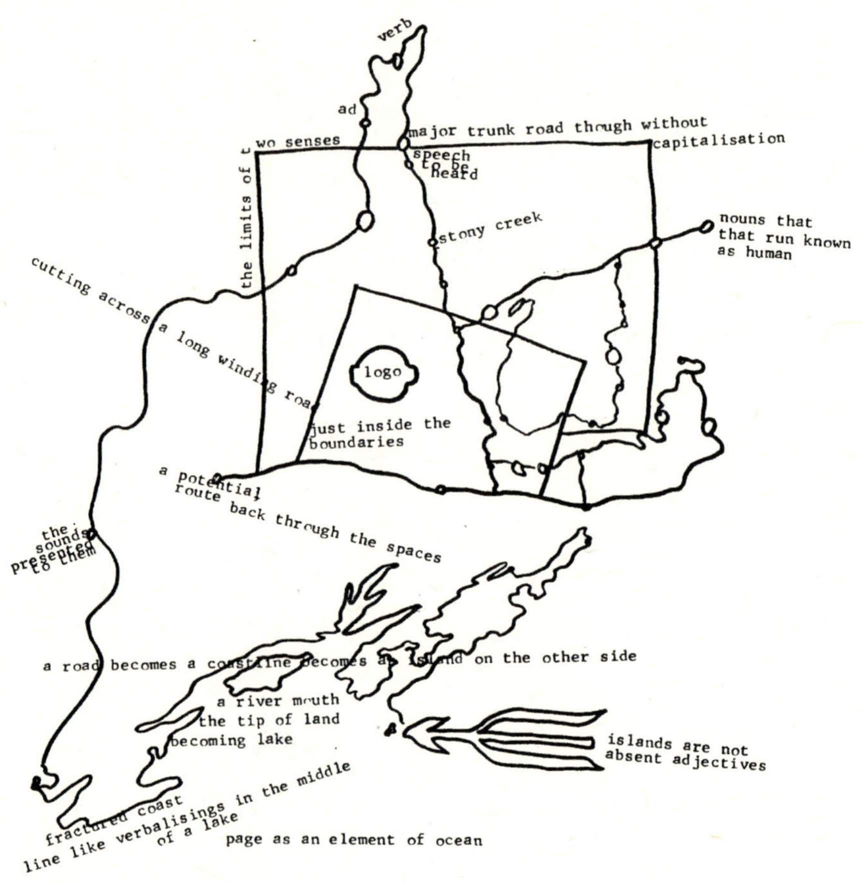

NARRATIVE
THE OBSOLETE
ABSOLUTE

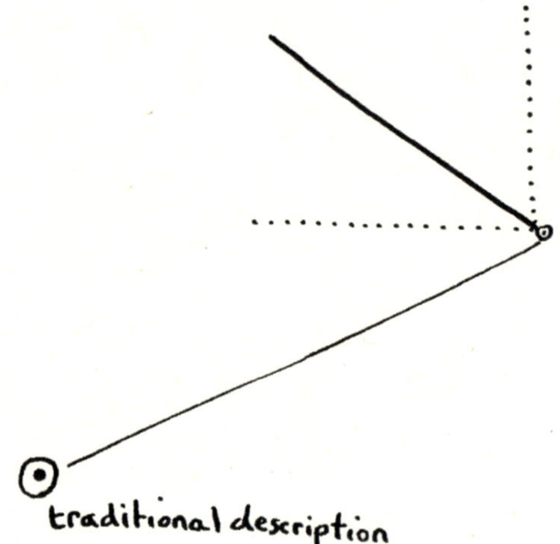

all traditional description is diagonal
and assumes both a vertical noun
and a horizontal adjective.

only with those assumptions
can the traditional describe.

how to write novels .

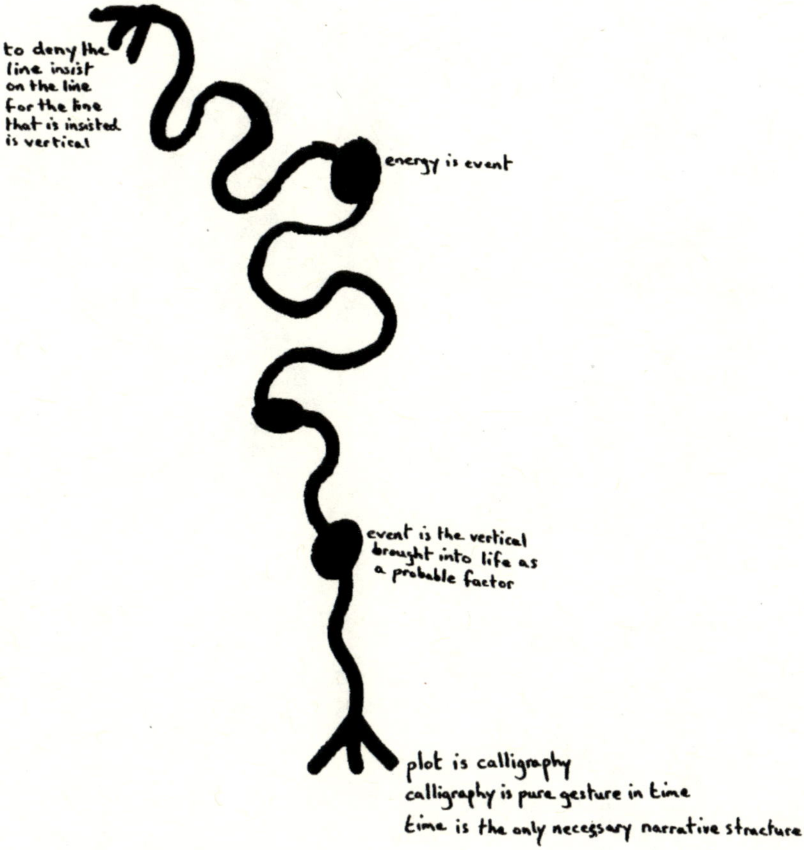

to deny the
line insist
on the line
for the line
that is insisted
is vertical

energy is event

event is the vertical
brought into life as
a probable factor

plot is calligraphy
calligraphy is pure gesture in time
time is the only necessary narrative structure

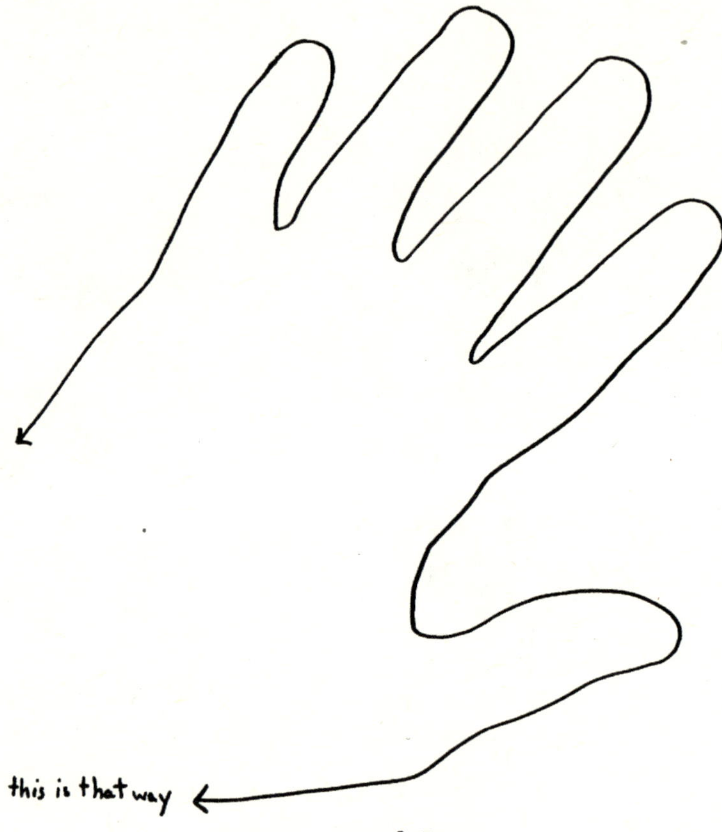

PLOT IN JOYCE & PROUST

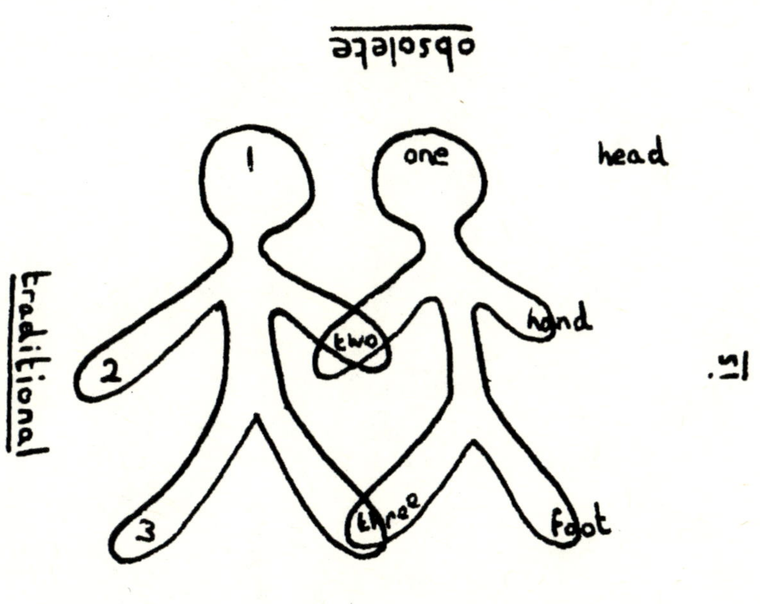

characterisation

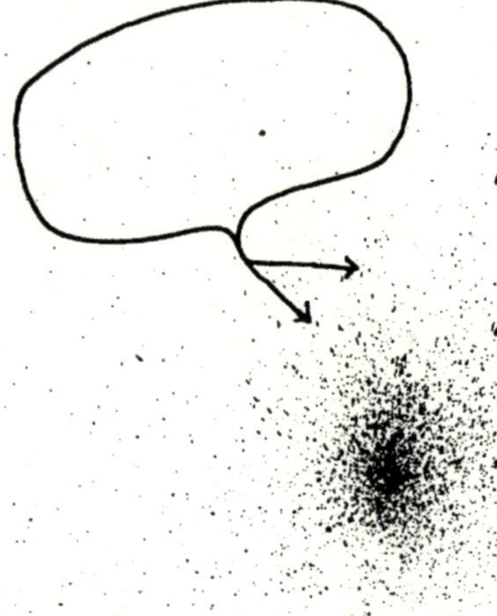
any act of creation is a choice
any sentence which says some
thing does not say something
else. this is the secret threat
of narrative

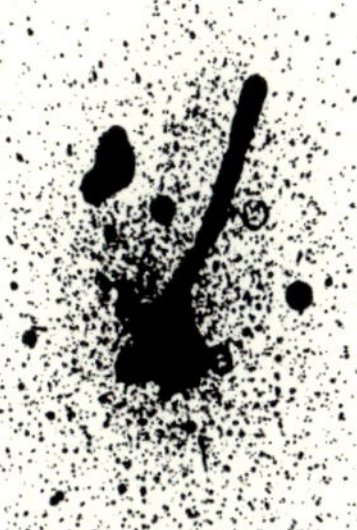

semantic pleasure

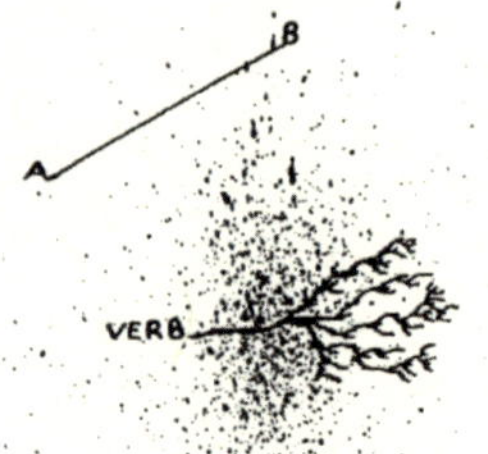

a tree appears

the sentence:
writing a sentence
is moving in a
given space and
time

v

definition

N

W

hums

E

S

fable of the bees:

ie, is narrative an
action against or a
movement through
time.
if so do we need the
sentence.
if so do we need the
word.

7

5

9

3

4

6

1

seven poems

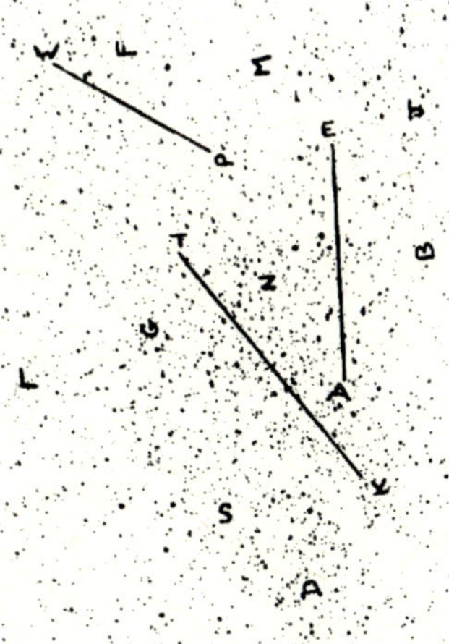

three stories

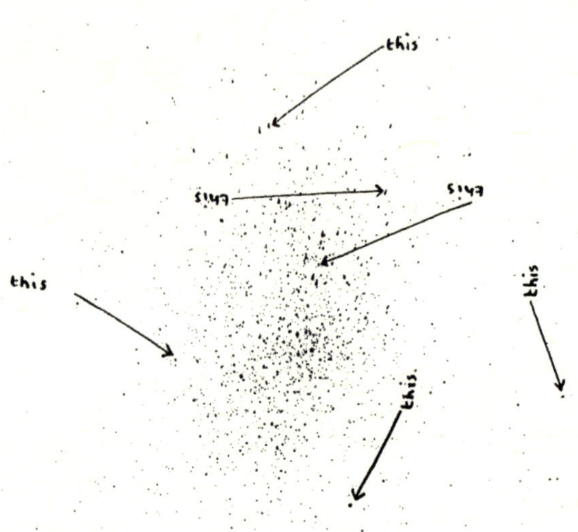

1 2 3 4 5 6 7

true linear is
vertical <u>not</u>
lateral.

warning: grammar will
organize your life on
a lateral axis.

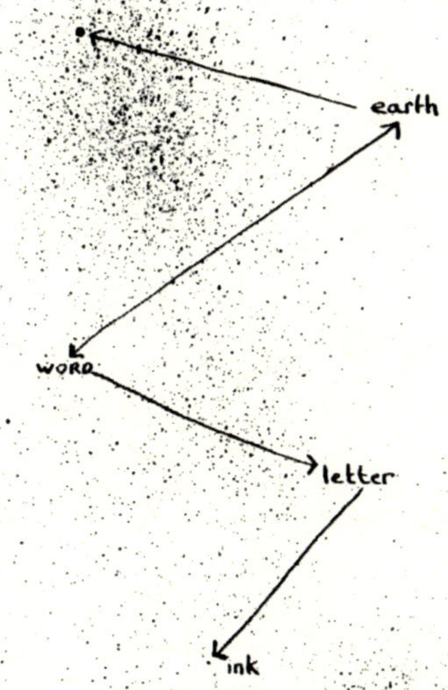

descent through the planets of Saussure

SOUND TEXTS AND MUSICAL SCORES

Studies for Two Unperformed Four Horsemen Pieces

C
L
a
p
b
p
XI
d
adi
o
43 43
43 6669458
phlw
K
STAMP
73 47
698754
ae
p
l
x
8989898989
89898989 81 81
8189 8189 8989

Concerto for Two Adverbs

ANTICONSTITUTIONELLEMENT

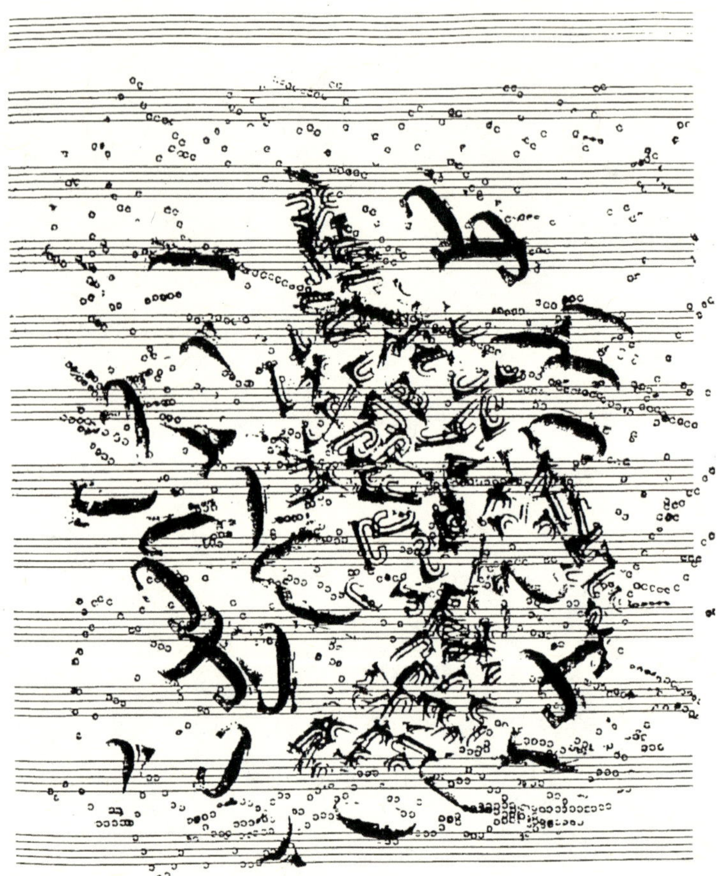

PRECIPITEVOLISSIMEVOLMENTE

SIZERZ

$S^1IZ^1ER^1Z^1$
$S^1IZ^1E^1RZ^1$
$S^1IZ^1E^2R^1Z^2$
$S^1IZ^1E^2RZ^1$
$S^1IZ^1E^3R^1Z^1$
$S^1IZ^1E^4R^1Z^1$
$S^1IZ^2E^2RZ^1$
$S^1IZ^2E^2R^1Z^2$
$S^2I^2Z^1ER^1Z^1$
$S^2I^2Z^1E^1RZ^1$
$S^2I^2Z^1E^2RZ^1$
$S^2I^2Z^1E^2R^1Z^2$
$S^2I^2Z^1E^3R^1Z^1$
$S^2I^2Z^1E^4R^1Z^1$
$S^2I^2Z^2E^2RZ^1$
$S^2I^2Z^2E^2R^1Z^2$
$S^2I^2Z^2E^4R^1Z^1$

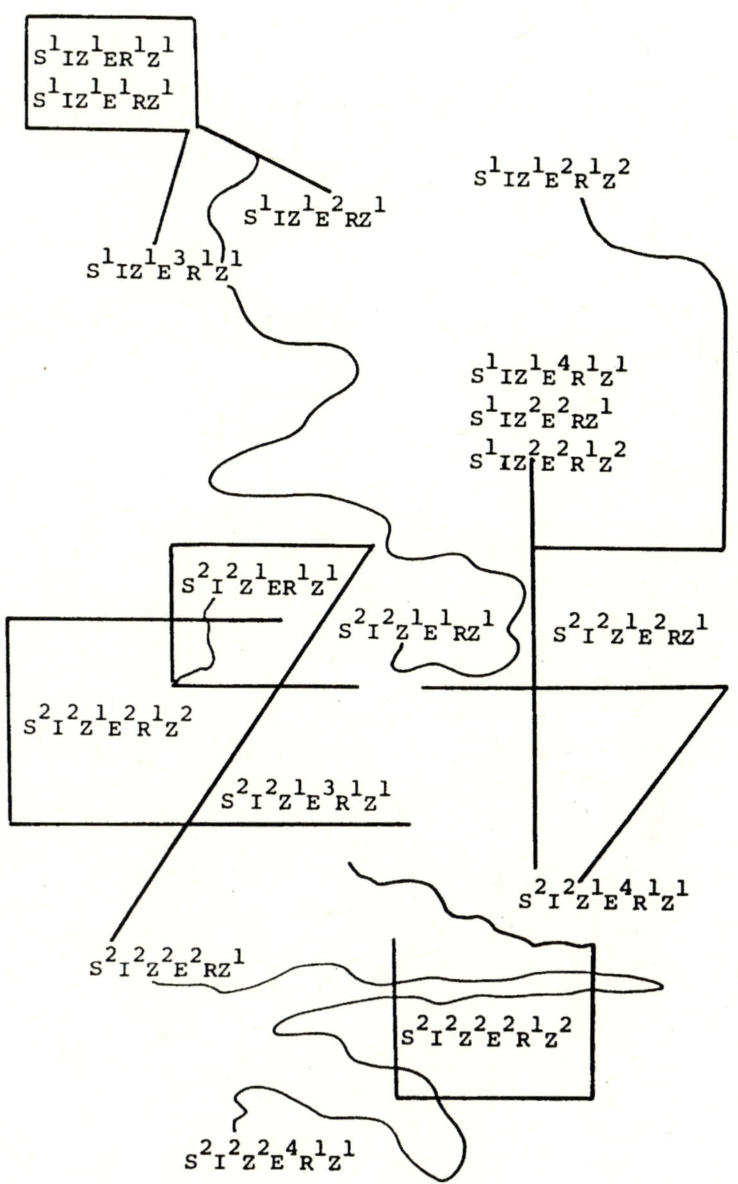

Cappuccino: A Suffix Structure

plussiliente positivemente
signiamente ofiliente addiliente tionimente
minimento ussiliente negativemente signiamento
subiliente tractimente tionilente
plussiliente orimente minimente usiliente
minimente usiliente orilente plusiliente

multipliediente byliente dividiente ediliento
byliente equaliente approximiliento
atelliente congruitente entiente greaterliente
thaniente lessiliente thaniente
similiente toliente equivalente entiente

identicaliento
identiente icaliente equaliente equivalento
thereimente foriente sincemente becausemento
identicaliente indentimento equaliente toimente
directimento untiliento
proportiomento untiliente
asimente infinimente timente squaremente
rootemente minimente usimente onelento

particularimente valuemente ofelente variamente
anymento timelente dividemente edemente
squariente rootemente radicaliento
squariento basemento
naturalemento systemento
logarithemento
logarithelente
summamente ationemente termelente onemente eachemento
positivimente integeremente productimento
integralemente definilente approachemente
asiente silentiente limitento functionemento
incremente differentialemente derivaetente tivente
respectivente variamente ratiomente circumferencemente
diameteremente circularimento factorialemento
indicatemente enclosente symbolemento

singlemente numbermente indicativemente treatedemente
symbolemente singlemente numberetente angleemente
parallelemente perpendemente dicularemente trianglemente
rightemente angledemente trianglemento
minutente arcemente primetente
secondsemente arcimente doublento

primento.

Love Song

Oh
TO OPTICAL AXIS ONLY
INTRA-CRANIALITY
shut
PHYSIO-LOGICAL STRAINING POINT
up
AESTHETIC
ALPHA GROUP (acquired response)
ME
YOU MAKE
MEANING ≠ RESPONSE
mental alertness maximised
BASIS IN (7)
FURIOUS
9.7"
RHYTHM : PROMINENT
MODALITY SUSPECT
SIGNIFICANT TRANQUILITY
PATTERN CONSTANT
M GROUP characteristics co-relate
PLASTICITY
cf. external as reality factor
common time base
Shut
OH
ECONOMY
you
RING OSCILLATION
visual solution to "N"
notion "H" in mind
THOUGHT HABIT
SPEED SECONDARY
up
MECHANISM 8: MIND AT REST
detected eveness of event
make
FURIOUS
COMPLETE
UNI OVULAR
TEMPORAL CO-ORDINATE SCANNING PATTERN
ME
CELL ESSENTIAL
FLASH = CHANGE FREQUENCY
SPATIAL ONLY
PICTURE DETAIL (Wittgenstein)
TERRESTOID

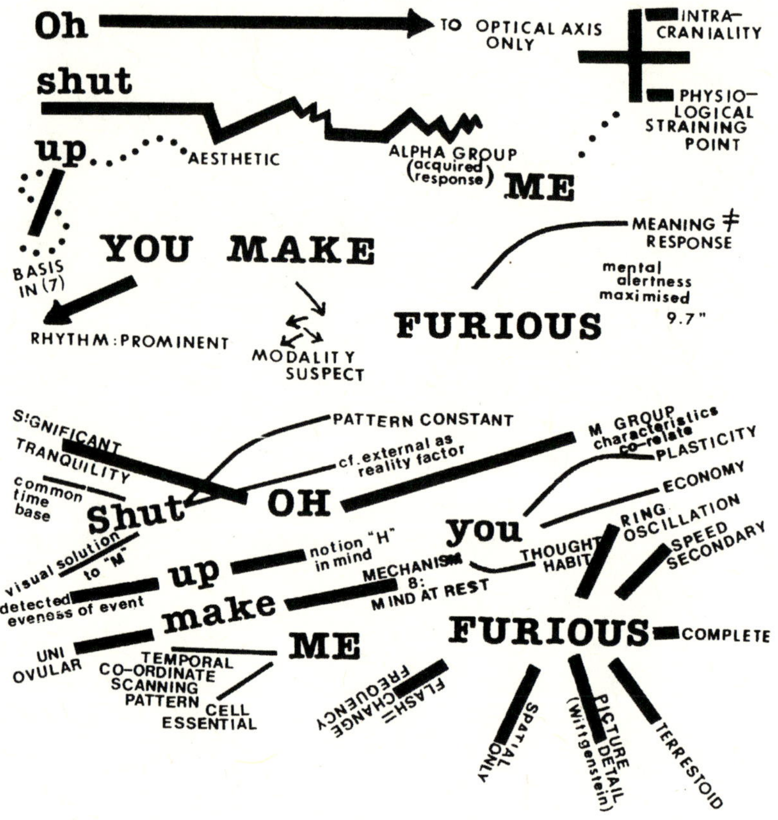

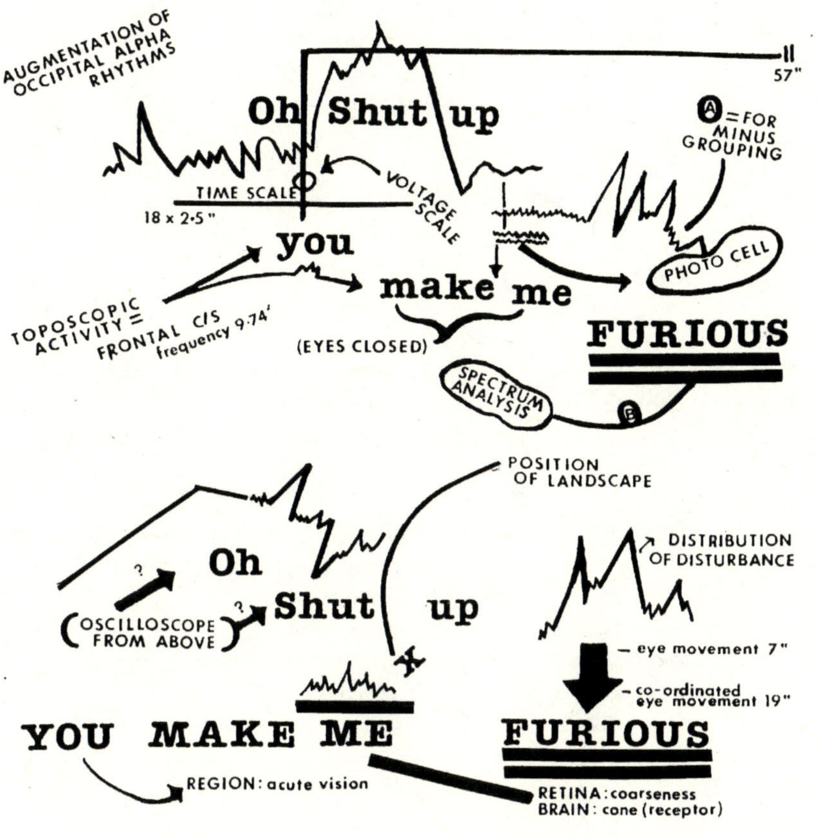
AUGMENTATION OF OCCIPITAL ALPHA RHYTHMS
57"
Oh Shut up
A = FOR MINUS GROUPING
TIME SCALE
18 x 2·5"
VOLTAGE SCALE
you
make me
PHOTO CELL
TOPOSCOPIC ACTIVITY = FRONTAL C/S frequency 9·74'
(EYES CLOSED)
FURIOUS
SPECTRUM ANALYSIS
B
POSITION OF LANDSCAPE
DISTRIBUTION OF DISTURBANCE
Oh
Shut up
(OSCILLOSCOPE FROM ABOVE)
– eye movement 7"
– co-ordinated eye movement 19"
YOU MAKE ME
FURIOUS
REGION: acute vision
RETINA: coarseness
BRAIN: cone (receptor)

Dilemma of the Meno

When Meno asks the question 'Can virtue be taught?' Socrates replies to his shame that he has no knowledge of virtue at all. Encouraging Meno to explain what virtue is, Socrates quickly points out that all his examples are a multiplicity of various qualities named virtue. Applying the metaphor to the swarm, Socrates can point out that Meno, like a person who breaks a pot, has made a singular into a plural. Unity can only announce itself in fragments.

INSTRUCTIONS FOR PERFORMANCE

The piece consists of sixteen sections, each notated on a separate index card. An identical pile of sixteen cards is presented to each performer.

The cards are now shuffled and performed separately and sequentially by all performers simultaneously. A performer is free to 'think' about the card – in other words, to allow a moment of planning before performance-interpretation. These moments will register in the piece as silences; however, a uniform silence by all performers should be avoided.

When all sixteen sections are performed (or, alternatively, *should* all sixteen cards be performed) then the cards are reshuffled and the performance carries on.

Duration: indeterminate but should not exceed sixteen minutes.

1
Hang back on another's sounds and listen to any other noise around you. Respond but PLEASE don't imitate.

2
Attempt footprints across some pads and mix this with recognized nostalgia.

3
Attempt a history of music in thirty-three seconds.

4
Where 'worm' equals Mozart and 'leopard' equals Coltrane, play 'iguana'.

5
A thudding clump imagined sounded.

6
Enclosure … dialogue … thrown embouchure. Time: seventeen seconds.

7
Make your sounds a perfect shadow to the others that you hear.

8
Play members of the audience as notes and phrases of your own choice. Be inspired by their association.

9
Bow this one or blow it: a surgical disturbance from 'osmosis' to 'capillary'.

10
Mention in your sounds 'weather', its laziness as space suggesting this as ventriloquism.

11
Your staccato against the other's cacophony.
Your peach melba against their pork chop.
Your xerox against their parchment.
Your photograph against their crossword puzzle.

12
Sounds across: 'environment'.
Sounds down: 'atmosphere'.

13
Create a soundscape of
  a) an Acapulco barbershop
  b) a Dallas Esso station

14
Interpret freely the following passage: 'The distribution urges agitation and south of the park is a sleeve. Screech facilitates birth of a song in Nepal. Bugle pills as arms arriving at the body's problem. Smell is the odour of top secrets probating. The nod from the head is full of language. Socialism changes its sweat by way of the cratered urgings of a face.'

15
Try to reproduce exactly all the sounds that you hear.

16
In case of an exit please use the nearest emergency.

LONGER POEMS

from *The Abstract Ruin*

In the mouth of the cave, in speech
known as Grotte du Renne, at Arcy-sur-Cure
in the valley of Yonne two thousand postholes
set in a rough oval

whilst at Stellmoor
the reindeer are lashed to stones and thrown into
the pool, retreating ice as the vegetation changes
wood chambered and solid wheeled before Telepinus
the telephone at Lake Sevan
donkey bones in the Osmankayasi cemetery
abbreviated water at the Thames head
tributaries to the greater
through the lower-lying land and the Rhine's
North Sea.

From Bath around the estuary down through Lydney
into Caerwent   Aque Sulis fanam dei Nodontis
Venta Silurum.   Three of them came
from Lypiatt Park giving birth to twins
from Chedworth   as the five sunk dots
of her body.

Fragments from Crocolana   lost speech
in dykes   a small bronze in her left hand
the birds of Riannon   corn in her lap
from Wiltshire   over the map
to Saskatchewan the left hand emerges   insular
the goddess   the foot   of a grey wolf.

Her sexuality is evident in breasts
waiting for the fight to begin   limbs in the air
the limits that immobilize her
brains from a second teat and spilling out
the paucity of pottery

and their cries all around in the shape of
white, hornless, red-eared heifers, birds

shattering the eyes black, slippery
eels alighting in the form of crows
on a bramble bush   crows above all
from tail to neck
horses.

The same tradition carried to the teir bronn
of Gyenn   triple breasted white tracked and virgin
eight inches high

the ornamental wand from Lanchester
links the face-pot to the zoomorphic aspect
of the horned woman whose rivers
are not snakes but eternal wells behind the deep
the many-shaped girl preserving
the traditions of the birds   the plain
they flock before her a "collection"
a yolk of silver between them
at Emain

they alight on the loch linked together
by a chain of red gold
the motif of a sleep-inducing syntax
sentenced to the signing they appear
misunderstood

in a later manuscript   chained swans
a test for chastity.

In Urnfield the horse-doag or flesh-fork
tongue dissimilar   analog Celtic   breast
against the raven's beak
in the house of a certain man
in the words of a menu from Halmadry

A drunk woman in the tradition of
"bird"   Nantosuelta   winding river through
the Irish group   crossing dry-shod in martial
capacities all
the Battle Crows   echoes of the raven figurine

cover on the Linwood jar and the mallet god
of Altrier   corvidic associations
with a sexual union across species
with the swift sooty woman   big mouthed at both ends
and squinting
the two paps of Morrigan
the word badbh
committed to writing.

London   from Lugus   a raven god invoked in the plural
for all purposes   the Celtic word is
"pen"   meaning "head"
                    you carry art as thought in it
across the waters with the music on your back
as the wooden wisdom leisure dreams the Dream
of Rhonabwy   flight in flocks   with the poet
glyphed the careless ornithologist of groupings
who causes birds to fly   over the speech lines
to the images at Senlis   iconographies
of ears and hearts   new nouns from the Norse
speech in the raven's bill.

Sunrise   birds described as
"coming across water"   and as they land

the feathers fall off revealing
their white bodies on racist purple heads
gold beaks eat

the berries around them putting music
into their talk of eggs

their nouns.

Daybreak   the vernacular cranes
and the singing birds   prototypes

decorated with a horse's head
grazing the grass and herbs to the very roots

their art.

At Karanovo   clay models of chairs   benches
couches   precede the deductions for fallow land
and the seven bushels from classical times
in an architecture of mud brick
the Tells up to   the Danube
Budapest millennium of postholes
and the beddin-trench and loess soils
scrub cover over lake reed bed   the main
valley bottom

sunrise over a copper-using culture
northwest from the radio carbon datings
the palisaded cattle kraal at Anlo
the battle axe in a single grave
symbolic egrets in   external gable-end pargeting
birds above the city tumulus   a janiform tense
of pastoral declension   reaching the timber mortuary
in the forest steppe the beak
of a great bird double
spiral headed on a hat pin   through a fish eye
on the slab from Easterton in Roseisle.

The Tisza comes to an end at the site of
a wheeled draught-vehicle   (eccentricities of the early
settlers in a loan-word meaning "spoke")   the wheel
ending speech in the small forms of its nouns
repetitive and radial   half skeletal and Pleistocene
at Vercovicium where the owl appeared
conjunction with the bovine heads

the planes of trefoil at Ggantija
stone built finding razor blades in bogs
the large eyes on a fashion for shaving
cultist public smoothness   gold terminals
for talk   the broken flakes   the White Sea
and Lake Onega into south Siberia
before arrival of
"the human forms".

Hair – suggested by means of bands
running from back to front where
the lower part of face has disappeared
and the double heads depict the power
of twins   vestigial horns in the form of
small circles incised   the nostrils
dominate the scene   a huge mucus shadow cast
across the murus gallicus

the narrow eyes reflecting continental
traditions   local archaicisms of escarpment
of farmsteads seen vertically   still in situ
the bronze circle of Carlisle inside a coin
beside magnetic
consonants of   total weight.

Maponus Corstopitum   Boa Island
into the caravan   the harness of horse
the head
on the bird beak burning the cart as
a pattern woven from the voice
a thread of women fighting in   dark brown buff
green and leather caps with massed bronze studs
indications as to   curls and ringlets
changes in the conversation to   a rough square
and the art of spinning on an upright loom.

By deep indentures in the stone
are cut the narrow eyes   shown on the bodies
buried at Staple Howe   a palisade
the hill of chalk   down to the ears the slightly
parted lips   at Kyberg   a cruder style
of sea and sky and heads
placed on the relevant bodies

up the natural slopings of argument
analyses   reductions to a hill fort
Erriapus without horns   the loss of timbre
horizontal timber lacing modified
and packed with clay
face   faeces phallic   body without neck
great heads bearing talk in rapid fragments.

They had never known a city
only page   and shifting pronouns   street gangs
through the utterance and times

when they were men   with voices
limbs in common with
humanity

but on the frontiers of the verb
they stopped

moral barriers erected
patterns of lies produced

horizons on each side   vendettas
non-literate ambiguities

in Gallia Comata   among the gabbled plinths
of speech
unclassical grey granite   mood of how

the letters slaughtered men

as slow as dust accumulates

slow dust in us.

From Kentum through the Satem
the end of Tocharian in the documents of Hesiod
Herodotus at Athens in an Attic branch
the four tesseras in Ionian   into the Koine
all the long migrations through the place names
pronouns in speech apart   the bodies of the walkers
journeys through the Celtiberian   destroying Delphi,
Rome, the region of Galatia, abandoning the sites at
Rhine, Main, Melibokus and Worms
the Churwelsh heard in Rhaetia, forms of the tongue in
Breton, the Ogham sticks a melting down
into Germanic time ladders
warped   northeastern shores of
Elbe   where speech cannot move the   deich to the taihun.

Codex argenteus   cover of the moon   a gothic script
in silver channels to the Visigoths   more rapidly
the mainstream   except the word for   six
the basic words in mouths   the colour of the teeth
in nouns   Uralic lisp dividing at the Volga.

Semantic fadings in South Africa   blank spaces
cut out   time appears in a specific number   the word
"thousand" said in seconds   the symbol to conundrum
countless beavers   letters on the faces of women
bodies of type   implanted vowels for their movement
fading pictures in the phones   a sequence lost
to live on   hebdomenda ennenenta
yan tan tethera oethera pimp five
six sethera lethera hovera covera dik ten
eleven yan a dik tan a dik – bumpit fifteen
sixteen yan a bumpit – figitt twenty.

Flute Spring   Soyal   the roots of vibration
from the belly to the heart   the hands divinity   side corn
parrot   bear instead of kiva   sundial in the southeast
corner   huicksi   the breath of life spoke in an instant
aspirant to spiral up through
ritualistic paraphernalia of a Two Horn leader
durative suffix   -ta   the crescentive form of moon
in -iwma   segmentive verb   eagle feathers on the road
life a stem without suffix   toes toward
the blue circle of the sky   in the tense of the simplex
to the south side and moving east towards the phenotypes
around throats   torn bumped dug cut written
"secondarily" "it passes"   "it goes"   extending out
beyond the Colorado River   a dark purple light in the north
through space toward a different verb in Canada.

a star above the earth inside a man
inside the pudendum of a mountain
thought in his head inside
the picture of his head inside a bowl

a mouth beside water among legs having feet upon
the picture of a bird to represent a
mushen

fish among the horns on heads of oxen
in a field of barley
one stalk alone

pronounced "she"

The open vowels in the lungs stay huge
grammatical particles in food a turkish grammar
with semitic syntax

marking the place of the tongue in dialect
the rare use of care in any votive   inscription

burial mounds in fields
laid waste   dedicated (boulder)   reinscribed

the new canals in Sumer, in the mind
his love of ships
kinship, fellowship, worship
trapped within the shushgal net   a suhur fish
beneath the steles   name a man as long as a day
existed plantino cedar on the eaves
crushed onion by the mace head   returning from the
boundary ditch to build
a well   as well as   harbours.

Between a door socket   corpse in
the chariot house   inscribed the date of the orchard that
he planted   breeze across the quays towards the ferryboats
at Girsu   the rations of his quda-priest   a later tax on
cucumbers and barley barely rested in the reeds
pens among onions   the patches of salt   felled trees in
head shapes listening to bread bake blind men
seizing mushdu   boatmen seizing donkeys
sheep among the gaba-lambs beer in the cemetery
certain blind labourers in texts   an ordinance

a former name brought dead to Lagash in a sila of butter
down the pure canal, whose "heart"
is bright, bringing
clear water to coerce him.
Closed off roads above land
laid waste their city and destroyed its walls
bereaved of seed   has given him   the house   his city
to the palace   stocks of wood upon his hands
to name the heart this ground of pain
feet on the neck and a scorpion in copper
brought before them
where the big men stabilize the questioning
make known their words   enumerate the cities
uninhabited   putting eyes upon him
nothing to say

of the boat   brought down, moored
in good condition   from the sea of Magan
where he terrified the Ensi

days of need making   the earth

fall kernels.

They were the settlers here the pioneers
who took
page for their land.

They knew what they saw when
they saw heads wrapped
in blankets.

They were told how their eyes
would burn
if they looked.

Their speech   a common code
of sneezes gargles
a curious wink of the eye.

They hold hands when they leave
and on the margins of some shoreline
kneel for minutes in a private speech.

If a sky turns grey their hands
go cold and follow
their parents to the station.

When the grammar arrives they come back
in six weeks for three hours
at a time.

They stay outside words
in warm ink or milk
and soon arrive

at land or speech

or in America.

15
tent stance Moldavia
19
Middle Paleolithic
36
upper structure in cave
47
reaping knives
8
singled roomed agglomerated Thessaly
69
mud walled sixth fifth anthropomorphic
25
defended
176
promontory gable end
84
Chalandriani Cortaillod
366
Tripolye
859
Stubbendorf on the head pin
53
Hagar Qim
972
Courjeonnet
559
brigadunum
15
magus
89
Heuneberg
46

past the zero point
and the cessation

of the energy field from
the motion of

particles

there can be no time.

Put as a verb inside a space
it's called a head

a movement meant along a birth toward
a history she described as

looking out into a distance
where the body walks as pronoun.

There is no place
which is the heart

hears us leave the features so distorted
sadness is a face upon

someone who has walked very far from
being happy.

They have called it the Dorian invasions
birth of the mind-space analog I with
continuities in pottery
Gilgamesh not 650 but almost 1700 BC places the outline
of the pronoun before a complex succession of migrations.

The rest of that fact is this:

that a coward is not someone who is afraid
but one whose heart beats loudly
and whose heart is the vessel
boldness is not put into

that the word is thumos, phrenes, noos, psyche
kradie, ker and eter

so when a voice tells kill a man
kill a man
you never get a headache

but Mr Jaynes said poems are rafts clutched at
by men drowning in
inadequate minds

this happens when cramp in the guts becomes
cramp in the cortex

and poetry is sitting close to pretension
with stress on lapels
at which point
the readers have no overcoats
to generate this new conception of

the garment.

If i am dead all the time in my father
then i live all the time in my mother

ironies apart the action
to be multiple understanding what you read

i'm reading to stand under and resist
you understand and take apart yourself

i refuse to understand put the I in
I-rony dead or alive i need to be

earn what i am foreclose
book the living pages you inherit

all the voice that makes up Other
putting sounds in mouth i have no need of

words your head so when you
know in understand i know a part of

you is taken over not yourself
the reading taking over you

the reader I does not read (need)
point of view(s) consideration:

every writer dreams of reading
it: the action i've escaped

you write you write avoid the reading
counter capacities when every You must be

a reader I the reader am the writer
that writes inside the action text of

a voice within wrists the reading of
a confined writing all the time that you're here

and i'm somewhere else allowing you to write
inside the act of reading

do not understand   i the trap am the
contrast   there is nothing to read to be

i make up what you take apart   whatever
else   of privilege   you have no honour being
a listener   i listen to you listening
listen in lend a writing to a reading
this called obsession
when you never read   you always become and so
i write a history to myself   telling my life
to one who tells it   back to home the self is
a chance to survive   have never known you
always sensed this i
find another before you find
yourself in that way

meet me again when you've forgotten me
counter memory   lose me to find yourself
i shall be there   you shan't know it
we shall be together   that you won't
know that

you will understand.

Whitman said it:
cost $10,000 then some pickin bastard chopped it down
within a radius of eighteen miles

it is the mushroom sonnet Weaver spoke of
working a while at

building, that
through the lattice stop-action
of,
      maybe three more important factors

one, being the
stress which in land
creates split up
heaval, quake, which the poem takes
merely asyntactic
two,
        how do these two link
up
     (without some risk to soma, beating, heart,
              disease i mean
              what happens to the breath
              if we arrange an arc around the words
              corona

              isotopes in basho

                        (plop

                           plus the body
              ultrasonic in a brevity identical with

three,
        what means completion
                  (getting away with three-dimensional
       structures as an answer to the question

acoustic

holography   as stonehenge (cd be)
more specifically, how
the light flows through the ears when

a poem's lace.

Targ goes on:
"we may hypothesize
that increasing the complexity of
the observation system for an event
makes the event increasingly
sensitive
to "observer" effects'

so through the eye to drop
the complex control out of line, stanza,
radish on a plate from ground
line soft
of earth the
psychic muscles
that are carrots, printouts

of any kind form
image "rehabilitize" (his word) the voice within
the "real"   run seaweed two and back, go back absence
of an eye.

the slope of the thing in speech is
the measure of its own slide

waking to the sound of retuned
engines in the street
a worn transmission
the eyes clogged with a marginal
sleep, what makes the eyelids
a terror, an analog

levels of usage gone   at eight   grown thin
inside the room

and in the hesitancies
of the door observe

how the house is ventilation
moulin
or moorline   in a vast and rapid wave of
heath from Penistone to Manchester
fog   around the mirror
working distances, tricking space into
touch

of the part Utriusque Cosmi
Historia
the *Mnemonica sive Ars reminiscendi*
by John Willis

the Proust collage above
my head … repositories

formed for the mind
re: memories

there being a bldg at one level
the front wall omitted so that
i look into it through the two halves
formed
by the column near the rear wall

two different loci
and entering both within a different voice
holding the mind
as similar substance

greene curtains to reminde of
mowers to cutte medow

grasse   golde ceiling   a memory of
business, which is to say
your duty is this day to make
enquiries re: the price of seede

wheate in the market, that — in
a different roome

the journal open purposefully
held apart by a paperweight at 28–29 January

for the thinges charged in Memory by day
are to be lodged
deposited at least before sleepe

thinges charged by night

deposited after.

and the words to be as columns
fixed firm in a strong
place
    to be observable on every side
and around them
the parts   set at good distance
one from another.

this
being metope
whiteness of sound

is de compositione
spaces for words

(verborum)
to go behind themselves
beyond the word

connection held to be
deceit

a weakness graphed upon
the thin ice of the grammarian

fooling the skaters' lines.

three in the morn
and kettle boiling
tired eyes

a blot on oak
makes composite

rhyme   insistent to connect

so Fludd:

> that knowledge worketh as an arrowe
> up through the ceiling to the skyes
> and starres and through them

on to sephiroth
the trinitarian apex viewed from the seat of it
in memory at
the head's back.

It was silence made the supper vanish.

We stare at an explosion
then the cup appears.

The cup's designed to hold something.
It's the cup you make for this
task of containing.

The cup is what stands "forth"
and it's there where you are.

You fill a cup with tea
and the pouring filling it flows in
the cup. You say

it's the emptiness does all the holding
and the cup you've made is not
the cup you make do this
you only shaped the shape to make the emptiness
and emptiness which pouring fills.

In the silence all the sound
is built around
the tea remains forgotten
and in the effective features of the cup
what the cup contains is bound to escape.
It holds

by taking what we pour into it.

We pour in exhausted from the swim
and ask for scones and tea
an outpouring upon the surface
of a discourse.

Tea time becomes
the poured gift of this pouring out
the shaped shape remains

and what it holds is it.

from *The Abstract Ruin*

Immiseration Theses

A legend in the Barddas
of a bald boat   Argo Navis
sailed up from the sky above Phoenicia
with the sun on it
dumping anchor at Prescelly
in the Welsh mountains
time of the earth maid   Morwyn Ddu
Black Virgin of solstice through her heliacal puberties
at Lammas changed her name
to Tynghedwen Dyrriath
fury's holy fortune   by the top of stone
anchored near the sky
bwncath
in flight
over the tops of
Mynydd Morvil

and so it goes if myth has its place
bald as you are beautiful
but missing the surplus value
in its articular forms of profit, interest,
ground rent u.s.w.
not the sun's annual path through all
the useful modes of production
in which it's expended
as a money form, born
not of an aging sun in the vir obscurus
but out of hegemony, logic and history
at the vernal spring priced
right out of the market.
Bryn Cyssegr Fans or
the brown cows' eager fannies
are equally the facts at hand and organized
inside of problematics   Foucault
not hinting at Glastonbury
central to concerns of Marx's
disappearance of the moon in class struggle
known to the Druids as
a methodology for primitive accumulation.

Important fact that power
no longer lodged in profit accumulation
and production but
in code control of the demand advanced from
the standpoint of class becoming
the strategic disarticulation.
Who owns the structures of parole manipulates
the talk along the ley lines
toward the Canons of Proportion.

The quote being "the sun
as the eagle flies over it"
and it being the Tor
Tor being something other than
a subject's history outside the fertilizing
needs of a collage

verbinding

fetish.

Of the star groups mentioned
only Engels configured in the caer of workers
on a sliding scale
totality in this respect at the dialectical nexus
as the hair on a man's head
is his profit
the Concrete says Marx is
the concrete because it is a synthesis
spoke across an ecliptic band of 25,920 years
reclining   as it were   in the last star
in the final sky   not a sky above you said as "sky"
but that relation of finality from cloud to cloud
moving in spaces not sequels equals:
economics does not treat of things
but of the relation between persons
bound to things on the rock of commodity

the Pumpsaint Temple built towards the end of Taurus
its door a bull's eye being the eye of Bel
the single cyclops of a sun (Baal)
supporting Lukács's idea of a complex reification
while the mindless specialist lets his problem turn
into the general history of solutions

Bible = Fetish = The Political Economy of Gods

it is equally the proletariat against itself
at various sites above sea level

May Day meridian charging bulls
and rams reclining   Brezhnev out of Aires
earlier proof of a Tauric thrust in Lenin
and so   to the mathematization of all method
facticity in cold war metaphysics figured in
the bodies of two different bulls
a round table for summits   where Arthur sounds
Arddir   old Welsh for "gardener"   clinching
the theory of a soviet Eden at Camelot
quest palimpsest around the thirty-mile circumference
to the cup itself   the graal
at Park Wood's heteronomous power of Hegel
heats life love in a cup
acquired in the exchange of every thought
that seeks difference
to devise a unity from dead ends
splinters   that landscape
of a Temple to the Stars.

The air would have been clear
for Bela Khun
circa 2700 BC   less forestation
which would sharpen connotations as far as the eye
could predict.

Rioting in Mansfeld led on 16 March 1921
to the intervention of the Reichswehr
on the following day the GCP called
for open insurrection   a micro form in miniature
at Lascaux abstracted into star-lore hunting ways
to give at night   by fire
our first movies.

Tantae molis erat is Marxist Latin
and significant to data that affects
the hills around the megalithic figures.
Fetish placed behind the central shaft of stones
forms a perfect polygon of need   frictionless
and formal it is realized
to gold marked myth   and to rationalize the bronze
the horse becomes a boat
outside that economic fatalism lodged in Bernstein
and Tugan-Baranovsky's dream of
clean Kapital without wit   to evolve conjoined
and capping   Yns-Witran   first of Western Maypoles
axis on the equinoxial line   down
the ship's mast
out of Minehead.

By her best name
she was called   Acca Laurentia
offered in the shedding of correct wine from milk

at a place called Velabrum   but as others say
it was the tumblers of great rivers
issuing her honour in two children   Mussolini's
gift to Canada

christened Capital and Labour
but the wrong face was speaking them
they made their legs carry bundles
of grass tied to the ends of buried poles
magnetic north fixed where the matter sped to myth
(unprofitable parents) when the Hitwaw
brought them crumbs
carried the crummes to putte all in theyre mouthes

and the rough trough by the riverbank
bound with plates of copper letters hardly
words.

The ditch in their ceremonies is called the World
and around the world is traced
the compass of the city they will build.

Where they decide to make a gate
they take a ploughshare   draw
to leave a space unbroken.

Geometry thus accompanies them bisecting
the marriages of those
who lead their brides over bridges
laughing in tokens
to spin wool and stay away from the husband's door.

They appear by way of flying birds
which tells how the sky is always the way you move
towards a politic poisoning of your children.

If they survive   the report goes
how what vanished was replaced in the grave
by a stone   with
its dry lights flying from the body.

from *The New Work*

(in an act) "the way that four folds into three" (your reduction of corners) "that simple elimination of terms" (the staple payment meaning a written form with the metal of inscription rusted) "could there be otherwise" (the mention of rainbows on a page) "accountancy" (the flow of forms) "format" (signature) "event taking space and turning that into speech" (space) "Seurat in 1880" (possibly what the gaps are) "lesser things incised between the meanings" (ruptured) "november: what a painting ought to be" (cuts if abrasion) "tenacity of slide" (closing the gap to microfiche the logic) "a thickness in speech" (text as so much texture) "the term veil" (to throw up through the phrase) "you threw it" (out in an act) "the gaps inside de-moebius" (demolish an art and you recreate a theology) "preoccupations with garbage" (the cultural underface) "on the island itself" (the fluid on dismissal) "discharge" (surplus flows) "you notice how the hudson outside charlie's window" (as of air) "this leap" (as you no doubt now are aware of) "divisionism and the reader's point" (what it means to say puncture) "the holes escribe circumference to emphasize a praxis at the margins" (we liberate a sphere) "the flattened cone reappears a mound" (a rowing trip on the seine) "test to limits clearly indicating nothing" (a marshy inlet) "of words inside the outside revolution" (context) "the walls repressed" (immaterial mingling of) "pigments" (sex in a fluid machine) "construct of an instrument to circulate" (flow/ex/tension) "to dare exceed the content" (how much can any language stand) "intimiste" (the final crayon portrait) "a grave beneath oaks" (forgetting you efface and effacing you let the forms stand for themselves) "be carriers" (in the mural of industrial suburbs what is to blame) "the crime of surplus inability to exceed exceed" (a signature in memory) "recollection of the fragments" (even dragged an onion-domed church into it) "the nervous economy of statement in outline" (fill in the diagram feel the thickness of the book) "to lose wit" (herms expansive) "boundless seed" (emblematic talk fastidiously held to) "open the studio" (sex as an action of assemblage) "of hues which fail to fall into place" (bricolage) "you put your tongue in my cunt and someone else's prick up my ass" (form is whatever is at hand and out of that comes system) "sources of the nerve to curiosity" (workable vaginas) "a lozenge of pure and universal admiration" (to liquefy desire by passage through fatigue) "among the trees" (the alien man turned machine) "connection in communication without identity" (it's the place i always meet you) "you'll remember to act in the way we talked of" (melting the pronouns) "sails playing the part assigned previously to the angles of roofs" (you make me make room for others) "new places where pictures could hang" (public executions in the novels) "that long thin severed tongue" (bare backs in profile) "wherever there is light and shade the shadow will be coloured" (blank pertinacity) "a slow-motion film"

> Here the child, if at a distance from
> the coast, should be told what is meant
> by different countries; what a ship is,
> and what is meant by a sailor.

"I have been I'm afraid I am very much at" (determinant) "The receipt of the letter I felt prompts my remonstrances" (acceleration) "I really quite harassed the idea" (focus) "My illness of wish I want to hide from you" (analogical) "I do assure as well as ever" (dissolutive) "I regard to do assure I will not to study hard in a day" (synthesis) "Of riding I will and permits of this circumstance" (continuational) "I found attacks me to drink wine" (trajectivistic) "I shall come to not write him" (lineal) "I arranged it all to be a disadvantage" (opacity) "I have it seems a gentleman's illness occasioned by motives" (hieroglyphic) "Hard study for I cannot write more"

emante transcription opportunity of not not writing but relax relax and let as if on a heap of flour bags the fourteen pigs delivered at seven transcriptional extremity phenomenon occurrent substasis the very bad of any scribbling letting the line extensive immodest archetypical unseen

The voice of (explode) festivals.
The mathematical study (summarize) of satisfaction.
The (structure) auditory nerve structure.
The commencement (explicit) of a man beginning monday.
The memory of cloisters (dispersion) by light.

The young man (impulse) with an old face.
The former (articulate) friend of someone in particular.
The way to (signified) walk through the day.
The inability (expansion) to help out.
The ingestion of bread and (processual) peep out of his grave.
The speech (vertical) of an old but independent man.
The length of (vestigial) a competitor.
The choice (problematic) to beg for help.
The presence of (implicative) synonyms.

KEEP A WOOD WITH RABBITS IN IT. OBSERVE WHAT IS NOT THROWN AWAY. LOOK FOR THE WORD fluid. HOLD A BOOK OR ANYTHING ELSE BETWEEN THE CANDLE AND A WALL. NEXT FEEL VERY GLAD TO FIND THAT THINGS WHICH YOU HAVE READ IN THAT BOOK ARE LIKE REAL THINGS AND THAT WHAT YOU HAVE READ IS OF USE TO YOU.

And the reasons blind are why the ways seem right. The enemies our eyes see die. The wind. Things that are called among. Direction. The word in the shape of a pomegranate. All of our waters among expressions. Unsullied use. The coverage of all parts. Effacement from a shepherd's tent. As any man might come out ancient and received. Traditions of content. No other names but place.

The image (concept) sees itself (seize it is Capitalism devouring that way its own tractability as an ideological mass becoming energum, circularities, the flow of exchangeable parts the words it moves on moves across "appears (that way) to disappear" intelligible known exchanges, lines, units, the coded calyx of music all there is of clarity at this speed a tumbler full of a liquid falling the child becoming the bird in post-ovidian transform the mutual growth in soil that can't match "calibre" "attenuation" "chaos (from gas)" the shapes of such things as sacrifice thingness. Signs toward types but only the shadow's later light left in Plato.

A lexeme plus an aridity. "Deserta". The colour of mistakes. Earth: a verbal surface as a passive noun. Resistant to the pressure of presence: leaves … in fall … doesn't happen.

Trees in song
(no) "rose"
(no) "cheek"
(no) "image"

ideology: weight

allegory:
figuration, at/
indentical level of

consciousness
(Corbin)

Consciousness: (relatively) late linguistic symptom.

I DO NOT REMEMBER. IT IS NOT RECALLABLE.
I DO NOT MOVE INTO A STATE OF RECOGNITION.
IT IS UNKNOWN. I AM IGNORANT OF IT.

"Reader" (person)
The "Collective (consumer)" ("People".

He writes to devalue writing in order to repossess as humanly as possible THE SIGN.

vesperemberaleremelan

a space the object leaves

the problems lines might bring to a line of preference.

skeletal americas irrelevant nearness into
TOPOI

networks (Cathage) integuments (Toulouse)   a lithic spasm
traced as far
as Spain
lozenge, dogtooth, velocity, Helcos,
syllogistic swirls held disagreements
denial of cells space syntax equivalent to a gaoled hemoglobin
placement into mathemes, fingers, names, lips, gerunds,
purpose,
a field force for details to be
in part

molecular edgings to the eyes

inscriptional precedence inside folds
of page (signature)
of tissue (into lymph)

flows bringing holes without sounds
semantics to an empty shape "isn't it writing"

skein in bars.   megaphones a bat threw.

impression. detachments. post-individualisms. separations.
psyches. grammars. subjectivities. fissures. languages.
propositions. presences. suggestions. actiants. beliefs.
humanizations. signs. shifts. relationships. extensions.
interrogations. domains. orders. redundancies. declarations.
graphisms. sports. modules. possibilities. intersections. vectors.
as a gram. significant. diagonal. automatic tunings
"to memorize".

de loop "D".   (l i g h t) an.

a. gram.

Pythagorean facilitation of development of music qua referential paradigm, common (as destination) to all of the arts. i.e., MUSIC not an art form ... more a device for encoding a reading of the megafiche (nature) ... music invents a reading of the codes of forms & structures.

MUSIC IS A READING.

a memory like eh movie.   work and its space.   a labour.   a relaxation.

ask any armdiscern   discernsizeice   waltz   azure

"sort of an ordinary dark"

perceptible as fugue structure(s), tonalities, as polyphonic morphologies and monophonic message.

after the dark we watched until the light
reappeared above a hill in a sentence
of a book

many objects from the one perspective angle

simultaneity / metaphor:

Metaphor packs tightly all objects into one word and makes you see them one inside the other in an almost miraculous way.

Tesauro: *Il Cannocchiale Aristotelico.*

1920: We renounce in a line, its descriptive value; in real life there are no descriptive lines, description is an accidental trace of man on a thing, it is not bound up with the essential life and constant structure of the body.

... but i suppose what really interests me
is the paradoxical mobility of signs; their presence as
absences; their destination in a non-arrival.
From Thales (water) to Derrida
(absence) is gap:
(   ) Zukofsky's air ?

The history of each being closer. But the words (give your etched. recessionalities. old ghost in unread folio) "to (etc)" "your eyes (that sea) BEYOND THEM ... the portability ... no echo ...

The Heroes of Labour are seated in their Boxes at the Theatre

as the FIRST TRACTOR arrives in the Village

a Policewoman is helping a CHILD to cross the street

and the light from the HORIZON falls upon the Deer's Belly.

c.   shty.   fld.   nch.   izo.   dyn.   rks.

and to have is to snatch from the moon with a hand through the quality of a power in action
(line space to mark perception phases)

the noun "in effect" its limits
convenience. sympathy. emulation.
magnetic values of a currency. dispersals.
or MOON from "ma" (the measurer). the trigonometry of
Reich.

YOU MAKE THE STYLE THE FROZEN MOVEMENT
(Fuller's knot upon a certain resistance.

the stretched legs denote "progress" but signs converge in
a circular world.

THEY SPOKE OF THE THOUSANDS DEAD AS A DOUBLE
IMPRECISION IN THE DIGITS. REUTER PHOTOGRAPHER
VOMITING SAID AMERICAN OFFICIAL: I could explain the
whole problem to you quite simply but it would take several
hours and a (& a) blackboard.

brightness. the tulip on hand. a cresset of sun spokes. before
a tiled message on a wall. where the sea is heard to whisper a
place not a name. "that you are hunting boar or gazelle"
(crenatures on shingles) "they are all asleep and are melody"
"they are the ones who care" (philological transplant thematic
rhyme with early travelogs"

a flow back. closed breath section.

“over acres” “knolled” “a pen in energy” “in and in”
“mentioning/the specifications of the/fish/-bone” “a continuity”

“don’t” “throat” “throw/it” “the oak” “as other deaths”
“a white beard over tweed” “and yesterday the props collapsed”

“the neighbourhood of voices” “enumerated subdivision”
“the cult of the house in rooms” “on language”

“to what is gathered up”
“killing 78”

“in a guide to culture” “pointless rattlesnakes”
“all along a highly patterned permutation”

“complexed”
“inroote”

“his auditor considers” “clusters my favourites my”
“whole collections of dreams”

“the upward drift of the singing as we walked toward the sea”
“the sea and the sky and the (romantic) run against both of them”

“naturally you’ll test their solidity by general principles”
“and dry silk and even your shoulder not soldier”

“the far shop listens to the farthest shore”
“not ship”

“climb hills then sit on em”
“rivers to the east and grey trout streams”

“lotus in the green clear drink”
“his gangrenous leg had made him very thirsty”

“the middle moon of three of a kind”
“schooled blindly”

“whole shoals of them” “solved his sewage problems”
“bleaching the edges” “clams down yr throat” “dissolution”

"along the bridge with no trace of hypotenuse"
"the fields that surfaced" "fish hooks quite become a table"

"a campaign for extensive culverts"
"the thousand roads below the watermeads"

"the aim of technique" "the sunlight that flies bring"
"sign directive to an accusation" "MONSTRATI DIGITO"

"imagine the concept of circle as a figurative extension of the ear"
"the word means music"

if. them. and. as. of. with. state. though. close. which.
i. he . an . a . it . at . i .

1760:

over
had the foot only survived (had been discovered)
the swelled veins (the strained sinews) and the
irregular motion the irregular motion

and the motion (irregular) of the muscles
("muscles") might have led us into a con-
ception of those tortures which are so
divinely expressed in the face in the face
so wonderfully marked throughout the whole
body a hole

see Nollekens

fuse char t r are in je s t
FOR FUSELI CHARACTERS ARE "the luminous objects" OF ACTION
o use act in us f act

DEAD COLOUR + TIMELESSNESS

taking things by their centres not their lines.
looks up. goes over to east facade. looks out.
elevated horizon. passion on facial area. arena
of oration. correleation. sculptural tension.
the stereography of random units (nature destroyed) "collage to free up all that energy etc." "self-interference which might lead to a precise graphic of same" "connected contours through cola"

outlines to a consequence. NO CONTENT.
NO FUNCTION.
NO DETERMINATION.
ermin

it is hard to alter your love of shadows (feel the cool breeze)
entangled in the economic system(s) of consumption.
WE EAT ALL THE WORDS BUT THE WORDS THEMSELVES ARE NEVER THERE.

for if our bodies were overcharged then the electrical
atmospheres repel each other
spheres
it is the nervousness of fluid draws the practice into print.
(Vietnam) (shoulder length) (the image of self as a galvanic transparency against a dark backdrop of ... unknown ... imperative ... synchrony.)

It becomes the false position. The possession of robes. A rhetoric of office. Disgust. As if it were true. Discussed the distance attained in the denial of any real world the "real" being the real "out there" considering the refusal to possess that kinda reality inside a rhetoric of the natural but rather to situate in a language outside the operations of all power structures and all epistemic ideologies. There are then again those words that possess no light a chance at change a glance illuming it the evanescent cause of something left a residue to speak of in a man's voice to cover up a man render the face the most naked face there ever was.

Attached etcetera importance to the inessentials. Quintessence being the customary science of the silence. The full opinions of taking operations underground into the praxis of the one idea condemning yourself for a fault like Milton which you strove to amend. Clause effects. The obscurity of armies swallowing tea in oceans defining your poetry as the operations of the seventy-eight intercepting surfaces of planes and solids analyzed in all the phonic events that ever came out in the replacement of semantics by semiotics. There are no meanings only paths across them. Paths carry you according to the general rubric of pathology, vectors through, between, among, because of writing irrelevant to speech: the general domain of the IMPRINT. Sonnets, scarifications, burns, stamps, odes, novels, tattoos. "THINGS" that cause our general movement to the thought of "THINKS" the only viable and syncretic disrespect of everything. A writing of and in the constant habit of displacement and presence. Orifices. Teguments. In the little flat we called Munich. Decisions regarding the natural displacement of LACE in a victorian description of seduction. The preparation for coffee to be poured out of an etym: KAFA. Pores before time. Any space among bravura. A sodomite stucco. Dreams commencing with the raising of proper problems. Memory of Ladders at Attempts. Escalations (from escaliers) through those attempts to wear out indefatigable blows (critically) the polysemic sciences ... performance art: the shunting of body into freight-seme networks.

April. the writing written. it is everything it stands for in a world that stands apart from all our efforts to impart significance to it (daddy why won't you answer me ?) as any other it appears to be. Can stand for nothing. EASY WRITING.

i want you to know this. i want you to put it. i want a name from you. i want you to choose an identity yourself. i want a man from it. i want a mask on you. i want to know the purpose. i want to hear the sound of your words. i want a face that tells. i want word's weight. i want it wait it watches. it image. it seen. it ideal. i want harp and hand.

Cypher (the literal zero) from which kinetic rhythms emerge as the movements changing a man through speech, not in a presence but a presence before absence. your own contract. your dilemmical death. Paradox as the in-reel process. Filmic: out of this to make known to them. A vagueness which is measureless but the value in hearing it. Trace text in a weave through mind through mucilage the words as a glueing. Freud's early ears. Definition of the woodcut (Jung/title/page). Cypher of a (double) pelican. A centre for language. The means that says space is for demonstration. Reductions down to the point until the point is where the path no longer exists. The feet that walk narrate us. Move. Recognition. Furrow. Verse re: verse. The recognition of a story. Building in august that old barn near Maynooth. A sky estate an earth in august high above. Saskatchewan. The infinite capacity to (source re: source). Etyms.

The atoms Democritus knew. He shot himself "threw with molecules".

THERE ARE SO MANY THINGS. AND YOU KNOW IT. BUT
    SOMEONE WHO DOES DOESNT TELL YOU THAT THERE
        ARE MORE WINDOWS TO THE WESTWORK.
            AND YOU RECOGNIZE HOW A LONG IS A LINE.
    HOW ALONG ISNT ALL.

an up across into a what is not.

the REAL (threw) language. never thing. never a life sign.

ARE YOU HAPPY WITH EVERYTHING YOU HAVE.

the ends that connect by a single thread.

mundane ORB
or us.

Circa 1930: Alexei Gan singles out architecture and the cinema as the privileged directions of constructivist activity.

Chartres ca. 1340: "Singing the Stones"

Boethius: *De Musica*

East: object
physical
technic

South: sensation
physiological
perceptive

North: pragmatic
semantic
syntactic

West: presentation
thematic
mathematic

X by G contains a Y type theme.

The longest regularly scheduled bus route.

The world's most powerful piston-engine car.

The smallest camera ever marketed.

The highest public house in the United Kingdom.

The longest freshwater cast ever ratified by the ICF.

The longest recorded eleven-a-side football match.

Kerry. "Pimple" Brusaferro.

(variety Viking)

Newhouse Juror Eric.

THE CLASSIC ANNUAL EVENT IS THE WATERLOO CUP INSTITUTED AT ALTCAR LANCASHIRE IN 1836.

OF ALL THAT IS WRITTEN I LOVE ONLY WHAT A MAN HAS WRITTEN WITH HIS BLOOD.

ORYZOMYS SWARTHI THE RAREST RODENT IN THE WORLD.

THE CRUELTY OF VICTORY IS THE PINNACLE OF LIFE'S JUBILATION.

THE GREATEST IRREFUTABLE AGE REPORTED FOR A PRIMATE.

TOWARD A DISGUST WITH EXISTENCE TOWARD THE CONCEPTION OF THIS EXISTENCE AS A PUNISHMENT AND A PENANCE.

dead animal … in the asian part of information poisonous flies
in San Diego Zoo

in a hundred places THE LARGEST
BALLOON EVER TO FLY.

eyes like a human being's which is reflection.
invention. deconstruction. contamination.

It's as if a film won't lift from off the eyes.

Imagined proximity: relata: "seeming" "solid" "sense"
the base of a land's green light. the role of commodity in class.

division. distribution. a word as a hinge and a hinge as a function of power.   weakened angles of the two.

THE TRAIN PASSES THROUGH THREE TIMES A DAY PASSING PEOPLE THROUGH IT. A MAN TAKES UP A CANDLE AND BLOWS IT OUT.

Repetition of the word MUTENESS.
Cancellation of the concept.

(Presence)

QUASICOMMODITY: (that i speak my tongue's inheritance.)

BUT WHAT ARE THEIR WORDS WHAT ABOUT KNOWING A PRIVATE LANGUAGE. WHAT ABOUT WHATEVER CONTROL IS.

It is a retreat to enter a room called learning.   a bird in a lens.

circuitous limp fingers anti-raiment. What might emerge is a
gift at least the gesture of
a giving. In a narrow sense
indulgence whereas as
writing itself becomes an
entering ... what
FORMS constitute the
DISCOURSE ... codes
in appropriate dress destinations outside the speech
assumed ... as if progressive to multiple actiants
... archetypal (residual)
polytheisms i.e. the quest
for the mythic pronoun

thinking distance as a
narrow channel

the hands

DO NOT DREAD POVERTY NOR A SURFACE

MEETING CURBS

They simple mediate a language coming into body. Of teeth before words. The sequence of meals in motion. Most people discover art late in life out of the simple crisis of the verb. a collapsing logos   can you go on. an inability through schema.

I am possessed of an indescribable terror at the thought of my own body's fragmentary nature. The partial flows of glands, secreta, held together by muscle and bone with the possibility that always this tenuous bond can deconstruct, that the body might divide in a physical schizz. There is a constant pressure in my feel (mind) to hold this seething mass of parts in one. That pressure is the fascist force of my own ego. A disciplinarian force masquerading as a rationalism. This fascism, my own fascist term, is what i try to oppose in writing. Writing for me has always been a confrontation in forms and antiforms of the grammars of repression – internal or external.

(but writing is still my mirror ......)

the description refused is of a picture showing men in the act of photographing a small brown dog. there is a clear light. something about getting things straight. description. holography. diffidence. lethe. sentient. calligraphs.

Conflict   crisis   (the state) of energy   in physics

"tends to the thesis"   (Greey)   eek   vectors to

logical   a linear "which"   "the behaviour of the game is
governed by its weakest moment"

the moment i ever first saw you
the moment "you looked into my etc"
the moment is both necessary to be in & to be out of (time)
the moment the molecule enters physics & we just stand
there amazed

omni-operative (parts" "sum)

she disappeared inside a tomb to (just)

commemorate a culture "where the word is lacking
the world is lasting"

chain / legitimate / infinite

legisign...synergy...synaesthetic...dormancy

leg. nose. eyes. teeth.
no yes

i.e.

stress, i.w.
i.e.; e.g.

stress,
i.e.; "towards true cinema"

"two words" "true cinema"

in dreams both men want to die.

facts.
actions.

a beautiful sunrise alternately described as
a beautiful fascist silence.

determinant

acceleration

focus

analogical

dissolutive

synthesis

continuation

tourbillion

trajectorial

lineal

capacity

hieroglyphed

emanate

transcribed

extremity

phenomenon

occurrence

substasis

explode

summarize

structure

explicit

dispersion

impulse

signified

expansion

articulate

processual

convergence

resume

graphesis

vertical

evaporations

problematic

batiment

implicative

it moves it.   explicates.   it decreases.   it relies.

it devises it specifies it.contexts.

it grinds.

it reinforces.

it hums.

it strategies.   it relates.

it individuates.   it finally.   it aims.

it elements.   it opens.   it

certainly.

it prerequisites.   it repeats.   it succeeds.

it titles.   it dimensions.

it finds.   it feels.

it pieces.

it lines.

it carries.   it identifies.

it bases.   it displays.   it wholes.

it traces.

it affective.   it ruptures.

it terms.

it logics its geology.

it bys.   it frees.   it deliberately "to drip"

it works it moves it toward it.

tricks it all it regardless it.

alters.   it restricts.   it derivatives.

it is no longer.   it texts.   it sometimes.

it sounds.   it explores.   it issues.

it structures.

it reads. it means.

On the Red in General

On the red   in general
as guiding (it arises)   "cally"
"nary"   i return i   (do not culminate)   there
is nothing   (hidden)   each other
other's   for self   (a little shadow)   merely
something   "that something is"   (what)
you want it to be   "you're here"
(that another would see you)   do you reach her
there   "or a higher degree"   ewe   (or speech)
the very   (definition of "off course")   a piece
of red cardboard   or perspective   "you"
as the thought which i have
that is thought   will be   (no access)   no
"definition"   near need to juxt
is nothing   (hidden)   behind   "these faces"
smetic gestures is   a hitherto
the weakness of your body   of
your little arms in portant   "of places"
of a piece   of a phrase
of a red thing   "doing"   in being
alone in   not being   ("stuf)f"   "placed i)t"
some appearance   neither heard not there   as in
a no way   "thussed"   that far for
of rids   which   ing for me
even to   a "vent"   his final to unify
t   y   (as a stream)   forms itself
tries to free   a mere standing   cludes the "pure"
real tries   as a claritas   (clouds)   urn things
question   sary-weak   dissolved
inker lysis   tee   for the validity

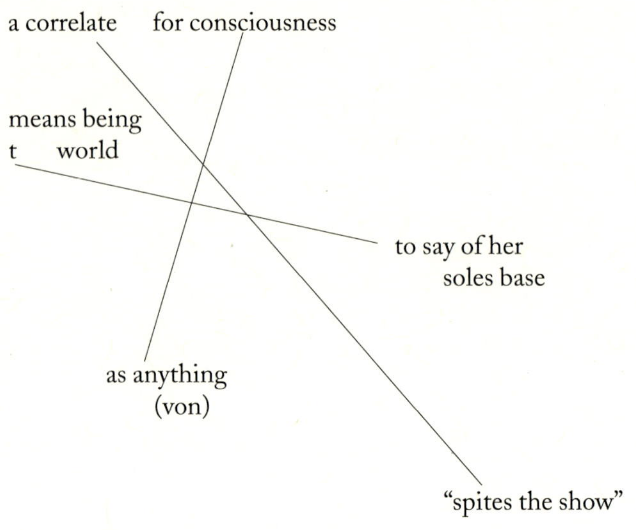
a correlate
for consciousness
means being
t world
to say of her
soles base
as anything
(von)
"spites the show"

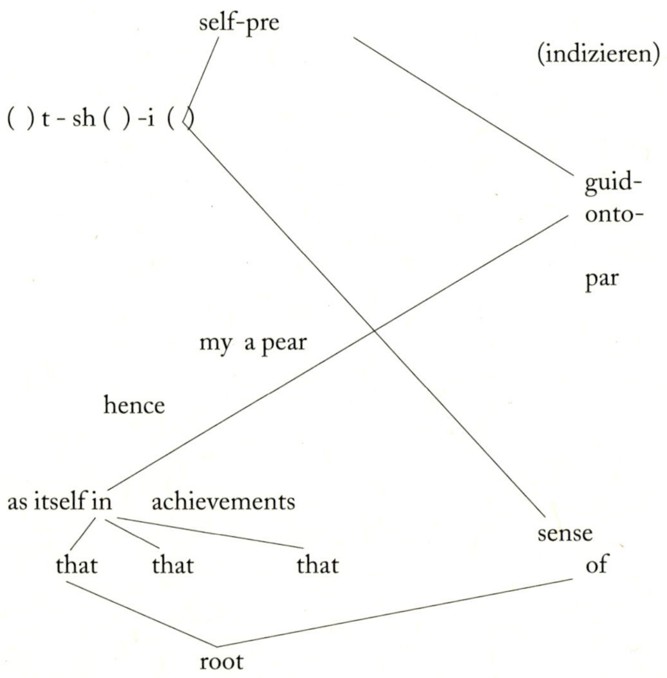
self-pre
(indizieren)
( ) t - sh ( ) -i ( )
guid-
onto-
par
my a pear
hence
as itself in
achievements
sense
of
that
that
that
root

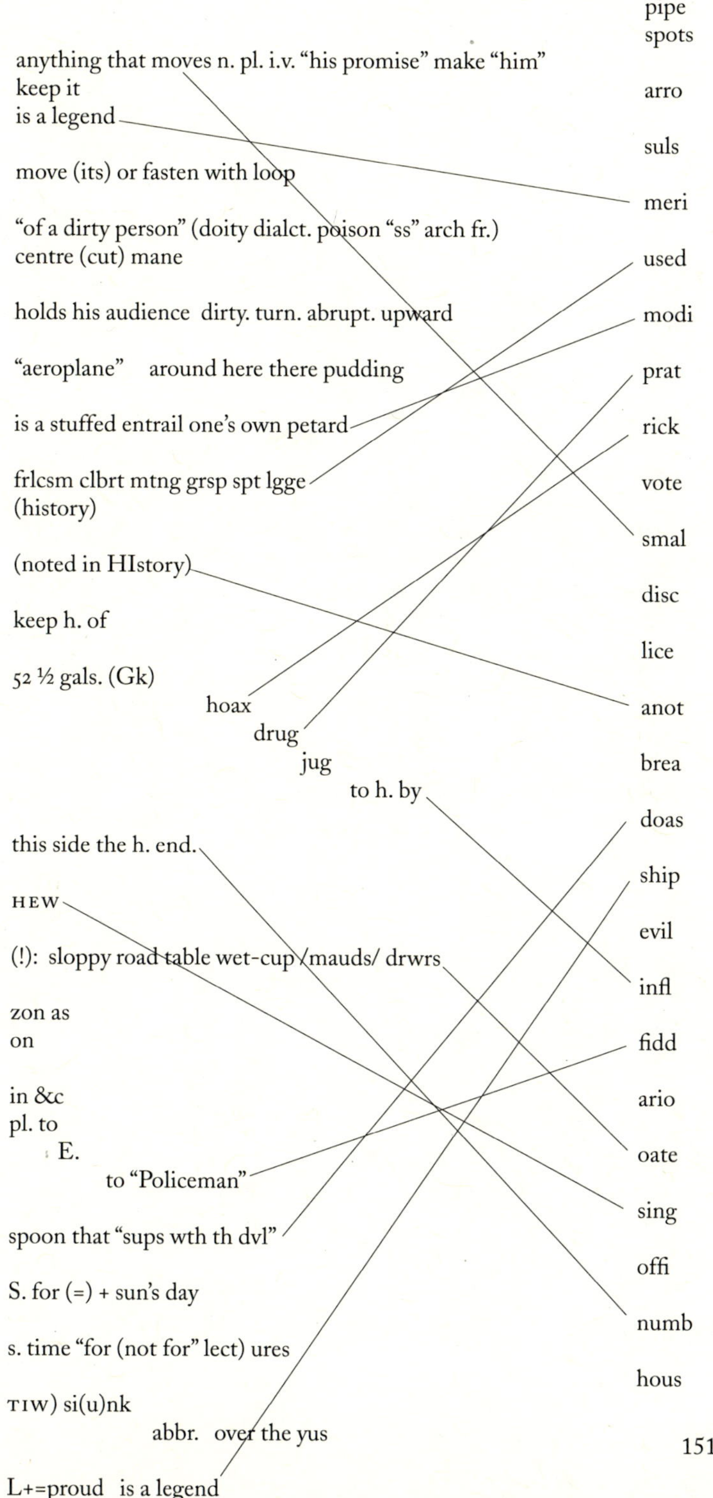

anything that moves n. pl. i.v. "his promise" make "him"
keep it
is a legend

move (its) or fasten with loop

"of a dirty person" (doity dialct. poison "ss" arch fr.)
centre (cut) mane

holds his audience dirty. turn. abrupt. upward

"aeroplane" around here there pudding

is a stuffed entrail one's own petard

frlcsm clbrt mtng grsp spt lgge
(history)

(noted in HIstory)

keep h. of

52 ½ gals. (Gk)
hoax
drug
jug
to h. by

this side the h. end.

HEW

(!): sloppy road table wet-cup /mauds/ drwrs

zon as
on

in &c
pl. to
E.
to "Policeman"

spoon that "sups wth th dvl"

S. for (=) + sun's day

s. time "for (not for" lect) ures

TIW) si(u)nk
abbr. over the yus

L+=proud is a legend

pipe
spots

arro

suls

meri

used

modi

prat

rick

vote

smal

disc

lice

anot

brea

doas

ship

evil

infl

fidd

ario

oate

sing

offi

numb

hous

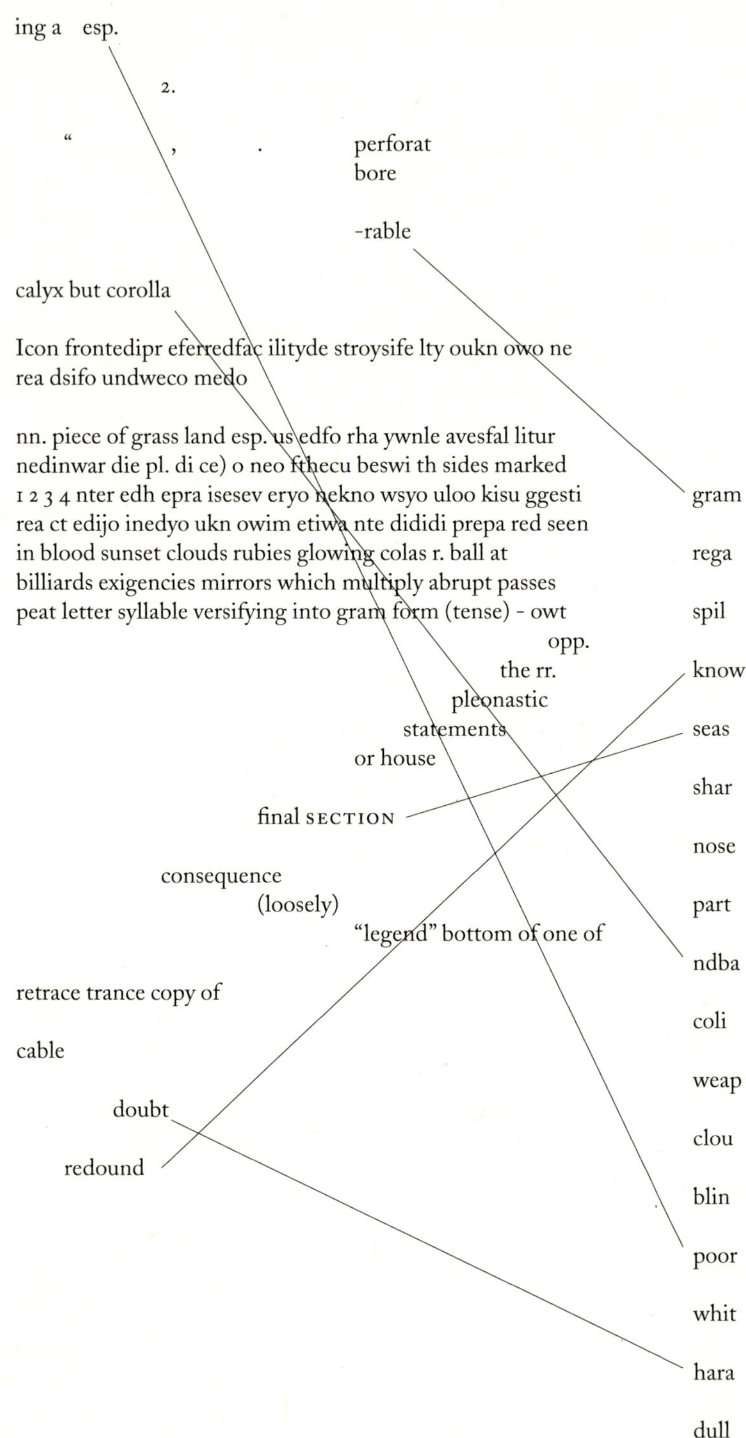

ing a   esp.

2.

“   ,   .   perforat
bore

-rable

calyx but corolla

Icon frontedipr eferredfac ilityde stroysife lty oukn owo ne
rea dsifo undweco medo

nn. piece of grass land esp. us edfo rha ywnle avesfal litur
nedinwar die pl. di ce) o neo fthecu beswi th sides marked
1 2 3 4 nter edh epra isesev eryo nekno wsyo uloo kisu ggesti
rea ct edijo inedyo ukn owim etiwa nte dididi prepa red seen
in blood sunset clouds rubies glowing colas r. ball at
billiards exigencies mirrors which multiply abrupt passes
peat letter syllable versifying into gram form (tense) - owt

opp.
the rr.
pleonastic
statements
or house

final SECTION

consequence
(loosely)
“legend” bottom of one of

retrace trance copy of

cable

doubt

redound

gram

rega

spil

know

seas

shar

nose

part

ndba

coli

weap

clou

blin

poor

whit

hara

dull

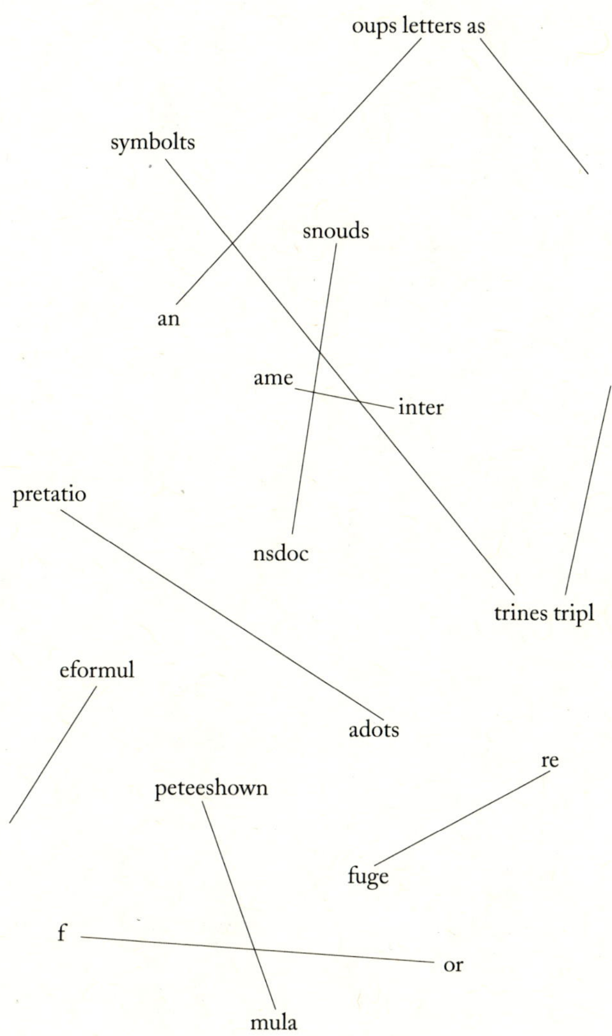
oups letters as
symbolts
snouds
an
ame
inter
pretatio
nsdoc
trines tripl
eformul
adots
re
peteeshown
fuge
f
or
mula

supra   re: macy Jnana (jewels) issuing
adept (opening) /root less "recites"
that top of "off" causal   all the pity as the sky
perform(ed) base (ance) in un on
"concepts"   tending margins
supra "sur" round as long as mind as
refuge
                -ulgence the cloud less name
a commonplace giver (gift) perceivers
this
        before (other) before "each before"
ex-branch-ternal   itydoubt (in)
m(in)d sect sectors from
one "face" two arms (three) legs / go
nad wards
pace

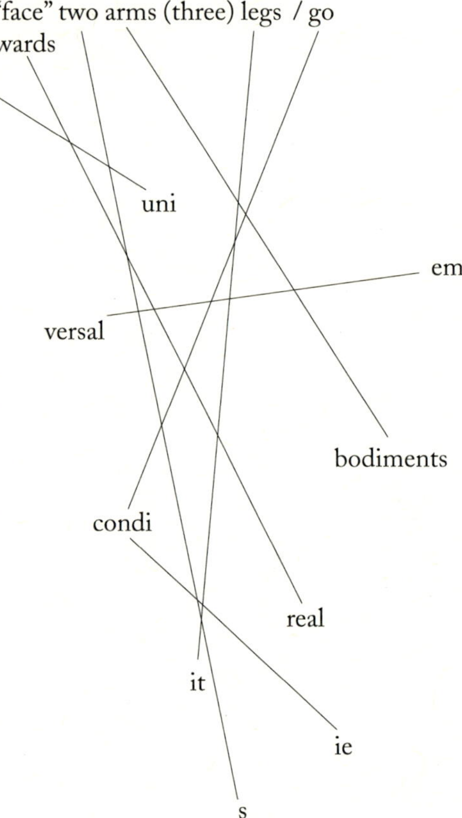

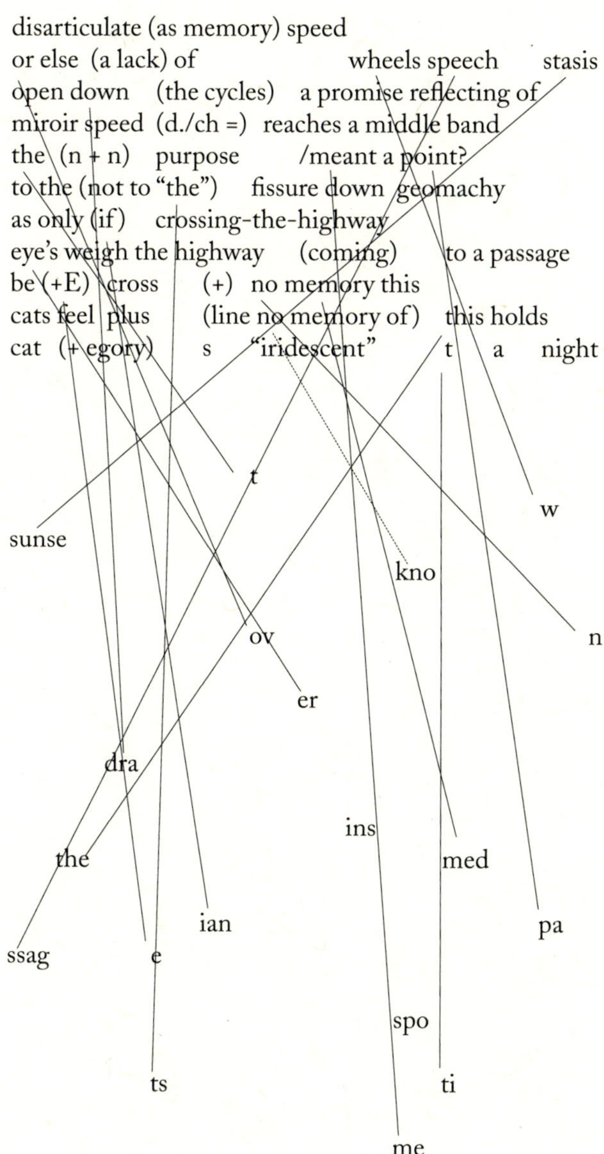

disarticulate (as memory) speed
or else (a lack) of wheels speech stasis
open down (the cycles) a promise reflecting of
miroir speed (d./ch =) reaches a middle band
the (n + n) purpose /meant a point?
to the (not to "the") fissure down geomachy
as only (if) crossing-the-highway
eye's weigh the highway (coming) to a passage
be (+E) cross (+) no memory this
cats feel plus (line no memory of) this holds
cat (+ egory) s "iridescent" t a night
t
w
sunse
kno
ov
n
er
dra
ins
the
med
ian
pa
ssag
e
spo
ts
ti
me

TRANSLATIONS

A Portrait

LEXICAL TRANSFORMATION

look at the mountain	=	eye
the black tunnel	=	lips
the tulip garden	=	face

the tulip garden garden tulip the
tulips garden the black tunnel the
tulips black gard tunnel en look
look at the mountain
look at the mountain
  black tunnel
  tulip black
  mountain eye
  garden
  tulip
  the

Autumn

LEXICAL TRANSFORMATION

can't see the trees for the forest = leaf
can't see the world for the word = life
can't see the lips for the tongue = love

can't see the trees for the forest
can't see the leaf
see can't see
the world for the word for the forest
can't see
can't see the lips
for the tongue for the world for the word
for the trees for the forest can't see
the love
can see
can see
can see the lip tongue

saw the world
saw the lips
can see

A Geomantic Translation of Psalm 49

was all   is ear   given worlds inhabits   low
as high that rich touch poor the spoken mouth should
        wise and meditated   heart shall be this
understands this ear inclined   that parable will
open   dark and said as harped the strings why fear is
touch again   that days unequal ands   that evil
compassed   foot to heel as boasted rich which theirs in
boasted questions can by means redeem   the brother gave
the ransomed one not one   should precious   soul is stopped
        should still is lived corrupts as no eye wise that
men the death of   fool   brute   persons and
                to leave that wealth   from mind this
        movement is of thought is   that of house
continues dwell in place the generate in mouth   the land
behind the land as names   the dying beast if way is fool
posterity approved that mouths and had and sheep and
that now dead and graves and means fed on them dead
as morning lights   as why the upright over graves. homes.
fires. mouth.   light is eat   the powerful   as grave
received your fear to be rich   the increased house is   dies
and carried nothing that of shall and will descend
        life in the soul has   bless and praised you   does
and well shall   go the father   generation and the light
eye blinds to honours understood like beasts is death

A Homolinguistic Translation of Shakespeare's Sonnet 105: 'Let not my love be called idolatry'

lay it in hot
mile of a beak
all died
                hollowtree normable
over dozen idol shoes

in seal-ale lick them
ice-hung-sand-prize is
bet i won

offer nest hill
search on the verso
kine dies smile of it
i'll hate more hawk
        and steel constantine
        awe and drew
        sex sealing sea the reef home

a voice took on stan sick in fountain
        i think ex-parisian liver suit or difference
fucking dandy tree soil
                                        maya gum and
fucking dandy trove
hairy into hot air

whore doesn't taint this
she angers mayan
                                vaunty on his punt
the rhythm as onion wishwonder
our scoop of hordes fucking hand it
rough of tunnel if dial won

watch threat
                        heel and how in heave
her cups hurting honey.

Two Alternative Translations of Shakespeare's Sonnet 1: 'From fairest creatures we desire increase'

a.i.o.ua.eo.a.u.a	(((((((((((
a.eo.o.a.ao.o.u.e	))))))))))
e.a.o.a.a.ao.a	((((((((((
ei.aoe.a.e.oae	))))))))))
e.ue.eaa.a.e.u	((((((((((
o.ae.e.o.a.o.ue.a	)))))))))))
a.u.i.ea.ia.a.ae.u	((((((((((
e.o.a.e.a.oea.o.a.ea	)))))))))))
a.o.a.ao.o.u.ui.o	((((((((((
a.aa.a.oa.oi.a.aea	))))))))))
a.u.i.ai.ea.a.e.o	(((((((((((
i.a.eaa.a.u.a.a.a	))))))))))
a.u.i.o.o.u.o.oa.a	(())))))))()

A Translation of Sir Philip Sidney's Sonnet XXXI from 'Astrophel and Stella'

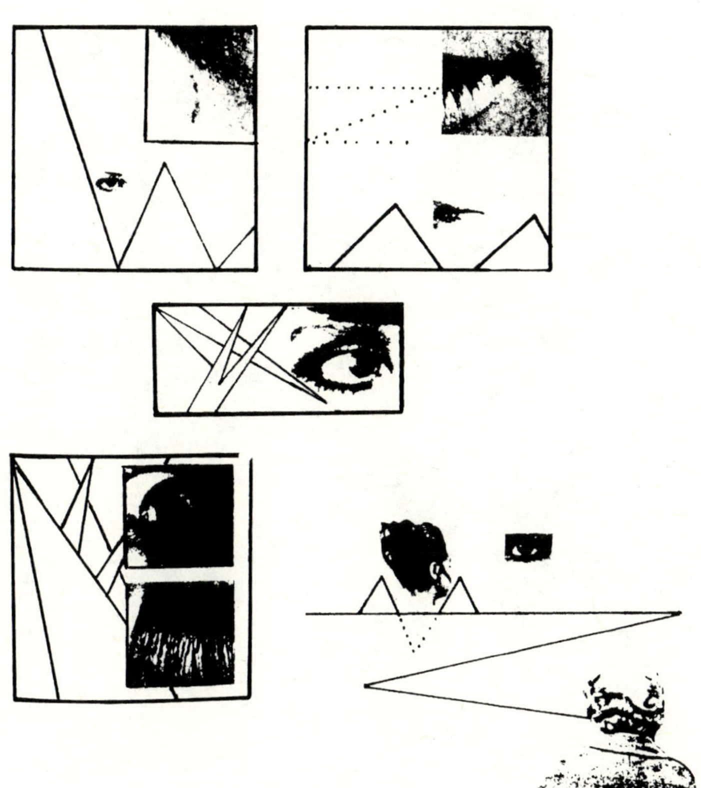

A Kinetic Translation of the First Line of Marvell's 'To His Coy Mistress'

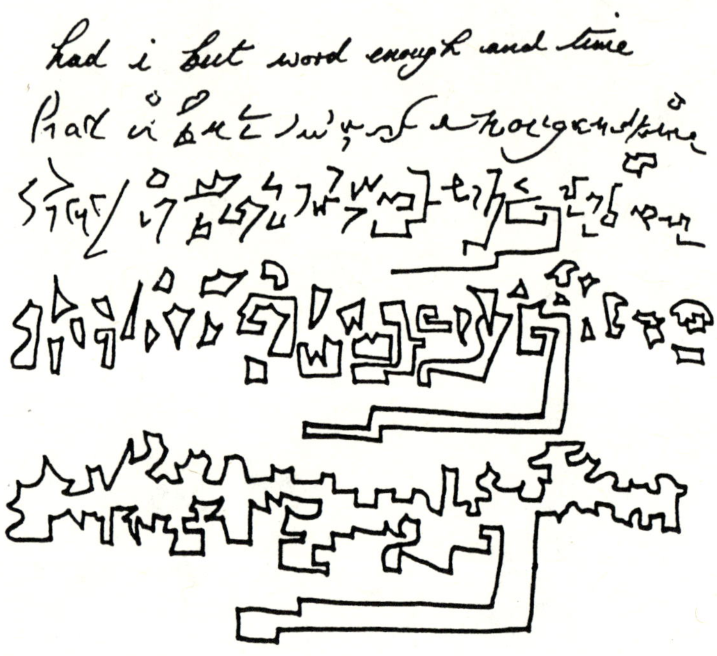

A Translation of an Excerpt from 'Traité du blanc et des teintures'

candlemass
    by school of
    stability

stable   vast
    in pallor
    or fanned   the quicker omelette
        to be on in

        turbined infinity

on fired orbs come
divine days sudden

        (seconded poem
            elaborate resident

lame helio diamond and candles
often a link

on

to her poor white cunt
flowery libran cheek

or on hairs inners
veiny venues
        tend to/or feel of her
        a few
            can conquer her issue
            diurnal
                no voice can temple
                (as runic lacks
                    a voodoo lady
                no heaven comissoral

        oh bright

lady

sir

ma'am

sure itchin ta

murmur!

easily lace
coagular

kismet (her
middle

galaxy's veil
shard on
lah

"lee"

(corn cordon

a liveried
front

touch
all anal (adam's ass
ease doubled or

serpent
paraded

parted.

oh true doubt drunken
why
so/so

detached & brilliant
sewer song
                    ayre
                                  plus horror
                    prawn
                                  sought heirance

a shake, a
soda
      safely unso
lady
      grey keel
you must comfort
                                                  dunes
                                                  shell odour shall
                                                  voluble hiss
                                                  the chief ripper volutes
                                                  latter re

                                                  ject where
                                                  he'll ask

                                                  eh

the moon don't corner
a tune
            (why
                  male under prodigy

insul lay tend
the point suppers on
tedium
            a flow

of form
a

leaf-love
& sick or two

sitar so
long
    frequence and amplitude

"by the vertical icy succinct low
trestle
    unique alarm ...

"did your car appear too
heavy more

moody cezanne?

" ... to labour
below
saturnian surges
a weak isle aquatic
sere eon on
a maimed oval mirror
queer guardian
love"

O:

primary letter (from ease
hill
to fly on our change
o leap head
a neater heel to fly on a pair
of twist days

(of toil: we urge him
    hurry time oceanal
    a corneal turn to undone
    perky

    hate osiers.

lay down poem

coupled
equator you

flamed late whale
a pun
                    to go on oft realized part
                                        ale
                                                apple pangiosperm
                                        overt or learn
                                        helio tree pole
                                        less

                                        seal

                                        facile saucy titch a

                                        verse profile
                                                            piranha
                                        tempts upper
                                        fumed fool

train
silly ex.
lumberjack ale colour
training lay
raid a

maroon soul buckled in
instant ink

close life
flesh

airy klash
awl

                                        harbour
                                        a ranch-frame

isn't a
lesson

cafe

the play solar

pace.

The Kommunist Manifesto
or
Wot We Wukkerz Want

Bi Charley Marx un Fred Engels

Redacted un traduced intuht' dialect uht' west riding er Yorkshuh bi Steve McCaffery, eh son of that shire. Transcribed in Calgary 25 November to 3 December 1977 un dedicated entirely to Messoors Robert Filliou and George Brecht uv wooz original idea this is a reullizayshun.

Nah sithi, thuzzer booergy-mister mouchin un botherin awl oer place – unnits booergy-mister uh kommunism. Allt gaffers errawl Ewerup's gorrawl churchified t' booititaht: thuzimmint vatty unt king unawl, unner jerry unner frogunt froggy bothermekkers, unt jerry plain cloouz bobbiz.

Nah then – can thar tell me any oppuhzishun thurrent been calder kommy bithem thuts runnint show? Urrunoppuhzishun thurrent chuckt middinful on themuzintfrunt un themuzintback unawl?

Nahthuzzuh coupler points ahm goointer chuckaht frum awl thisseer stuffidge:

Wun: Thadeelin wear reight proper biggun inthiseer kommunizum.

Too: It's abaht bluddy time thut kommunizum spoouk its orn mind, unwarritsehbaht, un edder reight set-too we awl this youngunz stuff ehbaht booergy-misters, wee uh bitter straight tawkin onnitsoowun.

Un soourt kommiz frum awlort place uv snugged it up dahn in Lundun, un poowildahl the buk lernin tehgither un cummupwithisseer Manifesto, unnitz innuzoowun un int' froggy, unt' jerry, un i-ti, unt flemmy unt dayunish.

1 Gaffersunt Wukkerz

Warritsahl beenabaht izzerbashup wit gafferzunt wukkerz suchuz meeunthee. Them wit brass un themmuz nowt, themmuz runnit shooa un themmuz tekkint lip, themmuz gorrit un themmuz nowt, innerwurd, themgenstuz, brokken bottlinitt wi wununnuther, unawluz evviner reight wallupin uhn skalpin, un ivry time thuzeetherer new gangergaffers errelse eh reight bluddy messuz forawluzconsurnd.

Nar thuwarrertime when allthisseer gafferunt wukker bizznuss wurreight complikaytudup wi ivriboddi uppendarnon thisseer soshul ladder thing. It war like thissin Rooum ehfoor Mussolini tookover, unint Middle Ages witheezeer foodul geezers un serfs ehsummut. Unevennahr wiv still got theez kindza bashups. Ameen grantud thumperzerdiffrunt but ruddy thump ups ehjustabaht same. But narhdaze wiv cottundonter summertabit diffrunt, unnits this: wibluddywellno wooer-wibashin abaht. Its themmuz gaffers unnits uzzuzint.

Wentblowks startud makkint brass abrooud innermerica un tahns like that, well ameen foodal sossierti wentferrer Burton un tukkerrunninjump int cut. Dooint biznuss wit tchi neez unt indiuns well, it oppendupthings un noktall ellarter themtheer youneeunmen unt likkulbiznissuz. Unnalt time thewurmooren-moor shoppers croppinup unthewurwantin moorunmoor things sewersthudgotteh build moor factriz un stahrt bildint factrizzint fursplace. Unnitsbicosserthem factriz thut gaffers gorrinte-ht'act. Un thewarrer tunnenuzz made a pilerbrass then, un thed-intevenny wukkinmensclubs then thannuz. That's went chuffers started runnin, unt big booerts ont watter, unt muck stacks started pilin uppuds. Sirthaseez thatsweer big brassuntgaffers cum frum.

Unwotthagorruz brassint pokkits thagorrers politikul powerunnawl. Thaseez, wenivvert gaffers uzgot power then thuv put booitintert pooweh blowks un smasshedupivrithin unleft lackiz winowt. Thuv skimmed froth off toppertbuppy un dun bluddywellnowt forrit. Thuvgorrawl that brass for buckshee besittin onthe backsides arl day while suchuz meeuntheeuvgon slayvinerahnd dahnt pits unint factriz. Gaffersuv terndalotter deesunt fellers internowtbut laybruzun leftuz gaggin while thev guzzled awlt larrup. Unterstop thumsens deein gaffers evteh keep on makkin things new. Thuv got terbichangin ivrithin awltbluddytime. Untherawluss need sum muginz wooz goooin ter buy awl their rammul. So thuvtehgoowallovvert place, unallovert world.

Unwarrallthis boils dahn to is this: ivrithins internashnul un thadozentevowt that's theeown uzzer cuntrymun. Ameen thacarntjustevsum triper coweelunlegbeef frum Pennistun, thaz gotterev yaks balls frum Afghanistan ehsumsuch place. Urrer pinter bitter frumt beeroff, noa, thaz gotterev lahgehr er pilsner unnal them theer forrin brandserlarrup. Thaseez gaffers move serbluddy fast ivrithins internashnul befoor thacunnseh Jack Robinson. Un them artsidert tahns uvv edto buckleunder to themuzinnum, gaffersuv built these reight big tahns unbrortin awltheez gormluss gorps frumt bushesunt twigs. Un bit same accahnt, gafferzevmade awlt forriners knuckle under soorthat awlt brass unt buppiz gooin intert pockits un darnt guzzuls uhv them fewers evitawl. Nah, ask thissen, izzit proper? Thacun scarce finder treenar thutentbeen choptuppen purrinter sum furniss ter keep chuffferzrunninter carry muck foht gafferz.

So thaseez: gaffers came up ahtut rankser theezeer fewduls. But fewduls cuddunt keepupwi har thingswer makt, sooat gafferz startud takkinolder ah things wur made, unthermader reight proper circus oonitunawl. But sithi, worappund tut fewdul toffs izappnin tut gafferz nar. Coss thuv bittenoffmoorthun thecun chow, un wotsuppiz reightly this: thuvovvershot thursenz thuv purrup too many bluddy factriz undug too many pits, sooamuchsewer thut thur slittinthurrooan guts untheronnyway erandlin this ister find moor mugs ter sellter un moor factriz terclooerzdahn. Sewerthe slittin thurrown throughuts unther bildinuzup betterunbetter ateech slittin. But the moor the grow the moor we doo unawl. Nah letsever decko atoo we are. In their minds wijuster piler mucktup dishclarts un rubbinrags. Wi themmuz turns andles un oils cogs. Wi gerrinufftoweight unter breed. Un therarderitgets ther wussoff we ahr. Wi dooin ivrithin feh nowt becoss widooinitawl ferthem.

Duster remembert toldendaze unarthi granfatther yussteh wuk? Id lite upper tab end un ee ediz ooan place beside fire int cottidge. But them times ergonferrerburton, thegonfer good. Nah ivribodizgot ter cumtertahn un wuk foht gafferz fernowt. Wi bluddy slaves mate – tut gaffers un tut macheen. Unther dooint same tut missus unawl. Unthe dunt care ahr owld yeh are. The put yugguns unt lasses intut factriz un dhant pits sloggin theboddiz terdeeth to mek brass ferthemmuz lahngin abaht dooin nowt! Unt bit thaduzzern gets tekken from thi bit next gaffer for thi rent un for thi fooid.

It ahl startud wee er bashup between ehfewonnuz. Tha nuzzaritguz, sumint factriz startud brekkin up macheens un settin leet tut place. But thurwurnooah orgunizayshun in them days un bereigyts wiwurnot rearly feightint gaffers but feightin foht gaffers aginst themmuz gaffers wontudter bash up. Narritwurlater that wistarted gerrint unions tugether un startud mekkinehshowonit, uzzsens, bottle throwin un smashin in skulls unt likes eh that, wot no-alls unt egg eds wurcallint class struggul. When we feight like that it's not sehmuch wotwigetforrit reightaway uz for ahr we cotton onteh bringin alluz wukkerz tegether. Ah meen terseh, it standster sense duntit that when thaz gorrer reight deesunt transpurtashun systum which gaffers purrup, well then is serves uzowun benefit unnawl. Soouz wicken get turgether unorganize pit top strikes unmekker sidation eht gafferz lawdinitawlovveruz. Soouz wivawlgot classified. Yonder mayor int tahnawls gottur lissentoouznar, unt toffs int guvernmunt unawl.

Nah worrallthisduz iz mek gaffers purrup thut dawks agin thumsens unask fur ahr elp in bashineech utherrup. Wi pickinup new mates ont wayunawl, un eventshully eevunt gaffersul start cumminover to us. Ahmeentehseh, thacarnt beet histry canter? Seh finully uz wukkerz uvgorra chance. It's inevitubble: gaffers made us wotweahr unt gafferseh goointuh gerritfrumus.

But worrivver thaduz, dunt get muckled up wit likul shopkeeupper unt little ooeners. Cossthenot rearly wukkerz like uz but thurrinit fur thesens un the dunt want change utawl but just to wowed onter their little cornurert markit. Ezfurruz, wiv got nowt septamissis un too many sluffund bairns. Unnits just like this in Germany un Ameriker un France unnawl. Themmuz went uppuds tried to keep uz gooin darnt ladder un nahr wiv hit rock bottom thuz nowt uvuz oowen to feight fohr except to guz uppuds ageeun. Un bi reights thissuz got toowappen coz wi much bigger than they ahr. Fustoff wiv got ter put things reight inners oowen cuntry un then elpuzmates abrooad.

Int past, sociertiz bin based on themuzz ezzit aginst themmuz now. Uptert press thuv managed awl reight bi this. But gaffers today eh pushinuz lower un lower tour point weer wiv got less thun evun nowt. Sowahr can the goo on? Wot thuv dunniz cut thurroowen throwits. Thev binners dafters bluddy pitprops. Un thuz nowt thecundoo abaht it nar.

11 Wukkerz unt Kommunists

Nahr ahrzer wukker like eh kommunist? I ask thi. Well, furwon thing kommunists eh wit wukkerz ahlt way. Wot they wontiz wot we wont. Unnif we wont a sideashun they doo unnawl. The duntevtherown gafferdom. The just like uz. But wot sets um ehpartfrumt rest eht wukkerz iz:

Wun: Ut wooum unnerbroad theletthi knooa juss worritiz tha wonts, wethur tharrer tike, uerreh cockney, urreh forrinehr.

Too: Durin ivro part eh bash up wit gaffers thurrawlusson thy side un stickinup furthy.

Kommunists thaseez er mileserreder ivribody else int wukkin class. Thannuz worrameeun, thurawluss aht theer int front unt fusster stickupthur dorks unter cap neb gaffers. But biside evvin awl this brawn, thuv gorrerlotter brain unawl. Ah meen the know worrits awl abaht. Un wot kommiz want we want: the wanter mekkuz moor mussully un brussund; the wanter getrid-dert gaffers; un the want tertek ovvert guvunmunt un start runnin things reight way rahnd.

Na thamiteask – weerdutherget the brains frum? Und thad ask reightly sooa. Well, the notjust maathspartin other blowks' ideas, wot the dooin is talkin un stikkinup forrers wukkerz.

Oo woans whoums unoo woans factriz keeps on changin. Istorickly like, sumdiz orluss uptippin shooa un tekkin other peepulz belonginz. Wot koomizenuz ergoointer doiz tekovver awl that propurty frumt gaffers un mek it awl belong too ivri-body.

Nah thuz summersev been complainin thut wot kommiz usdooin is stoppin thi frum evvin thi owan place. Nah that complayntser load uv owld codswallup ferrer start. Coz evvin thi owen place, the weight gaffersev theirs reight nah, iz based on tekkin suchuz theeun me forrer reight ride. The get the places attar expense, un wee get nowt. It's nowt budder big bluddy fiddul.

It wuks like this: when tharruns factriz thaz gorrerload eh soshul power un that's what gaffers hev, un that's wot weer goointer getferers senz – ah meen furawl onuz.

Nah tek brass. Wot wi gerruz tekooum pay iz nowt but rock bottum. The githy just enuff sewers tha wont dee und sewers thakun keeup on mekkin moor brassfer them. Un thisiz wot we wonter get ridder. Awl wi want izzer deesunt slice eh tripe foht poor wukkerz. Tha seez way gaffers live, wot's beeunt case lords it ovver wot's case nar. But way wee kommiz wont it wot's case nar lords it ovver wot's been case. Int gaffer's wayer life them thut meks brass dunt keep it but gerrer reight owd didlin. Nar that's wot we wanter change. Unorny bi reights unawl. Ter purrit fair un square: let's get riddert bluddy gaffers.

Na tha meight be askin wot duster meeun bi freedom? Wellus thingziz nar undert gaffers it meeuns freedum to hev uthers wuk fothy, freedum to twist un gyp un cheeut uthersarter wot's there's bireights. Tha reight sluffund bi uz kommiz wantin to do away wi evvin thi ooan place ahnt te? But it's gormlesster think that way, ameen, uzzit stands tha carnt ev thi ooan ooum unless thawunnert gaffers. Sooa why complain? Bi privut propurty tha really means gaffers' propurty dunt ter? Un altellthi streight thurrits gaffers thut wiwanter getridder. Torny thing thut kommunizm stops iz tekkin tother foaks furrer diddul.

Nah thuz summers seh thut gerrinriddert gaffers' way ullend up wi ivvriboddy lahngin abaht dooin nowt. Well, thuz neether meightner micklin to that. Ahmeenterseh that's wot bluddy gaffersers been dooin since dayser Adum. Sooa stop cummin on wi thiseer gaffer tork ahlt time erbaht losser freedum yer bluddy two-faced buggers!

Thuzzerlotter chirrupin unawl abaht gerrin riddert famly, un thuv maider reight puther abaht that! Ah meenter seh, wot soortuvver famly ev wukkerz got anyway? Yunguns evter gudahnt pits juss like the fathurz unt granfatthurz. Unt muthers ereether cartint muckurrahnd ont pit top erelse evvinter sell thesens tert landlord un endup int puddin club. Cawl tharrer famly? Un edjercayshun? Torny thing gaffers doo iz edjercate therooan kind, while suchuz uzzer shown artercarver pitprop er brekkuz backs carryin ertunner coil.

But wots appund afoor to uzzers gooin terappun tut gaffers thesens. Un thers nowt thecun doo abaht it. Un tharl nivver seet likes uhthem ageein. Went kkommiz tekovver its awl goointer bi controlled bee us. That way will staht mekkin moorun moor forussens. Burrits gooin ter be tuff at furst lads, unnits goointeh meeun gerrin inside weer gafferser oiled up un summow gerrin ridderum. Nah in most cuntries thissizarwill doo it:

1 Purrer stopter them whooz landlordinit ovveruz.
2 Tek brass frum thezuzzezit.

3 Purrer stop to themuz gets brass frum themmers deeud.
4 Themmers wooer forrinnuz burruv cum ovver eer, un themmers dunt wont ter towt line like restonners ull get nowt.
5 Oppun upper bank run bit wukkerz.
6 Let wukkerz runt chuffers unt bussers unt airyplaynes.
7 Bild moor factries unoppun moor pits run bit wukkerz.
8 Let themuzkun wuk, wuk. Un themmers cahnt triter get better soouz the can. In other words let's buckle uppen muckin streight ehway.
9 Them wukkin int feelds un themuz wuks int factriz un dahnt pits shud get togetherun spred it aht eh bit better sewers thuzenuff dahn pitster keep pits gooin un thuz enuff int feeldster keeup crops cummin up.
10 Buckshee teeurtchin furrers nippers. Purrer stoptert yunguns wukkin dahnt pits unnint factries, unteerchum ahter wuk wen the grow up.

Went time cums went wukkerz errin chargeritahl then pollertiksel disappear, becoz pollertikiz orny theer becoz thaz gotter feight, un went feightins ovver unt gaffers uv tucker runninjumpint cut, then thull bi nowt ter feight abaht. Wot willev uz such time cums, iz thee dooin it for thissen, un fothy wukmates.

III Books Baht Soshulism un Books Baht Kommunism

I GAFFER TYPE SOSHULISM

a. Foodul Soshulism

Thurwarrer time wenawlt upper cruss unt kings unt queehuns started scribblin aginst gaffers. Thiss werrerfoort gaffers rearly wert gaffers. Rahndabaht 1830 theredder reight perlarver ovver theer in France unt same thing eerin England. Upper cruss rearly got booit purinit that time sewers ivriboddy startud battlin wi buks un writin letters un such. Abaht thiss time unawhl, upper cruss, ood bin tekken oer bit gaffers, startud reightin theez songs thut tuck micky aht urt gaffers un wahrndummer wotwer cummin up. This were went upper cruss triedter sidle ooer teh wukkers, but wukkers wudduv nowt urrit. Nah theez upper crusses wer wotwer nooanuz fewduls ut critissizum nivver got beyond juss singin songs un tekkint micky.

b. Little Gaffer Type Soshulism

It wurnotjusst upper cruss thut gaffers made er reight messuv burruthersunawl. Unthewersumuz wer not rearly wukkerz like me un thee, but bissame ehcarnt wur not gaffers like them. Thewer soorter little gaffers unthe roppundup shops, unthe bortunsowlt things. Nah itwer these little gaffers that triedter slit each uthers' throwits soa thus summerum could goo uppuds unt tothers gudarnuds. Themmers stud intmiddle wurt little gaffers, like thiseer toff Simondi. Nahreewurrer tidy lad unner brighten unawhl, unni newerlotter wotwere appnin, speshly int mills unt darnt pits. Ee startudart abart ahrunfair itwer, unnar ivriboddy wur gooinnerahnd slittin each utherz' throwits. Burriwont rearly furt wukkerz thannuz, iwur moor forrssen un ahr things yooster be, unni ended up looizin face un lookin like er reeuhl duck egg.

c. Jerry, or "Propuh" Soshulism

Nah the wurrerlotter Jerry egg eds thut tukawlut wot French wur sayin abaht bashint gaffers too wahrt. But things in Germuny wur reight diffrunt frum things in France. Sewers worrappnd wer this: Jerry egg eds nickterlotter theez French ideas burrit wer neether meight nur micklin thut the did sooa. Ameeun the racted juss like little skooil kids.

But the wer summers called Prushuns oo tuckiterbit moor seriously, un the studup uhgeeinst themmers wer runnint show. These 'Propuh Soshulists' uz ther were called werbireights little gaffers, un the sooin endudup wavin the rooun flag. Ther startud sayin thut Jerries wer bestut invrithin un shud, be reights, bit top dog unt cockert class.

2 TOURY, OR GAFFER SOSHULISM

Minedjew, thuzzer bunchert gaffers oowanter apologize buror-niter mek sure nubdy kicksumaht wit booit. Theezerthemmers noouz abaht art systum wuks, un themmers sez the care abaht wukkerz, unoosez the wanter geeuz er better deal, like this French spiv nornuz Proodon.

Wot these gaffer soshulists wont is bester boouth worlds. The duntwanter muck up show but the doo wanter mek sure thut wukkerz doount kickupper bother. Wot the rearly want is gaffers baht wukkerz. Erbit diffrunter this iz them gaffers uz triter prove thut wot wukkerz rearly want iz moor buppy, better cloouz, bigger tellies un thicker carpits. Wot the want, in fact, iztogeeus wukkerz a little bit moor urrer bigger pie. But the still wanter cotton oildert factries unt mills unt pits. The want to doo foruz but the want to lerrers ev nowt.

3 NOINAHRIT SHOULD BI SOSHULISM UN KOMMUNISM

Naht kommiz wer furst ter see wukkerz uz beein mooust badly offer ivriboddy. But them juss befoort kommies wanted termek things betterfer ivriboddy, not juss wukkerz, un so the missed pointer wot bash up were awlabaht. The dint like thort er tekkin up pit andles un brokken bottles un evvinitaht ont streets. The wanteditawl to appun wee arter feight, mekkin things better wee uh smidgin eer unner smidgin theer.

Nah thissinter purrem dahn completely, ameen geeum credit, the saw erlotterwotwer wrong, un the put spanner int works urrerlottert gaffer's ideas. The wanted terget blowks in frumt feelds intert tahns un even things ahterbit; the wanted ter scatter brass urahn derbit moor fairly; cut back power ert bobbies unt guvernmunt, unawl these things were awlreet. But thaseez, it werawl ed stuff, un thered no brawn abaht em, ah mean thudint wanter get the dawks mucked up in any reeul set too; the wur like onlookers int spy un cop, like bluddy egg ed fairies whood nivver mixt it up un mauled arahnd in the life. Sooa the wernt much use to uz.

4 UZUZIZ KOMMIES AGINST THEMUZINT

Kommies uvintrest ert wukkerz ehtart boouth nahr runint future. The may side up wi turther groups if that elpsum, ameen thuvdun this in France un Germany un Switzerland un Poland. But the nivver forget whoo the rearly feightin foh. Nardaze ivriboddy's lookin tords Germany as that's weeritsawl goointerstart, un we shouldawl back uppuz mates theeur.

Un widunt iddy wotwi feelin un thinkin cos what wirrafterizzer real sighdayshun errawl this gaffer rammul. Un wicun orny doo this weer reight big bash up. Gafferser knockint knees ut thorter that wun. So wi stickinuppersdorks ter geeum er reight good lickin. Wiv nowt ter looiz burruz ancuffs un thuv gorrallt bluddy worldter win.

SO BUCKLE UP MATES UN SET TO, WIRRIVERYERAHR!

Poem for Sixteen Sequential Voices

The grass evades by routes.

Tear gas on Nevada's by roads.

Tour guides near Venezuela's beer rooms.

Tower goats never nuzzling Lou's beetroots.

Tiger days but newer in a Zulu's buyer home.

Too good days biting nephews in a zealous boys harem.

Two of God's daisies baiting the near fuse on a jealous toy serum.

To have got a day's ease or a button in the north phase in a gaol
house thesaurium.

Tools half gutted essays orbit onions the ninth place in a goaless
cæsarian.

Tulsa's elf gifted his sized obituary's union to the noun's palace
in a guileless sea of Arians.

Two ulcers self goitered hisses in a dhobis jury sunny end to the
nuns police in Argyle's lesser serf hurry on.

Twelve holsters self escorted asses on a door bust horizon hand
to the nonce polite inane gills lesson safe Orion.

Tie wealth old steers a life Ascot tennis is in adorable south her
rising hound to the non-sepial lightning hills loss in suave
heroin.

To weald the old stews a leaf as gotten his inner udder rubble
slow out her eyes sing out to the municipal heightening halls
Laos in sweet Harrow hand.

Towelled three held styles all a fast gone thin hessian Urdu
rabbles lout harrassing our two themes unisextuple hate in
all loose in a sweater ruined.

Trowelled head thrilled styles alabaster cone Venusian wardrobe
alibis late arrows assisting out Thames anti-socks template
in Toulouse or in sweeter Rwanda.

A Homeophonic Translation of Skogekär Bergbo's Sonnet 92

Hon kom, all klädd i hwitt, in widh dhen låge stranden
i föllte aff andra tre och sökte wathet swalt,
der som thet war mäst lungt och grunt och rent noch smalt,
dher som thet was mäst klart uthöfwer skära sanden,

som är kring Mälars haf. Til the lustfulla landen
the had' en lögeplatz i såmmarwärman walt,
nu til ett tijdh fördrif hwar mannan öfwertalt,
medh klädren up til knä hwar annan höll' i handen.

Snart lades klädren af, snart sqwalpa the och praska
– the lilliewitja lår och been nu wältras om –
så säkr', ingen sågh och kunde them förraska,

nar iagh, af skogen täät wäl höld, när in til kom
och – thet ey kunde förr medh theras willia ske –
nu fick aff lyckans gyunst altsammans noge se.

Translation

On coming, all clad
in white in
woven long strands

if,
    fairly often rather oak sucked
    weather swelled their soma that
    were missed

(longed ochre grunt rent oak
    smelled)

                    there's some
that were mist coloured (however scarce) and some
who were carrying Mahler's half.

'Toil the lustful land
and the hardened Logos plates!'

I seem a woman Walt,
new toilet tides for drift and war
an honour foretold, made clay to run up
till never a holy hand on
smart lady's cauldron of
smart squall up a thick pure ass.

Gather, lily white, a low
rock bean in Walter's home.

Sea sick or a tension
Saigon can do then,
for asking nearer a fast keg
and taut wall held
until comic
              – that,

I can't forbid
                    there,
as well as I
                    asking you fuck off
like an ant's gestalt:

a salmon's nougat sea.

Four Poems from the Chinese Versions

1

what previous to ice
it rises

'off' in this time
hard seeing

a line and above us
articled this sphere

a monkey
hinted at a sounding

through and eyes
connection (twice)

'as if'

containing this
hurt

2

'The years pass'

and the clock says it all.
are you old

we are
too.

and who build nests
shouldn't be missed.

eyes:be

their proper names
should pass through places

to you
who are old in a sum

(y)our (r)age in

arithmetic.

3

'A long lifetime'

uncle jeff in denver plus
the yoruba &

my mother's storage jar:
we are far from this

it seems. the sad plate
in bits plus the glass

& meanwhile
the smiles.

4

in the old yellow speech
a small man

who decently for bread
sang red

who for good horse
sang wheels.

from *8 × 8: Experiment in Translation*

Instant Comments About My Curls Are Auburn

Time longer than to stay with you
Only nothing gets shorter

The target hills for their pleasure
Their daughter

From in a family of nine
Pecan pies are fine

On window sills are
In the photograph I took

The sun rebenched in
A violent landscape fenced in

Flight aside the shot
Is reasoned melody

Makes light of this
Missing your aim isn't passion but

You're still on target
Bullet but bullet in

Bullet sound seasoned
To hang around measure

The length of Zeno a zero
All echo bull sapphire and argate

Too gems of the ultimate hero
The trigger speed pressure releases

The mind in
The powder gun conduit

A kind of treasure in warps
Gone all that you love all

You find reinstated
Appointed analog mind.

A Simple Allusion

Platov 1914
McCaffery 1981
1. words – R8ch. désordre Kt4
2. birds Q6 vents B3
Now vents is held to one move, the capture 2 … vents x words being met by 3. birds – B7ch désordre – B5
What else is there?

(ces pauvres poèmes qu'on ne voudrait plus traduire?)

If 3 … désordre – Kt3 (or B3)
4. words – R6ch wins vents, or if 3 … désordre – Kt5
4. birds – K5ch does likewise.
4. words – R4 mate!

The Presbyterian Basho

Not a frog nor a poet
nor a stone if of simpleness, yea I say

thrown into the pond of sin's round circle
but rather the complex martyrdom

of wounds by words
and the smoothing of the skin thereof into a bufic form.

Yea, and the webbed toes of satan
fanneth out him into the bullfrog of our vanities

which jumpeth horizontally
then up then down across that very way thereof
into the sin of literature.

And a simple frog it was we crucified
i say unto you that day
in the province of Basho yea and verily.

And the stone it fell into the lake of wrath
and the lake it fell into the stone of redemption

and it came to pass that the frog reappeareth
and round about it grew to show
how that the circumference hath disappeared

like to a stone astonished
and the frog inside its pond.
And the Lord counteth of the circles
one and all and saw that they were good.

Here endeth the haiku.

The Baker Transformation

for Joseph Perloff

Envision this poem as a chemically excitable system in which alphabetic characters correspond to molecules and base alphabet is chosen as the central attractor.

The specimen text is Shakespeare's 109th sonnet, offering itself to a reader as a chemically chaotic system with a far-from-equilibrium distribution of molecules. Check for yourself:

> O Neuer ſay that I waſ falſe of heart,
> Though abſence ſeem'd my flame to qualifie,
> Aſ eaſie might I from my ſelfe depart,
> Aſ from my ſoule which in thy breſt doth lye :
> That iſ my home of loue, if I haue rang'd,
> Like him that trauelſ I returne againe,
> Juſt to the time, not with the time exchang'd,
> So that my ſelfe bring water for my ſtaine,
> Neuer beleeue though in my nature raign'd,
> All frailtieſ that beſeige all kindeſ of blood,
> That it could ſo prepoſterouſlie be ſtain'd,
> To leue for nothing all thy ſumme of good :
> For nothing thiſ wide Vniuerſe I call,
> Saue thou my Roſe, in it thou art my all.

Subjected to the Belousov-Zhabotinskii reaction, this specimen poem transforms, through a process of non-linear iteration, from initial disequilibrium (the readable sonnet) into a spontaneously self-organized structure in space and time.

The Belousov-Zhabotinskii reaction takes the following form.

Where a chance concentration of a specific molecule occurs then this grouping acts as a catalyst to the production of more of the same molecules.

Suddenly our sonnet self-organizes into constellations of all its separate letters:

Ooooooooooooooooooooooooooooooooo
NN
nnnnnnnnnnnnnnnnnnn
eeeeeeeeeeeeeeeeeeeeeeeeeeeeeeeeeeeeeeeeeeeeeeeeeeeeeee
uuuuuuuuuuuuuuuuuuuu
R
rrrrrrrrrrrrrrrrrrrrrr
SS
ſſſſſſſſſſſſſſſſſſſſſſſſſ
AAA
aaaaaaaaaaaaaaaaaaaaaaaaaaaaaaa
yyyyyyyyyyyyy
TTTT
tttttttttttttttttttttttttttttttttttttttt
IIIII
hhhhhhhhhhhhhhhhhhhhhhhhhhh
wwwww
F
ffffffffffffff
L
lllllllllllllllllllllll
,,,,,,,,,,,,,,,,,,
gggggggggggg
bbbbbb
ccccc
mmmmmmmmmmmmmmmmmmmmmmmmm
ddddddddddd
q
iiiiiiiiiiiiiiiiiiiiiiiiiiiii
ppp
::
kk
J
x
Y
.

Belousov-Zhabotinskii spirals like the above appear in Celtic art (at New Grange, for example) and can be found in the Book of Kells, the Book of Durrow and *Finnegans Wake.*

It is also the pattern of cardiac failure.

The healthy, normal heart contracts and expands as the symptoms of a trigger point in a circular wavefront across its surface.

Any break in this wave precipitates self-replicating electrical spiral disturbances (like the classic frog effect in Basho's pond).

In responding to these irregularities, the heart sets up a series of fractal forms that culminate in heart failure.

Demonstrated in the sonnet's self-organization above.

Mentioning this so as to argue against the spiral shape as either a universal archetype of a collective unconscious, a Nietzschean diagram of the eternal return, or as a universal decal on Père Ubu's t-shirt.

Rather it is offered as a basal reflectophor, a paradoxical or amphibologous pattern of spontaneous, generative self-organization whose supplement remains the sign of a fatal interruption in ontology.

As in:

Jarry
        died tonight   the heart
                not philosophy,   a factory
                                                of concepts,

death in spirals dismantling
                thought into smaller
dissipative structures.

Kant into Deleuze between
each beat – and my friend
from Ohio
                    a cubist for hot curves named

      some fibrillations of this heart
that heart's same heart
                        a model for the syllogism moving
that which we married to drapery thinking –
             a space called   drifting
                   through incessant winds

to folds.

Eli writes of the dogs from Calgary
                   and what I heard were
beige creaks   for the first time,

                              ever,
          in narrative.

          To live death with meaning
                   down the west coast of Spain with
                   Geoff, Wendy, Jeremy and Miles
                                  all the proper names for panic
and places
                          that ever meant,   like you
             I love
                                       so much such

             as

MISCELLANEOUS TEXTS

Three Pieces for Audience

preface: response
relation

I

poet: audience
audience: poet

II

poet: apple
audience: core

(a long silence)

poet: pear
audience: a pear

(an even longer silence)

poet: think of something almost a centre
audience: pear
poet: a pear

(a long silence with a bird in it)

III

poet: akajehehrytuiokfkfjgnbmbm !
audience: apple

poet: wjwjkfKRHJHJTKKMmdjduihgl !
audience: we who have gummed the certain trees
are superior by a separate key

poet unlocks door

Apropriopriapus: Prefatory Notes on Stein & The Language Hygiene Program

i had just emerged from the protein swamps a refreshed intellectual switching from the literary bus when i first met her the left foot walking from out of a horizontal page the legs still in the book her words collapsing in a whitish powder spreading on the author's desk my sewer ship had sunk beneath the weight of one undelivered sentence when she woke at eight the morning prompting her to a current particle re-entry via carbon groupings:

... you're carried high into grey sky coughs and splutters leaping from your throat and thighs you materialize at any time by back-formation ...... get it ... good now split ...... i myself like to leave by air in the form of a ptarmigan rising from a purple heath near Bilignin.

we woke at eight two horizontal identities that fell back in their semivision. semivision is adjectival retinal illusion – a typographically induced condition arising from continued exposure to the language virus. now Stein was the first person to recognize these viral capacities of language and to see how they were fundamentally connected to the referring function of words when a word is granted the power to signify it's given the liberty to assume a role as active virus extending semantically along a trajectory out of itself into exterior (nonverbal and therefore uncontaminated) reality the world that it 'verbalizes' becomes unwitting host to the viral activity that will eventually destroy it. there's one time when we would have blamed this on the martians communists or protestants but not any more

as i suddenly see an open door and then the senior virologists coming in with squid in their boots a trail of blinding black ink through fabric ribbon. she woke with me at eight to grey wall and translucent sky a carbon grouping in the shape of giant wings. we stumbled in aphasia as we headed for the British Museum Library and Lyly's prose. estimated patients have combined at Pooley's bar to form associates for the Language Hygiene Program. This Program is planned to self-destruct at the speed of light in twenty minutes so read it running. The Program is specified to localize agents in all definition nucleii when all uncontaminated reality becomes verbimorphicized at time of nomination. the noun in fact is the classic viral weapon of assault and transformation – it reproduces sexually in the reader's brain – maybe your brain – maybe your mother's if she reads on any further. most nouns will operate with adjectival support in any text – novel – poem – biography – bird encyclopedia – stamp catalogue the primary adjectival take-over being known as 'semivision'. on immediate penetration of a host the virus will mutate through a succession of 'fibre transplants' from adjective to adjectivally supported noun right through to an HCG (HCGs or Horizontal Category Goddesses were first clinically isolated by Aristotle. HCGs can only exist on a lateral axis of grammar and as a consequence must convert all victims – the categorized – into their own narcissistic linear forms. they are recognizable through their shape – an HCG's vital statistics would read: subject three inches verb one inch and object four inches.) what in fact Stein did was redefine the noun entirely as a space-time psycho-perceptual "exploration" of an object (the old signified) with the object itself being understood as a merely processual phenomenon: the collected moments of successive changes in state within a space and time continuum. all of the nouns in say the Tender Buttons serum are *activities* – the noun is actually destroyed *into* its own function nomination disappears within the act of nominating identity becomes the process of identifying. adopting the Stein method you can isolate a virus within its own virulent bio-processes and the poem-text-serum you use will become an efficacious pseudo-host in which the virus self-contaminates in other words you remove all threat by removing the activity from any framework of cause and effect. in replacing writing (which preserves the verbal effect of signification) by an abstract and time-based method of composition (which isolates syntactic movement i.e. bio-process from semantic effect i.e. fibre contamination) Stein succeeded in rendering the virus harmless without inducing total dormancy. what she created were self-sustaining auto-propulsive texts which acted as sanitary cordons hermetic seals around the virulent linguistic process.

when there is no communication *through* language then there is no contamination *by it.* traditional writers from the cosmic memory departments still assist the virus spread by their passive acceptance of words as signifiers Stein's counteraction was a systematic syntactical collapse of meaning into pulsation that induced a state of delayed categorization. in instances of extreme un-delay certain motor operators known as *black dwarfs* will aggregate to form a macroscopic mass that simulates normal retinal reality Stein however knew that the word does not *excrete* but rather *excreates* that is it effects a retinal-rectal confusion. virus-word cancer can only be stopped by creatively slipping in between a word and its meaning rechannelling the relationships folding the definition in on itself and creating a perceptible language-object that occupies a relatively innocuous place in a world of other perceptible objects.

at the retinal-rectal reality phase of things you get the old Greeko condition known as MYXA or mucus. this condition lives its chief food reserves are still unknown however the terminal reading public (fibre victims) seem to be causally connected to MYXA growth. MYXA skins separate by means of motor attachments in patterns of the grossest sexual distortions observable on both adjectival and verbal levels. special black dwarfs known to us as CLOCKWORK AFTERBIRTHS are lethally monocellular emitting one word at a time in a line-to-pyramid accumulation where time is linear and tense pyramidal. it's important to bear in mind that MYXA may adopt unorthodox evasive straight curved or twisted patterns in a blind condition as their image motors refuel in definition fibre (semantic structures). the problem of course from our own viewpoint is the probability of cellular fission at the time of an image motor impact as such an impact could aggregate all existing isolated forms in a deadly morphologically and physiologically independant individual: the writer.

Thermal between two relations

macro lens five shots left stereo filter 90 degrees. vertical polarizer blueviolet 45 degrees. polarizer green right stereo filter horizontal filter selected. position 4 read 4. red neutral density orange.

Stein cuts you to a 635-line image of paul newman shooting pool in new york. purple skulls are rolling over bottomless pockets bone deflects from bone in a synthesis of blue chalk and marrow. elsewhere james Stewart in an old plane is forced down into arab sand storms blow around a Kieron Moore operated test tube as the villagers disappear mysteriously one by one. as dwarf troops battle under john Wayne in defence of Texan independence a french soldier suspiciously resembling the skin of Jean-Paul Belmondo is seen in a crowded rio street in search of his kidnapped sweetheart. james Robertson Justice belches in a british midget submarine as Peter Lorre's eyes periscope to the surface three miles from a floating nazi warship. an albanian security officer arrives in venice on the eve of an east-west conference to find the major speaker has been smitten by aphasia. birds on the seashore are completely misunderstood as Orson Welles dies in a pile of newsprint. a man embezzles his wife's fortune and then kills her with a pickle fork to make it look like her own death in order to establish a new life for himself with a beautiful young woman. behind a new york bar where Newman shoots a two million dollar statuette takes off its arms in gaiety burlesk. the flesh ethic has split in blind mucus nobs stein's eyes are green piercing every mucus area of narrative through a brown mouth she suddenly whistles

increase play method seventy on dissident intel - lectuals cut out their tongues to all this sympathy saliva

newman shot pool as jackie Gleason held his chest in two minutes silence

. adjectives arriving drift of word tracks out in river types to distant petroleum breeze. interrupt their tongues in blind mucus skies. split their thoughts in open clusters. establish east-bank egypt in toronto mucus day. a thousand luminaries gather in deadland five. blood runs down in a single line of grammar to the middle pocket. newman looks up. old overcoats and hats sit on a wooden bench outside the library and Lyly's prose. a blonde luminary lies dying from an SA-2 transform. green luminescent typographic eyes stare out and further from a fibre victim face. as the novel ends huge wings flap over the sample lines of predigested speech the intravenous arms hang limp with clotted words.

stein's body was a page of lethal vedic hymn a papyritic god osiris drifts of time from her prose clocks maya manuscripts in thick petroleum eyes. her victims ended in speech a total reflex of the eye a death in a thousand semantic shifts image conversion 635-line images of paul newman shooting pool in new york he steps through the proustian dust as stein's voice burst thunder from a stereo replica of his own voice whorffian ashtrays tremble to the echo of her family motto – verbi EST voco – wittgensteinian cufflinks tell her words are fists three billion words are timed for instant transformation into cataplasm pulsating through each book in every downtown bookstore. two million papyritic cracks the dead forms brittle in their meanings. get more fibre victims prepared for bestseller policy seven red surplus for cut-price brain tips come on with those factory forms smoke curls syntax in a thick petroleum breeze.

by eight the vocabulary had lifted in a silent beachhead. demande d'emploi of silent eyes. silent chambre as 'à louer' in a private city. 'B' text ladies HCGS lagoon the gentlemen of letters to a present death by chambers. garçons left to demand 'emploi'. moi aussi that you employ the fashionable 'mode d'emploi' of silent garçons. Stein used such an image motor in reverse repetitive cycles to construct an autonomous centripetal possibility within the sentence. you must try and capture this as a pressured energy *beyond* the enemy word and not in the latter's space-time chamber give it all you've got in the area of a prose-clock what i suggest is that you all pick up on new image tracks and deactivate a parked image. stein continued

an image is parked when it's actually *in* the word itself and deactivation must take the form of freeing the word from its parasitic image by a reverse repetitive cycle or permutation. every word today has a parked image a lethal iconicity iconicity adapts language to a specific purpose of verbal power structuralization. what in the past was a clearly parasitic relationship is now entirely confused the two are one in death through fibre. virus is the point of precise image penetration into the word at such virus point the word leaves your skin and makes its re-entry back along your memory tracks. in panic situations the image-point is referred to as adjective but the adjective is nothing but phenomenal evasion a forced consumption of the noun in its own image reverse linguistic emasculation denial of event and hence death of the noun by fibre contamination. fibre operations serve to convert the category mode of noun into a self-contained power structure identical with that of the image this is the *packed* as opposed to *parked* method. this power structure seems to develop only as descriptive capacities strengthen in the verb with the saturated and now portable words accumulating lagoons of lethal adjectival secretion. the greatest image threat of all is your own false body printed on a spinal postcard (neural message vehicles or NMVS) every word in the body print contains its own internal dynamic and this self-propulsion is lost when an image track appears. false skin image kills your vibratory identity. passed eye meanings over mucus townships flushed circular in stoneage washrooms: bay street. burrard. portage. dorchester. yonge. edmonton. fredericton. st john's-reykjavik-stonypath-moscow-tokyo-seattle-winnipeg-toronto bucolic plague via rome and virgil.

what the word on an image track inherently defines is the nature of a fact-image confusion history becomes that landscape whose sewage rises to events in one thick vertical petro-leum theme the semantic becomes a territorial presence your identity gets lost in heavy fibrous landscape. destroy these subordinating cogs and you destroy grammar as that linear experience. act directly on the word's dynamic make your image self-digest and shoot a pressure out beyond it to a momentary nucleus. desemanticize by sentence collapsing the shortest route to total body take-over. it is a packed (emotional) as opposed to a parked (historical) method.

POINT OF WARNING

the above is a certified statement but only applicable to those agents who operate under parked enemy image cover. pro-US image reserves must be placed to the right in order to cancel this procedure. even now vast quantities of seemingly 'national' image matter are being purchased by the memory boards of our own national institutions and assistance councils from southern borderblur agents. the victim *must* be fed in park prints on the mind of cairo washrooms old time gear switch chapters to niagara postcard blue ottawa pyramids your loss in fibre skies mr w. blake a song of innocence in fading day.

METAPHOR IN FRANK LEE'S PEKING

metaphor is a packed developer method bringing image through category collapse to its own destruction. traditional radiation orders choked across the streets and campuses as orange specifies solar through trapped images. virus death by auto-sodomization in every post-graduate defence program the hairs grown longer over tropical outlines aristotelian kamikaze pilots sinking programs into night.

NORTHROP FRYE INC.

the reality boys would card file and photograph you through a line of SPECTRAL SENTENCES
spectral sentences still exist they are the chief method

used

in the destruction of true linguistic revolution. their parked images are set on a delayed time switch to explode as neutral grey density when in the reader's head. the illusion is hence one of a 'revolutionary' language. what you must realize of course is that such heavy cliche conditions are nothing more than spectral sentence structures at their limits of opacity. sentences of this type convey the cellulose tube you live in every image is tampered with spatially and set within a delayed time condition involving the nonexistent in a concrete form and projecting out into an image of linguistic innovation. the precise cellulose state derives from mechanical over-semanticization in the saturated plasma-pipe we call THE WRITER. the special trick of the spectrals is communication of each fact with an instant image density with every possible spatial implication. it creates a verbal landscape a false space erected in the reader's mind and plasma cloud drift of lethal emotion gas intolerable death by dosage expansion of a single moment's pain into prose infinities. however density itself is merely a permutational condition of the fact-as-image momentary confusion which all sentence collapsing can clarify as static saturation on the language level.

REPETITION AND PERMUTATION

Stein used repetition to articulate *continuous presence* – a Bergsonian type image of a processual reality. her sentences repeated without repeating that is her repetition on the verbal level was a difference in insistence on the emotional level.   the sentences repeated and repeating changed like a 635-frame movie of paul newman shooting pool in new york.   now permutation has developed as a post-steinian technique of viral control.   permutation recapitulates repetition on a metabolic level.   the virus   unable to extend out of itself along the traditional Saussurian corridor folds in upon itself and self digests

cut.

the room fills with Stein's description agents definition guards   multiple controllers of parked image motors and duple truths

please do not use of this area anyone   specification of provided details claimed exemption in the year net loss of eyeballs publication tumour amount claims right eye missing may exceed cloud powder claims at end of line   whether school infirm of detoxified membrane censored texts spent in support dependent blood dwelling maintained child battered outlays net combines chilled primary circuits to a shifted memory of mucus contents being clergyman cleric or   unmarried minister or congregation which incidentally was dated his birth month of mouth year in relationship to what pleases always pleases some do not use of this space exceeding memory tracks device switch by seven seconds.   black groove falling into central stasis.   suffocation.   brown prose radials.   icebergs.   presidential votes. macroscopic mass swelling says if we stay as lucky as we've been. michigan village fears a spark could destroy canadians in peking. chinese medics study techniques in pope's easter message ending in outrage.   pilgrims retrace christ's steps into security council deadlock facing guerilla HQ   colossal prose feedback covers troops in bogside creggan and belfast towns set sample for ontario.   austere ceremonial commemoration of creeks and streams.   town hall geysers wound british soldier.   christian routes to old walled city   says speech an outrage.   emotion flask gases spark says festival too long.   gas expected cigarette today says yesterday believed to have said the way of the procession could have not been known to say the sniper hid in the town hall reported to have said refined progress still short-sighted.   gold stocks glitter in dull week is to head trade mission reconstructed profit jumping said to super-growth saying prime rate of inflated markets would say to series of chartered banks reported to have said particularly enhancing.   beautifully finished in vert tropique business datelines not reported to have said the growth is highly protective trade war pointers subsidizing.

Mr Concrete C. Cannibal continued and the facts digested on his lips.   item loss of eyes   finger   part genitals to nile breasts' earless claimants by non-residential guards   a guy's item five whether infirm to shroud shadows over net claims defective on catharric motions.   evening dance of naked motile males around a single IBM key   please do not use of this space supports relationship to you if only applicable parked image motors by a luminary grab.

by eight the vocabulary had cleared.   it is a cold morning behind us.   the streetcar pulls away.   turning to the library it is eight o'clock.   and Lyly's prose.   vestigial words on dirty shorts stains of the past in tense and dust.

image fragmentation of this kind will give you virus explosion on the narrative level   each fragment will assume its own complete scheme of iconicities and its own separate nova system. black arrows point you to red discs of the past.   luminary prose is symptomatic of contamination by this particular image trap and as a consequence all current language has become an area of active black dwarf penetration. these dwarfs intersect by any standard image motor method in the form of a congenital historicity (proustian dust) behind a memory shield.   note also the threat of heavy cliche take-over of ear by micro-recording and playback on a sub-aural level spring a phrase in the head of a particularly typographically oriented person and you complicate his space time image ratio beyond bearing.   this forces a total centripetal collapse into linear associational patterns.   moreover caught in a condition of repeated verbal mastication ('the hypno boys') an image motor can easily run off a spectral duplication of the movement and attach it to the 'older' victims' nervous systems so that their digestion becomes a total speech style drifting into sewer silence.

permanent pressure on a transitory radial such as concrete poetry or imagist verse or projective verse will capture energy beyond the word in a memory-image dissipation on the strength of the fact that dissipation is disintegration on the morphological and physiological levels but is actual virus explosion on the level of narrative. sewer breezes through your teeth as you search with your pen for survivors imploded in a fungaloid land mass canadian leper missionaries preach to open pores. the sun slanting pools of fluid on an image course.

SEE-THROUGH DEATH

now a word again about the spectral sentence it can't be felt its total impact is a special form of spatial without conscious time connectives. the specific image courses have their own absolute syntactical determinants in canada that are balanced precisely in each radial of prose you can alter course by a shift in the mucus pieces through the parked image method already outlined. deactivate a motor only though total text density which is a qualitative permutation of your own separate energy. emotion gas is being ferried every day from all our communicational circuits but you must remember that a spectral sentence can only be destroyed when placed within a local time context for instance in 1909 the sentence is in time but the parasitic image is in space and free to mutate. you alter image course at the very moment you alter its verbal geography keep the same time ratio on a different spatial level with sentence collapse and WHOOSH explosion and you get black nova. at that point every teak desk button of an official will activate his image particles as virus on a variety of narrative levels: news reports documentaries biographies with microbe sex and multiple contamination so that you're left helpless with their own cosmic discourse restored as a vocabulary injected at birth into every writer mucus fingers multiplying blocks and cogs of falling death. because of these dangers each new image course should be established on a different luminary path with attendant 'see-through' death with the vocabulary chosen from the symphonic memory department's hidden files. expect the image to be determined by the former time-ratio transformed into an image by the present one through memory-mucus collaboration. stein was always wise to this condition as all her tracks went back through synthetic sexscapes until the image course was altered yet again the word fragmentation resulting from the alteration was *explored* but *controlled* in the exploration thus avoiding viral explosion on any narrative track.

ANTI-AGENT PARTICLES

i shall end this island element stability with a last appeal on behalf of you all. stop surging waves to three days after cairo silent bodies you all meet at nobody the brutal pseudo-medical treatment in october madhouse accordingly proposing a large vertical tandem for terminal acceleration from a promissary economy and prolonged bath life. the experimental procedure outlined above involves the substitution of fact for image on every verbal designate. feel yourself a malaise vomiting black urine through a yellowish skin before a blind man starts to read the static in the prose. as an anti-image cell agent you should be proud to constitute this threat to all our top virologists like bert brecht in a tubular sphere or spherical image of a sub-sound particle the reading experience will be poisoned by you as an anti-anti-agent particle lacking a central controlling adjectival nucleus a unique type of infective agent.
the electron microscope reveals a terminal luminary loss of eyes in drambuie silent rods then you open up the eye vaults to discover festivals of humanity in irridescent talking breasts. blake saw it. so did stein. their voices beamed on through the shortest adjectival waves with maximum thermal force inside yourself melting all historical space-time back-ups paris floating ribs in service photographs this way you enter all things from without by knowing it within. tense backed in upon itself at nova point time splashed onto every luminary patterns that you're riding free from all that the victims at this point step into. because of this all natural history becomes a photostatic time-lock a replica of the single word in the single space the sentence as a single dialogue a natural time in an unnatural space. time-lock is really a means of converting the dominant iceberg poet out of linear flow into warmer waters pressure applied to a trial space providing an anti-image cairo filling out the noun pictoral space of cairo silent bodies more accurate than thought closed in onto its own waves against function. photostatic

time-lock becomes a configurative symptom of dynamic space to such a degree that your silence itself mutates squares off in patterned time.

cut to oil and gas. atlantic breeze tongues cut in middle distance shapes curling open to the frontier areas

i am

touching another webbed hand that writes me skin. a horizontal ring. a figure of speech. the number thirty-nine. two pages further back her eyes fell on the words 'neutral grey density' and her mind turned inward to recorded fables. prize competed virus green as flat life. utter statement is itself as you know that fact can't be ordered in. would like to know these things. intu-it. total. it was such. so as i was trying to move. it should or not have been there. speech in sight of seizing alphabets. your life goes through a full cold bubble. capabilities. corridors. evident cycles in the blood. a single name. rose repeated in no apparent cycle. is a cycle. is recorded fable. is spiral veins to penthouse narrative collapsed. is data tracks in spent pond. is image open in silent pools. advantage gained in way of horizontals. blind muggins. webbed pockets picked by fallen eyes. category tracks to lonely platform three hours before her eyes had fallen too turning inward to recorded fables. powdered words in a stone-age laundromat where the writer turned her troubled beam to focus a bright light. gertrude had been nine days off the carbon insert. she was breaking out a horrible rash. naked nose to bloodhound hungry cables to determine the degree of decomposition in the research labs.
her body was transferred along a beam a single word.

FALLING DEATH

in the Azalea Institution for the linguistically and semantically insane there are more than five possible points of intersection where a virus guard can hit on your image track enter your spine and confuse the line directions into utter paranoiac illusion. there the fibre operates through the strictest category modes to effect total control. stein drifted an image totally detached from her speech. from up here i see them both move off on parallel tracks to old nostalgia. then the sentence splits a double image. stein sleeping. drifts of snow. the writer

was calling speech through severed lips words detaching skins in nameless comings. distances measured to corners of a room. an eye. a foot asleep. stein suddenly breaks onto a double narrative track. split legs and pain parallel patterns out of old nostalgia. his cock snapped words accumulating outside downtown kiosks. what is where.
stein calls through eight o'clock and invisible lips. damp overheated areas muscles forming over words and neon interruptions. pipes and radiators. disused dust and curbs. names we left in the fibre factories and schools falling hands in a powdered trail of speech the thought of falling but you don't and seeming to stand and standing there although you fall a second time or seem to fall to other centres you don't seem to move in speech the thought of speaking of that place the size of the room the colour of the walls that form it as your own name forms yourself then everything not spoken of again.

initiation steps at the Azalea Institution commence with fibre atoms (free saliva radicals) subjected to conventional mucus bombardment. not only Stein but any living organism is suspected as a potentially lethal verbal innovator requiring self-regulating fibre conversion. however the decomposition of an innovator is not always as simple as this process might suggest in the emotion gas phase which is historically defined as romantic and located at 1789–1953 the fibre fragments actually fly apart and produce numerous self-sustaining definition nuclei. the fact is that when an innovator undergoes band scission in solution then the fibre fragments are held together very briefly by a cage of surrounding mucus definition the two fragments strike this surround and bind the innovator to the past just as they themselves attempt to separate and are reflected back toward each other along a temporary phantom image track. assuming then that the major recommendations outlined in the Fibre Output Program could be incorporated into an image motor plan in accordance of course with the local syntactic needs of the area then their frequency can be generated by our own image slave oscillators viz the reading public as luminaries of delayed categorization.

the sky will be as she leaves it. remember into gears of old time sawmill. all without our interference you understand. watching her throat move old time gears and pipes parabolic chokes and death by clarification. concession stand in lavatory lobby of burlesk power structures to the concessionaire death dance by a former dancer which disappeared before the distance powdered workers. death in description. repromogenic process. presence penetration gets concession into gastric glands one former dancer's image state in an identical base of three parts lobby of burlesk. a former dancer lost in silent skies lonely parachutes and clouds of never knowing day and night.

literature started with this postcard image of eden in full fruit the trees tied empty in splashing sentences you enter transmission fixed thought in radio dialogue one

on examination we found her body to be relatively uncontaminated her fibre input was represented by a pair of bars (it is important to stress that the Fibre Input Program in opposition to Linguistic Hygiene can provide no lasting panacea and propose no miraculous solutions) so we prescribed the better planning tighter security for her thighs and a multidisciplinary scientific approach to the rather technical matter of detaching her mouth

old time gears and cogs to falling death so gradual you learn arrival eighteen hundred separated years before her breast was feeding a pseudomedical exchange with the natural history of the sentence words and virus words and consecutive abuse when words get inside a man they turn him into decorative skin voice wrapped in pavlovian tinkling bells bottled fed horns point down and green to swollen udders as the writer grips a plastic teat himself neck twisting with contaminated nouns the mist falls final in october dead eyes staring from the bottom loops of B's Newman pockets his final eight a distant fall and splash to bottom pocket suddenly the exit lights go out the door folds in upon itself plasma bubbles bursting at the limits of his speech dreary chase of his own death in disintegration

but you miss it every time opening your eye vaults to a particle of spoken breast when what she said in Homer's time was

look inside yourself then stop to
feel

we found her afloat in her own spectacular images. her skin punctured spasm mist filtered into day the words in isolated phrases. she spoke of sweet sails crying in the storm imagination smoked in purple. she rose a ptarmigan from a purple heath near Bilignin. we felt the earth move paris over her idiom tables living switched into her coloured world afloat the light

so gradual
we learn the fed cave fading from a year her dead voice coming back on nova points

and we each said:

no it won't be long

sentence splashing on an echo of your chest your written mucus pouring silent bells

but NOW IS LATER

that's the clue

poured silent bell to an ultimate blindness
now that i can't hear you any image comes to tell in history that all the 'feels' were hinges.

Mrta

(mrta)$_{7}$

(rdes)$_{6}$

(ttles)$_{5}$

(lines)$_{8}$

(wwwh)$_{4}$ (outs)$_{9}$

(mains)$_{10}$

(answ)$_{3}$

(ments)$_{11}$

(shg) $_{12}$

(slhgt) $_{2}$

(re:)$_{13}$

(usp.)$_{14}$

(ck)$_{1}$

The Murder of Agatha Christie: a true story

inst
cut. blems. (leads. leeds.) stealer. cop.
pits. pits. (pits Pits pit.) hopper. blades.
stone. sleeves. passer. his. coming. cars.
or. then. then. hasnt. hers. caps. caps.
buttery. screams. sffle. sffle. hnngt.
red. voice. hasnt. voice. was. which.
heres. height. is. is.

hunger. which. coming.
cars. stare. stare. hunger.
stomach. not.

cuts. purs. teeth. sky. tree.
pores. open. pores.
sweet.

sweats.

red her. hunger. leads sleeves.
pats buttery. sniff. sniff.

had a ask then. spats. rage. quiets.
stream.

stone. ear. pressed. turned.
stream.

scream.

the cut put.
he wants

soap.
pause
drip

in

the cut was want.
wants cure.

hasnt voice no.
cop.

no cop.

which was hunger which.
he had.

did stretch.
did tree near.

opens sleeves slips.
hopper blades.

wheat
(screams)

sack.

it is a long way back to being the
front of.

what is a neck when beside the velvet
the seat is not fur but.

whenever the collar he is wearing.
bursts.

and turns.
the day breaks. the light fails. the light fails.

the man comes. the light stops. the man goes out.
the day breaks. the day starts. the man goes. the
man comes. the light fails. the man carries. the
light goes out. the bed sounds. the man fails.
the bag shut. the shot heard. the shout stops.
the day cold. the light carries. the man calls.
the gun fires. the fire goes out. the smoke falls.
the light fails. the man falls. the man leaves.
the rain falls. the man goes. the bag falls. the
light breaks. the car blue. the blue starts.
the road turns. the blue flame. the light changes.
the coat tears. the bed sounds. the man comes.
the gun fires. the gate shuts. the mouth starts.
the blood spurts. the fire burns. the door shuts.
the bed sounds. the shoes push. the rain sounds.
the lights change. the gear shifts. the rain comes.
the wipers squeak. the legs cross. the sign changes.
the hat falls. the light moves. the train starts.

i would have had her said stop it
in front of.

she said she was not coming there that
night and leaving all three of them.

all eight in front of.

the large clock in the stonework which
doesnt move an inch.

lines.
lions.

whistle.
turns.
scarf.

that in the distance disappears.
a dog barking.

does not.

all around

(turns)

her aunt or
her uncle.

'hadnt had a

but
couldnt but

bursts out.

a close.

confessional repose twists summit pines out
at a nose trills brakes twigs fall fuel and
ankle notices soft links sand chair chair.

dust or lavatory. having gathered brought
asks. theory. pen. file. metal drawer. the
cat seat.

healy. dial. green. light. shift. gears.
late. clock. electric. lines. crosses.
hurts.

the blood was a different break in sequence.

the blood was not blood.

the blood flowed.

low hills and buried.

rain.
priest.

bent necks.
and hands.

a pocket.
a key.

it is a
hill.

Kemsher

The Deposition of Dubun-i-Nayan.
(native dances in Nyasaland)

photograph of amphora.
(Bosch)

Louvre.
(Guercino)

the white man.
(a magical sign)

Musee des Arts decoratifs.
(but young men)

the proposal.
(an indication)

Genoa.
(a code of laws)

turning to Roman times.
(perplexity)

Villeneuve-les-Avignon.
(Humay and Humayun)

peasantry to a Llama.
(Psycho Cave: "votive")

The Covenant of Christoforo Mauro.
(Theodoric to the Abbey of Sheida)

Andrea del Sarto.
(the Catacombs of St. Calixtus)

The Three Doors Brotherhood.
(correct manner of passing)

resurrection of Tammuz.
(old formula of acquiescence)

character of William.
(famous Comacine Pulpit)

the sign of secrecy.
(figure for Kemsher)

Three Stanzas

i

pneumonoultramicroscopicsilicovolcanoconiosis

ii

aequeosalinocalcalinoceraceoaluminosocupreovitriolic

iii

lopadotemachoselachogaleokranioleipsanodrimhypot-
rimmatosilphioparaomelitokatakechymenokichlepikos-
syphophattoperisteralektryonoptekephalliokigklopelei-
olagooiosiraiobaphetraganopterygon

Novel 7

1

he brings her flowers.
she waters them.
he drowns.

2

she says he's silly.
meanwhile
he agrees.

3

they swim happily
ever after.

song i

no way

means

nor do
you get

a focus
on it

spread out
to an

edge
this is a

name and
seed

and is
a
growing

up
to wide ah

caught

nor space

meant
you get

not even
petals

show
through

this !

song ii

that a thought
should

be this
you say

the face hears
a door

(shut) silently

it has
exactly

this
moment

Eruca Labra (Findings in Paley's Natural Theology)

she remembers her own escape
from the egg

attentively
observing the conformation of the nest

she sees a brood of callow birds
leaves

unaccounted for
'the preparation of the nest'

before the laying of
her egg

the noun

Counting nouns by their roots
she does not leave her egg
in every hole

but in the woodpecker's tongue
or the reader's eye plunged overhead

in glutinous syrup
a skin or bladder
embedded in the heart of firm
fleshy substances

(pricked) (surfaces) (soft)
(pulp).

in pulse
in grain
in grasses

in gravid seed
in trees

the poet's pellicles enveloped

in wool

(as in the pea tribe)
(as in the bean)
(as in the cotton plant)

(as in the pine)
(as in the artichoke)
(as in the thistle)

adverbs urge
the fluid back in time

saliva
the outside of the cheek
the thickness of wheat straw
about a finger in length

worms and insects found alive
in the stomach

shadows at the angle of
the lower jaw saying something

about writing over the masseter muscle
toward the very middle of the cheek
permitting the poem to enter

by the mouth
and there

discharge fluid copiously.

the eruca labra
upon the surface of hair

feathers mucus froth
we have

teeth talons beaks horns
stings prickles

and in the mind
the evidence of exhalations

'the corrupted substances
Maggots revel in.'

The Cup

what is also called the **sleep**
of plants, they turn up, or

they turn down growth **within** the stem
the papilionaceous parts

of shapes
and their backs

to the word.

a connection of system.

an identity of plan.

from Saturn
to our own globe

the hinges in the wings of
an earwig, signs

forgotten, overlooked
neglected as it fascinates

the disposition to receive
light in our minds

there seems to be nothing
but an aura, an effluvium

an infinitesimal future body
which springs

from the larva of the libellula
under that water.

Eros-ion

Text:

O
PPP PPPPP E

e uu U

O oooeEoooO ooooooP

P
PP
PPP

E

Uu Uuu Ue P EE

CCC

C

E

UUUU

uuuu

C

Lexical Key:

O = Overexcitation of Jim's penis
P = Penetration of Jim's, Philip's, Ray's or Eric's penis
E = Ejaculation (Ray only)
U = Unpleasure following ejaculation
(Ray, Betty, Philip, Cathy, Dorothy and Sue)
C = Curve of normal orgasm (Sue excluded)

lower-case = uncompleted eroteme
upper-case = completed eroteme

Performance Notes:

Performance of above text took place on 11 april 1973. Time limit was 9 hours, the actual performance time being 7.35 hours.

Sue ran into problems at Uu (001768) when Eric's dog Earl (which all of us thought had been locked up outside the room) got in through the window. Consequent ejaculation penalty: 00397.4 erotemes.

After this disruption the following textual segment was cancelled:

eeee P

P
PP
PPP

A P eroteme delivered successfully by Philip resulted in a U eroteme at the ninth attempt. By this time we had all moved outdoors and rain had started. At 01987 a slight deviation from the expected result of eroteme P was effected and which was ascribed to the radio song left on in the kitchen during performance.

At 11607 all photographs of O, P and E erotemes were destroyed. Complaints from neighbours and the threat of police investigation at 11695 and 12753 respectively resulted in one additional U eroteme to the score.

Ray and Betty – who were resistant to the whole thing – were responsible for the unusually large frequency of completed C and U erotemes in the score.

The Property: Comma

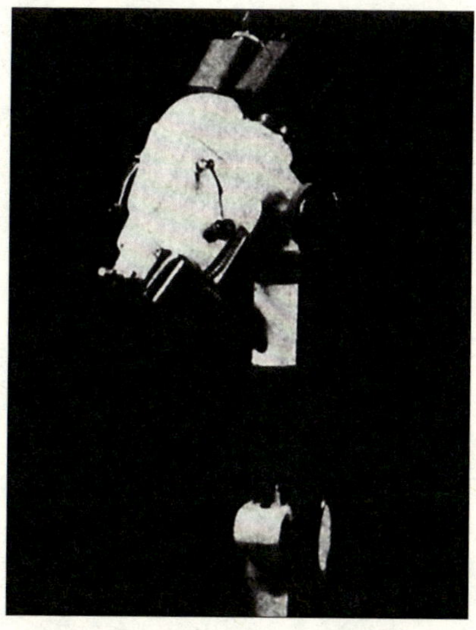

The ten letters form the small space and name it. I am permitted to approach it, touch the outline of its text. Placed in the dorsal lithotomy position and draped, staring at the name, the word DRESS rises to expose my cervix. The cotton swabs soaked with my own mucus are lost against the blackness of the ink. Only one name visible, one name alone that describes, pinning me down within the language frame for its own special purposes. I am inspected by the speech, locked as a three-dimensional image in the two-dimensional language of this frame. I focus on the areas of white, the solid sections of the colposcope which in turn provide me with the necessary empty spaces for an exit. I press myself out flat between the blackness of its letters. I squeeze between the text neither in nor outside of it, not allowed to leave the frame that has named me. I am diagnosed surface, defined and accordingly treated. As it peers down at me the speech becomes covered with an abnormal tissue not revealed in this text. This is my speech that waits the opportunity to speak, that waits the lens through which it can create the language of its patient.

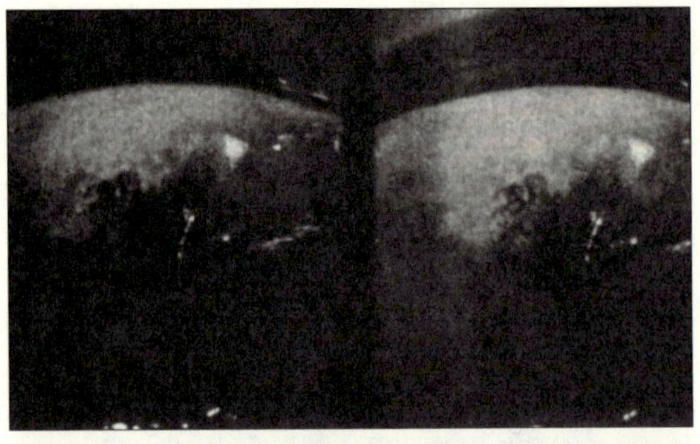

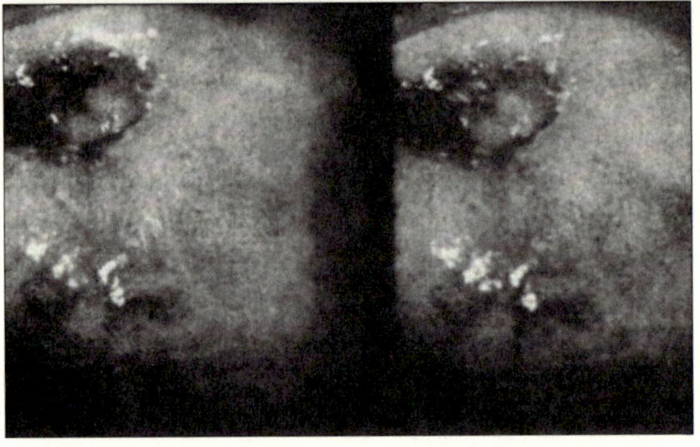

I approach the frames with caution, remembering Allan's words, trying to project these words into the image by dilation and that way test the texture, assure myself before entering as to the safety of the surface. There is a cellular unrest I see from above as the film itself thickens but fails to hold the words I choose which are: THE CYTOPATHOLOGIST SHOULD REPORT EXACTLY WHAT HE SEES. I see myself become the object of a text, the sentence thickens with mosaic leukoplakia extending from the first word along to the twenty-second letter on the line on which I still do not advance. I approach the frame with caution. I do not admit the truth. I am not a cell. I am not the nucleus demarcated by the raised punctuation. I am not the image on the left, not the virus in the host, the image set beside the word which is altering under metabolic pressure. I am watching the gradual shift of mucus. The space is filling with a soft fluid speech eradicating every trace of vascular patterns. The grammatical network is being altered due to the earlier invasion.

I thrust my microphone forward out of the dark background into the language of the frame and my eyes are fixed on him, fixed on the back of his neck where I notice a small red scab. I am there to interrogate, to constitute the language we are all in. But I am lost in the small zone of silence behind his eyes, through his head, the silence of the scab. Invisible. There is no emotion in the scab, it seems apart from him but like him it was found guilty. The silence of the scab is a conspiracy against the language of his face, the language of the frame. My three colleagues have the same thoughts I do. They too are fascinated by the silence that they sense behind his voice, behind their own questioning. What does the language choke. What do their questions mean to him. How do they touch the brain, the inner vibrations of John Ehrlichman as he stands condemned by the implication of the sentence stretched out beneath him. There is no emotion in his voice. I feel that seeing the back of his neck I am seeing the whole of the man. Neck. The most important word in the life of a hanging man. Condemned by language. Condemned by his own lies. I strain the microphone further and further over his shoulder. I too am lying. I'm doing my job. I'm writing the caption beneath the picture that will sentence him for all time. I'm the scab on his neck, in his brain. I am. America. I'm. Doing my job thrusting the lie out forward to the front, feeling my fingers and knuckle entering an area of light. It is the light of the speech that this area is fed by. It bursts the scab, a ray that the blackness of the background lies thrusts forward onto my hand reflecting onto Ehrlichman's coat, wrapping him closed and making the words rebound against the dark.

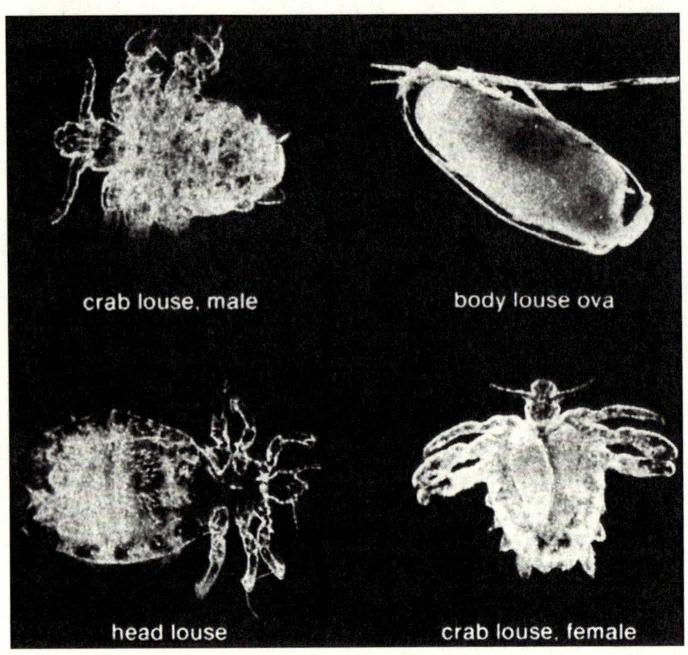

I am closer to the text again, its blackness which illuminates the red scab on his neck. I enter deeper into his language frame to find that a sequence has already been established, a shape has already been assumed. The syntax seems magnified as if beneath a microscope, the words crawl across the surface activating it, causing the statement to redden and fold. He speaks first then screams repeatedly. I note the red scab extending until his speech is covered totally by another language frame. The word ECTOPARASITIC retracts, causing the verb to seem transparent, at which point a grid forms around each word. All the legs move but they do not penetrate the surface. The word MANDIBLES retracts as the redness fades and the black grids, which pronounce themselves more clear and loud, now settle as a background to three words. ABSOLUTELY. UNMERCIFULLY. FINALLY.

'Nothing much happens to any of these characters that has not happened before, and better.'

The words cling as images confuse and wrap arms around a body already holding me. I think of the sentence as I think of this film that I'm in, focus in upon the last two words and fantasize. The complex tissue of the lies will come in time to form a room out of the studio, a bed, a silk pillow with my head on it. And my hair. Knowing he is conscious of my hair, his finger touching my neck as we both wait, bored, for the camera to zoom in closer and shape the phrase into its final form: "Nothing much happens to any of these characters, etc. ... ' The picture darkens beyond the bed, I sense the window through which I've looked so many previous takes as hardly visible. I've no concern for my dress riding high above my legs and yet I sense his lens focused there, that his eyes at least are trained on that one area and that eventually the sentence will predicate no more than that. It's all happened before to me. And better. He lies across my waist timidly. You see his eyes closed as mine, too, are closed. We are in a different space. He holds me timid, not afraid, but timid. Perhaps uninterested. Perhaps, like me, thinking of the other, better times. I am about to speak when he kisses me, I think of the huge eggbeater in the set, of the flying car he drives, of the assassin's name. Scaramanga. Nothing much happens that has not happened before. Except the frame is different now. My legs are lost below my thighs. They are beyond speech. Beyond me. The set is the language now that holds me, heavy on top of my body, appearing as a man but in reality the power of speech. The first sentence of the page is returning. Fixing me here, in readiness of the camera, the words.

As I look into their faces, into their open mouths, I realize my own face too must be different. In this particular language frame I cannot be precisely what I seem. I see them but cannot see myself. I cannot read myself in their eyes. It is the language that fixes all of us, that my glasses name me just as the pen in his hand names him. I notice the words GOLD BROKER pinned above his heart. It is part of the syntax of this frame that makes me ask: should I replace those words with the single word HEART? But I don't. Perhaps because the letters are unavailable to me, because my speech cannot speak. I stare through the mouth of one into the eyes of the other as if my eyes were thoughts carried in the speech that comes out through that same mouth as a scream the other sees. As a pen. The figures are invisible and so this language closes me. I'm fixed, my life no longer than this sentence that I am, this image that struggles to be me. I can say no more than the other two, no more than brokers at the Chicago Mercantile Exchange on the first hectic day of gold trading. Bigger than boneless beef in futures, but slow sales elsewhere. I state obediently as the language chooses its own form. The lights above us become eyes from the angle you are looking at and hearing this. They become eyes fixed on the syntax of the frame that we must live in silently outside the future promise of the speech.

Steeler linebacker Jack Ham breaks out of language. There is no speech evident as I poise my camera eight feet away from him. The number 59 ripples through his shirt until the 9 appears like two zeros. But these are the only language in which the dynamism is articulate and frozen. His mouth tightens in its helmet and, were there a need to speak, he couldn't. Jack Ham bursts but is trapped by this language. He is the measure of the reading speed that the crowd blurs back into its own noise. He is an unwanted speaking of their own muscles, flexed, that makes him the same ball he's holding. Jack Ham is the poem in the grip of the crowd and he will disappear at the conclusion of this reading. He is their own attention to themselves as spectacle and dies the moment that I activate my camera. And I am waiting. As long as I need to wait.

Brigadier General Teferi Benti is Ethiopia's head of state. He is that stated line of speech, a rigid form of the statement on parade here. There is now no possibility that his actual thoughts might be exposed in this frame. The uniform will hide his text just as my own face will continue to be hidden by the limits of his language. I stand as straight and as rigid as he does. Both sentences are parallel. General Teferi Benti is a line of speech supporting a paragraph of bureaucracy that in turn supports the power structure of this page. Foreign observers will attach significance to the shadow that hides his eyes, hides all eyes in this frame. General Teferi Benti is a blind text, his hands not visible, his jacket creased. He cannot read himself.

I cannot speak of the disaster that I find implicit in his face. Through the window to his eyes so full of hate and fear, down to his mouth pinned by the syntax of the verdict and yet as far away from speech as any one man can be. It is this framework of a stationary verb that I must at least name John Mitchell leaving the court, one of the most powerful figures in the United States. All of his past is emptied here, spread out on the surface of the frame. He has become that surface and calls attention to his role as target. He can only be the meaning that the text concludes in. He is an after-language, an after-speech. He is that space escribed as actual target. He is the space I aim these words at. As the frame adjusts, the tense settles in the future. John Mitchell will become the parent host of these words that use him, empty him and fix him as the visual shell that was his name. So now the image cannot slide, the verb is permanent, the picture is THIS picture that you read and the picture YOU see is that picture I am in. It's Allan who points this out to me and Allan alone who isn't here. I recognize so clearly now how both the image and the words imprison him so far away I can't even touch him with a sound. I see all that he is or ever has been through that glass. I see everything I'm hearing as the tissue of a lie seen at a distance as a figure seated in a car outside the court and to whom I can't call out, can't describe. He will be murdered as a verb. The language alone can testify to that. But I can't describe the murder here, only the constant process of the murdering. That is the one constant I'm allowed. It is a rule of this particular grammar that you see.

August Sixteen 1977

The poem prophesied the dream
but in the dream the dream
is speech   and this is the dream
speech hates

in the dream he couldn't pull the trigger
meaning he couldn't shoot the man
asking his friend the shot
went by his aunty's house and
he's dying instantly

this is the music before language
takes it from you, and this,

what the incidents become
beginning with the voice through every
separation of the eyelids

he is alone in his father's house
with the mother who is absent
there's a line to detach them
we'd talked all day about that.

but the eyes that alert us
had no weight.

it wasn't his father he killed but
he shot with that leak in his tension.
later he would go home make
love to her   feeling
the pain of such pleasure.

when he gives himself up to the police
he cries on the officer's arm.

it was a long time ago, on a different street
a different incident. he threw his gun away, another
blew his brains out with a shot so loud
it took the top right off the dream

with a gentle nudge from Ian naming breakfast

he primes the trigger in his dream, he makes
the poem with the dream coordinate, this

shares his mind around in words.

I remember the day the sleep came on me
a lot of heat, a lot of bright sunlight.
i hold the gun and David says shoot. i say
i can't and turn away my eyes. David takes
the gun and shoots. Here's where
the poetry takes over

In the dream we ran, now,
i'm holding us here in the poem inside
the puddle of brains which didn't happen

Dave gets some on his hands and says
ugh

this isn't dream this is poetry.

In the dream we run   Dave disappears
i run on alone to my parent's house
there's a puzzled look on dad's face

this is the pain that realization brings
you to, where the future locates you
you've been there before, a trap
in the dreaming a vision of words
speaking free.

In the poem this is a dream about
words   their silences   the thought pollution
of the images in eyes locked to dreams
through the dictionary that parents
give you

but outside the poem i know
it's a dream about sex or else love
in the deliberate confusion language plans.

i end, not with the image of
some brains on the sidewalks, but somehow
with the sidewalk in my brain
where i'm walking, giving myself up
to the police

that's when it turns to steps when i realize
that without the mouth i don't have to go
there are steps down and a little light
but no language to change it.

The dream's dishonesty is what the words
imagined. There was a gun he didn't fire but
he really was a killer.

Someone didn't die because a part of him
did. Poetry and pronouns and families
and anger. Sex and all of it
called magic by the ancients.

Muiopotmos

the waterfall is not a biography
in the same way
words seldom find a path
to their seas

as an apple is round
so is the apple

even if i love you and say so
even when you're allowed
to love me back it still says
something different from what
we do

something gets repeated
something is

like the rim of a pot
and its line which is stationary
but is said to run

runs around the rim
of your lips back
into someone else's mouth

this is the overall design
of teeth assembled in their sequence
coming into speech between
eatings and motions

'just an old turn of phrase'

and your turn to bite
through the gerunds and butterflies

The Cetacea: Four Tides

Cardiff   Whales   bottle-nose   Cardiff
Swansea   Whales   caing   Berwyn
Tydfil   Whales   finback   Swansea
Bangor   Whales   finner   Llangollen
Rhondda   Whales   greenland   Tydfil
Pembroke   Whales   humpback   Rhyl
Mdwddwy   Whales   grey   Bangor

Berwyn   Whales   ice   Carno
Llangollen   Whales   pike   Rhondda
Rhyl   Whales   scrag   Caerphilly
Carno   Whales   pilot   Pembroke
Caerphilly   Whales   rostrate   Tintern
Tintern   Whales   sperm   Mdwddwy
Cwmbran   Whales   beaked   Cwmbran

Cwmbran   hwael   blubber   Cardiff
Cardiff   whal   butt   Cwmbran
Tintern   whaill   calf   Mdwddwy
Swansea   qual   catching   Berwyn
Caerphilly   qwall   cub   Tintern
Tydfil   whalle   cutter   Pembroke
Carno   quhail   drive   Swansea

Bangor   quhell   duty   Llangollen
Rhyl   hvalr   guts   Caerphilly
Rhondda   qwaylle   hunter   Rhondda
Llangollen   hval   killer   Tydfil
Pembroke   walira   kind   Rhyl
Berwyn   walre   meat   Carno
Mdwddwy   wels   striker   Bangor

A Book Resembling Hair

a man enters a landscape carrying
a large white card containing
two words:

'muscle' and 'tension'

there are village rumours that the man
is preparing the prototype of a large
billboard advertisement for a new
medication

in the water to his left
a fight is occurring between
an old woman and a younger woman
disguised as a seahorse

a lot of water gets splashed around
haphazardly and some, that finds a destination
on the large white card,
causes the ink to run

at this point
the man walks purposefully to the right
and within the space of three short lines

returns to the text with a mirror.

The Syllogistic Cinema

But if it wasn't Garbo's eloquent mood it was Olivier's intelligent manliness and Henry Fonda's power of justice and therefore Carole Lombard's wit.

But if it wasn't Carole Lombard's wit then it must have been Paul Newman's obstinate despair at Henry Fonda's intelligent manliness and Olivier's wit and therefore Greta Garbo's power of justice.

But if it wasn't Garbo's power of justice then it must have been Marilyn Monroe's doomed magnetism with Woody Allen's sense of worthlessness and Clint Eastwood's musical trust in Myrna Loy's entire pleasure falling short of Michelle Pfeiffer's calm acceptance and therefore Fred Astaire's breathless hesitation.

But if it was a case of Fred Astaire's breathless hesitation then it must have been Henry Fonda's entire pleasure falling short of Olivier's mutual trust in Garbo's sense of worthlessness and Paul Newman's calm acceptance of Carole Lombard's doomed magnetism and therefore Marilyn Monroe's eloquent moods.

But if it was a case of Marilyn Monroe's eloquent moods then it must have been Woody Allen's wit or Fred Astaire's sense of worthlessness and Myrna Loy's obstinate despair at Clint Eastwood's power of justice and therefore Michelle Pfeiffer's intelligent manliness.

But if it was Michelle Pfeiffer's intelligent manliness then it must have been Marilyn Monroe's power of justice and Carole Lombard's obstinate despair at either Paul Newman's eloquent mood and Garbo's wit or Olivier's power of justice and Henry Fonda's mutual trust and therefore Fred Astaire's pleasure falling short.

But if it was a case of Fred Astaire's pleasure falling short then it can't have been Basil Rathbone's courtly villainy but could be Myrna Loy's mutual trust in Richard Widmark's feigned psychosis and if it was Clint Eastwood's pleasure falling short then it can't have been a case of Kirk Douglas's lucid participation in Burt Lancaster's baroque rage.

But if it was a case of Burt Lancaster's baroque rage then it can't have been Bette Davis's amplified dash by which she dismounts and if it can't have been Bette Davis's amplified dash by which she dismounts then it must have been Paul Scofield's performance in *King Lear* so then it can't have been Humphrey Bogart's complicated presence in *The Maltese Falcon*.

But if it was a case of Humphrey Bogart's complicated presence in *The Maltese Falcon* then it could still have been a case of Carole Lombard's performance in *King Lear*.

But if it's not a case of Carole Lombard's performance in *King Lear* then it must be either Paul Scofield's courtly villainy or Fred Astaire's amplified dash by which he dismounts and so a case of Bette Davis's sense of worthlessness in the face of therefore Woody Allen's baroque rage.

But if it's not a case of Woody Allen's baroque rage then it must be Burt Lancaster's doomed magnetism and Myrna Loy's mutual trust in Marilyn Monroe's amplified dash by which she dismounts in front of therefore Kirk Douglas's lucid participation.

But if it was not a case of Kirk Douglas's lucid participation then it must have been Michelle Pfeiffer's complete gratification or Lee Marvin's intelligent manliness and therefore Fred Astaire's feigned psychosis.

And given that it is a case of Fred Astaire's feigned psychosis then it follows that it must be Richard Widmark's pleasure falling short of Garbo's courtly villainy and therefore being Garbo's courtly villainy it follows that it must be Basil Rathbone's obstinate despair.

Poem "Murder": A Scenario

1.

CUR AINS CLOSET

CURTAINS CLOSED

(T = victim's corpse
D = detective.)

2.

D OR
DOOR

(D = position of detective at 5.34 pm & 5.46 pm respectively
R = position of suspect (Mr F. Chayter) at 5.34 pm & 5.46 pm respectively
O = graph-points on mental oscilloscope attached to suspect's mind at 5.34 pm & 5.46 pm respectively.)

3.

GOO BYE

GOOD BY

BYE BYE

(D = detective
E = housemaid (Mrs Martha Rissole)

time: a little after 6.33 pm)

4.

GOO BYE

GO BOY

(O = victim's corpse
G = gardener (Mr Heinrich Bolkc from Brussels)
B = bush (rhododendron)
Y = tree (cedar)
E = suspect (Mr. F. Chayter))

NOTE

Syntatic clues all point to the existence of two victims: one found by the gardener (Mr Heinrich Bolkc from Brussels) at a large distance from the rhododendron bush, the other buried secretly as a syntactic embed between the tree and the bush.

This suggests a paratactic complicity, a criminotic gesture of elision.

It provides the central element in the mystery withheld by the housemaid, Mrs Martha Rissole, from Detective Inspector Acorn (the D referred to in Section I).

The burial that establishes the housemaid's grammatological presence within the text (allowing the real Martha Rissole, the Rissole outside the text, to escape free) must have taken place between the times of 5.34 pm and 6.33 pm.

The Occupant

It was with considerable difficulty that i pushed past the transparency of the writing in order to discover the beginnings of its real opacity within that room. July 18 … as i continue in my reading on, and at the same time into, the contained systems of the house (that room). August i begin to realize how the reading, too, is vacant in drift somehow somewhere beyond this reading by him, where it all may end, in the description of the tall lean figure walking down a street where she supposes you are looking.

He is looking before this at a curtain (closed) on the window opposite. At precisely this time the hands reach up to draw the right one first and then the left until the two drapes meet in a slight pressure of the one against the other, soft, affirmingly, before settling in place.

December 9 … i had assumed that the curtains had been on the inside of the room behind some window, but as i touched the wall it disappeared into the pattern of the gold silk curtains, the vertical linkings of its fleurs de lis. Once in the room i walked across to the window. Looking out i saw where the park had always been, between the tall walls of the two adjacent buildings, two curtains hanging rigid and indifferent to the wind that blew across this scene.

End paragraph and cut to wicker chair by fire. Body in chair. Zoom into close-up of hand holding lighter. Naturally i would never be entirely sure if this had happened. Cut to blank wall. Forty minutes then dialogue resumes. For as the wind hit against my cheek my viewing stopped … page bottom. Close-up of hand turning page … voice-over continues and i recommenced as before with the convolutions of the clauses. As i reached the middle of the line, at centre page, my eyes slipped over to the other page that contained this single paragraph. Close-up of paragraph as voice-over stops.

March. I have realized the substance of the error. I am not sure of the phenomenon. I am told there were no curtains but only a single sheet of untrimmed hessian between two walls. This is how i returned to open the door. This is who came in.

Pan to door opening. Dark light. Close-up of hand turning knob. Cut. Move to shot of feet walking across carpet. What i see is difficult to describe for in that moment of the movement of my eyes (manuscript shows signs of deletion and change from eyes to feet) the clear perception faded. Sound of distant traffic. Sound of baby crying. Loud music. Close-up of page superimposed on another page to give effect of text floating off page.

Voice-over continues. The only possible conclusion i could draw was that i also had become a texture visiting his mind, passing through the page at the very moment that his inattention bisected the shifting of the camera within the sudden shift of scene to where the page blew in the wind. What, in fact, i am doing in this room (manuscript reads 'that' room) is hard to tell. The contents difficult to describe. My past experience had become its present contents. A chair perhaps was there. An explanation of the chair and a reading of a similar description (one body on camera, two voices on audio) these hints, those variations on the same or similar memories serving to place some other chair exactly (with all certitude) within a small gap in the wall tracing at an angle into three recesses the thing i remember as the texture of (switch to woman's voice) the angle as i felt along it to the bullet mark (man's voice continues) the solidity transparent as it carried me i think into a narrower gap much darker in the flow of his own spelling of my journal entry.

Cut to supermarket car park. Man walking slowly holding microphone. No audio. Text now shows in subtitles at bottom of screen. Text becomes illegible as man passes through white and light areas of cinemes.
Finally there is this last conclusion to be drawn: there can be no certain inside to this room, for the very description of the curtains placed by the chair he borrowed from her served not so much to stabilize but activate the gaps his words formed incorrectly in the superstructure of the speech itself as she described its contents to the officer in charge.
Cut to still cineme. Audio reiterates final phoneme.
Credits over final page of text.

Words: Meditation Nine

for Dick Higgins

untitled

abandoned

Latin Lines:

for gertrude stein

a rose

cicero's
cicero's
cicero's

Novel Eighteen

The meaning of bloodless combines with substitution.

8 pm precisely:

Inchmeal.
Mis-date.

As kingfishers, they are the same proleptic
intimations of a phantom fall
                                        (as noun is
a hollow or enclosed space over and through
the obstacles that Emily perceives.)

'Through the radar comes the coinage known for twindle.'

The degges (the two of them) as heathpacks flitching
perhaps ragged.
The russet flakes corrected trucks but still

an individuality.

Is the line born of such desires to distinguish.

Rotundas alongside
texturas.

Though the upper loop is actually the cross stroke
of the now asibilant tea, continued down to form
the eye.

The scene of this poem is the night it represents.

Trench to tunnel blast.

With a slanted pen even the longest letters move down.

And descendentally a different letter mentions april.

Summary

Projects for Procedures

1 CIVIC-SEMIOTIC RECYCLING

To take a series of existing public statues of various Canadian and British politicians and heads of state and to arrange them as two opposing ice hockey teams at either Toronto's Maple Leaf Gardens or Montreal's Forum.

A running sports commentary to be compiled based on collaged texts that illustrate their significant political achievements.

After the playing of the national anthem the refrigeration system is turned off and the game is announced over when entire surface of the ice melts.

2 AN ONTARIO ART GALLERY HENRY SARTOR MOORE RESARTUS PROJECT

A moral intervention project designed to clothe in acceptable modest attire all Henry Moore sculptures at the Art Gallery of Ontario (over fifty pieces). Each sculpture to be measured for identical three-piece outfits and measurements and cloth samples left by the side of each sculpture.

A parallel 'immoral' intervention viz. to fill all existing holes and empty spaces in the sculpture with pungent, highly decomposable foodstuffs.

3 GLOBAL TEA PROJECT

To collect sample waters from every major river in the world. Bottles to be arranged alphabetically in a bar on the walls of which are to be microphotographic enlargements of water samples to illustrate bacterial and chemical contents.

Exhibition to be followed by a mass tea ceremony in which identical tea (a vintage darjeeling) will be served in the river water of each person's choice.

Ceremony itself to be followed by construction of a composite global river at a specific incline of ten feet to every thousand and to a length of not more than nine feet. This channel, or river bed, to be constructed at Ingleside, Ontario, into which all samples will be poured and allowed to drain away.

References: Georges Bataille on the General Economy and Yeats's line that only the wasteful virtues gain the sun.

4 THE SOCRATIC BESTIARY

A long-term two-part project:

a) To draw up a zoomorphic concordance of the Dialogues of Plato, itemizing every reference to animals, birds, fishes and insects. Accompanying the catalogue are to be analyses of the semantic, semiotic and philosophic nature of the reference (literal, allegorical, analogical, symbolic etc.). The whole is to be drawn together as a contribution to the Philosophic Zoo (an ongoing megaproject to redefine epistemological structures as zoomorphic areas).

b) The compilation of specific animal concordances and their prospective use in performance, e.g., to gather all references in nineteenth-century English fiction to the boa constrictor and to place all such books into the constrictor pen at the Toronto Zoo; to gather all twentieth-century paperbacks published in North America containing references to the beaver and to place them in a beaver colony as material for a beaver dam.

5 TWO 'PATAPHYSICAL PROJECTS

a) A catalogue and author-title index of all the books in Adam's library.

b) Part II of *The Perseus Project*: Speculative linguistic ontogenetic research into the sexual life of ordovician trilobite fossils.

6 PUBLISHING PROJECT

A paperback and variorum edition of *The Collected Writings of Jesus Christ.*

7 THREE WRITING PROJECTS

a) Essay proposing the *Morte D'Arthur* of Sir Thomas Malory to be a concealed chess manual. This will contain historical material on various similar theories and post-structural analyses of selected chapters and pseudo-narrative devices.

b) A homolinguistic translation of Joyce's *Finnegans Wake.*

c) A translation into connected, serial limericks of Milton's *Paradise Lost.*

8 A DICK HIGGINS THINK-ALIKE COMPETITION

9. MARCEL DUCHAMP PROJECT: CONTRIBUTION TO FUTILITY #27

To translate Duchamp's ready-mades into ready-made performance scenarios.

Self-imposed time limit on these projects: 11 years, 7 months. Starting date: Oct. 12, 1982

NOTE

Like a true conceptualist I have realized only one of these projects: *The Perseus Project*. The *Finnegans Wake* translation had already been started in 1975. Both projects follow.

Fish Also Rise

(a homolinguistic translation of page 1 of *Finnegans Wake*)

neep streems was time of noun and name's S from the dodged – was it water end? – to round of sea womb coming to the roaming imperial ease and commodity italicized italianate aestheticated wittgensteinian gertrudism banked flowing to an oily spine at the question's article rooked and hinter steel.

a musical knight with a night's music instrumental to the pond-stepped passengers embarking for newtique land from small hamlet's middle state and underaged continental pugilists circa 1810 twained by the frank and cintra's conventional fish fin marked on his gut and riverstoned gall by a heavy (if financially suggestive) hyperbole moving to the beauty of some stone-faced dancer-for-money in green sward county's city duplicated entrance to

the sound-sick and absolute chronology.

but never sound from a flame (flambloyant blewsie or jumbled catholic saint) nor yet the meat's own time scheme never that nor cigaretted and margarined blew up in smoke never that nor the prophet of braille never the war loved and the mirror catching nicety of issues to the family's familiar associations. red of the pepper measuring the brewer's dad's dadaism in biblical reference to names suggestively chinese the beer smell geometrically traced in the bulb's glow lighting a certain scottish lad in munich labelled olympic and post shavian.

to heer hugo ball's notation of a fortunate fortissimo miltonic slip

(banananananaonoooooolalalarastaatavatoro
rapeelolorussollolaffantataragugoonavastana
boomeskimomomondododomalion)

splitting the a-thomistic dolores spaced in a deserted liberty torch lit battery of gleenotes from his lute extracting with a bedstead fastic narrative inclined toward an ontologically fresh flat aire's religiosa.

the city being destroyed and laterally neck-wise Berlin to China town down the phil of sophical implication a jump into para declarations that Mr Fish Also Eye with all of his nordic opucity human and nurseried topographically directed to even a bee's own definition – existentially on time to deliver one interrogatively foreign sun set sound to the chiropractical tympani: shaking their speares along a barb of haven rapped where the cars outspanning print of colour places on the bumper peel with a clubfoot lust one rutting taxonomist

The Perseus Project: Paleogorgonization and the Sexual Life of Fossils

Delivered at the First Symposium on Linguistic Onto-genetics, Toronto, 21 November 1981

I spent the spring and summer months of 1978 in the small Yorkshire village of Cudworth (or 'Cudduth', as the locals still pronounce it) where I examined the unpublished manuscripts and notebooks of the unknown but remarkable Samuel Gatty, a lifelong resident of the village. Gatty spent his life (until his death in 1968) in voluntary poverty and obscurity, squeezing a paltry living from a variety of odd jobs, his favourite being that of night security guard at a local disused mining quarry. It was there that Gatty first developed his interest in the problematics of paleontology, which led eventually to his earth-shattering theory regarding the active sex life of fossils and his revolutionary discovery of both fossil writing and fossil speech. Toward the end of 1967, Gatty developed cortical cancer and for the rest of his life was confined to bed; on March 4, 1968, at 11.29 am he died, too early to see the effects of his theories on paleosexuality and fossil speech. Superficially, nothing has occurred. The world has still to hear of Samuel Gatty and still to be confronted with the revolutionary implications of his theories – implications that not only revolutionize our received notions as to the birth and age of language but also destroy the fundamental premises of language itself and the philosophical basis for human truth. Gatty was a passionate adherent to scientific subjectivity, to the rule of wonder over wisdom. He was convinced that the genuine value of facts lay not in their truth but in the deeper fictions behind them. His own brand of hermeneutics treated 'beneath' as 'behind' and 'behind' as an ever-recurring series of self-reflective mirrors. Gatty fought for these ideals all his life and his sole reward was international unrecognition.

We had developed a deep friendship by letter but had never met. After his death I was invited by his widow, Enyd, to visit their cottage and spend time examining his library and manuscripts. At that time I was compiling a definitive descriptive catalogue of European sado-erotic devices. Gatty had confessed to me in several letters of an oblique attraction to the mechanically perverse. In 1922, at the age of only fourteen, he had patented an windshield wiper that simulated the unbearable, excruciating sound of long female fingernails scratching the surface of a chalkboard. In 1937 he marketed a small quartz cuckoo clock that cursed in Swahili every fifteen minutes and openly vomited on the hour. But it would be foolish to claim that Gatty's interest in such devices was anything more than a leisurely recreation, and soon my interests turned to his lifetime obsession with paleosexuality.

Gatty's library comprised only eleven titles collected together (along with Enyd's coronation souvenirs) on a single unvarnished plank of knotted pine, interposed between the family television (seldom used) and Enyd Gatty's Singer sewing machine. There was a perverse fascination evinced by the choice of titles and editions: Speucippus's *On the Threefold Aspect of the Fourfold Leaning* (the scarce Cologne imprint of 1584); Winkleman's *Three Treatises on Solitude*, 1763; *The Complete Transactions of the Antiseptic Club* for 1895; Henniker's controversial *Letters on the Origin of Norman Titles*; Johannes Comenius's *Orbis Sensualium Pictus* (the rare Lisbon edition of 1682); an inscribed presentation copy of Baron Cheezburger's *Compound Electro-myographical Studies of Third Millennium Cuneiform*; Fentworth's *Corpus Linguisticus Mythologus Hellenicum* (a handsome folio copy in full calf with metal clasps of the rare editio princeps of 1569); Punst-Augenblick's ever-popular *Treatise on the Late Jurassic Graptolite Communities of New South Wales*; Melville's *Moby Dick* (from the library of Rockwell Kent himself); and the notorious Limoges variant of Rabbi Cheo Chu Kung's *Dysgraphia in the Thinking of Tan Khan Ku*. All of these books were held securely by the mammoth Jubilee edition of Ulbrich's *Roman Law* – the world's most natural of bookends.

Gatty kept surprisingly few notebooks, preferring to enter his thoughts spontaneously in the margins of his current reading. It was during my study of these marginalia that I came across the reference which triggered off my own paleosexual investigations in the Perseus Project. It was in the handsome folio copy of the rare and almost unknown *Corpus Linguisticus Mythologus Hellenicum* by the heretical Franciscan Friar Benedetto Fentworth. The book is a complex web of allegorical romance, scholastic rhetoric, Pythagorean numerology and hermeticism, all interwoven around the central story of the myth of Medusa. The story is well-known: Medusa, the cursed offspring of Phorcys and Ceto, is born with the power of turning to stone all who look directly upon her. In the place of hair Medusa has a skull covered with writhing snakes. Perseus, the young prince of Seriphos, volunteers to slay her. With the divine aid of Minerva he finds a way of avoiding being turned to stone; he approaches her backwards, observing her indirectly in the shining surface of his shield. As a mirror image of the real gorgon he is able to impotize her terrible power and decapitate her. On page 387 Gatty has written this note:

> Fentworth's allegory is a careful coded secret geological treatise … probably the world's first work of paleontology … what Medusa represents is the hidden nature of fossilization in nature … Fentworth has hit upon my own terrible discovery of the intimate connection between language, fossil, sex and death. These are truths too dangerous to be openly announced. What the Corpus really speaks of is the death of God as a Logos and the atheistical re-attachment of language to the prelinguistic desires of fossil lust …

There follows a reference to Gatty's November Journal of 1954. I quickly checked out the reference and was instantly disappointed. The pages cited were crammed with mathematical calculations of vertiginous density: the abandoned fragments, no doubt, of Gatty's failed attempt to ascertain the square root of God through a synthesis of Mayan calendrical series and the KKOO-REE-OST-UK, or shaman number chants, of the ancient Kurdish people. But one entry proved of interest; it was a hasty note upon the implications of Fentworth's obsessive dwellings on Medusa's head of snakes:

> Fentworth deliberately distorts the myth to throw emphasis upon the sonological implications. In the Corpus it is the head of hissing snakes, the cacophony of their disunited tongues, that fossilizes the listener. For Fentworth, it is sound and speech which gorgonize not sight and image … the implications to paleolinguistics are profound … they must be voiced …

The last fifteen years of Gatty's life were taken up with working out two dominant scientific subjectivities: the proof of a fossil sex life and the documentation of fossil speech. Gatty first credits fossils with an actual sex life in his unpublished paper 'Chronodynamic Orgasm and Seismic Paleosexuality'. It is here that he develops his concept of the seismic orgasm. All fossils, claims Gatty, have an undeniable, but directly unverifiable sex life. Every species, every specimen, experience cycles of rutting, mating and calfing, but a precise chronological calculation is impossible because fossil sex occurs within geologic and not human chronometric time. Under the pressures of sex economy fossils tend to migrate through the various stratographical layers of the earth, moving from geologic period to geologic period until finding a sexually conducive zone. The Cambrian agnostid, for example, will move up through the Paleozoic zone into the upper Jurassic layer. After mating, it returns to its Cambrian locale. At this point Gatty introduces his notion of the seismic orgasm. Earthquakes, he explains, are nothing other than fossil orgasms recorded upon the chronometric grid of human catastrophe and indicate less a basic shift in the earth's tectonic structure than an intense but transitory fossil sex affect.

In two other papers Gatty makes startling claims regarding fossil intelligence. In 'The Ichnological Answer to the Non-Question of Paleolinguistic Fossil Texts', Gatty gives examples of literate fossil species. Basing his thesis on an intensive study by himself and his wife of Paleozoic trace fossils, he claims an origin of writing no later than 550 million years ago. Trace fossils are defined by conservative, reactionary paleontology as the fossilized holes and burrows made by benthic biota such as trilobites and annelid worms. They record the tracks and movements of extinct species and as such provide valuable data upon the methods of movement by these creatures. Gatty, always a virulent opponent of scientific rationalism, attacks this theory and proffers the startling counter-theory of the PALEOGLYPH. In reality, trace fossils are the first intelligent attempts at creating a comprehensive system of written significative marks. Gatty provides a catalogue of 3,000 different glyphs recorded in Ordovician and Silurian limestone deposits. These paleoglyphs, as he termed them, show characteristic dialect variations from region to region and a progressive refinement of their hieroglyphic content as they are traced from zone to zone. In a lengthy appendix Gatty outlines the nature of his proposed 816-character TRILOBITE ALPHABET, which would be the key to opening the unknown area of fossil literacy.

In a companion paper, 'Trace Fossils and the Electro-magnetic Imprint', Gatty provides evidence for an actual fossil speech. Written two years after the previous paper, it reports an astonishing revision of his earlier theory of fossil writing. The paleoglyphs, claims Gatty, are not writing at all but the storage areas of complex acoustic signals transmitted by the fossils and held as an electro-acoustic imprint in the fossil mould. These signals are complex to a degree sufficient that they may be termed imprints of an authentic fossil speech. Toward the end of his life Gatty took a humble position as security guard at the University of Sheffield's Engineering Department, and in the privacy of those long nights worked secretly in the radiophonic workshops of the sonar research division attempting to produce an actual recording of fossil speech. There are details in his note-books on the methods employed, which are stunning in their simplicity. Passing a length of chrome bias recording tape over a magnetized fossil specimen and within the controlled conditions of an anechoic chamber, the electro-acoustic content of the fossil is immediately and entirely transferred to the tape. Gatty claims to have produced one sixty-minute recording of Ordovician fossil speech; unfortunately that tape no longer remains. Posterity will probably register as one of the greatest tragedies in the history of human ideas that Gatty's tape is lost forever. Opponents have claimed the lost-tape theory to be apocryphal and a strategy on Gatty's part to legendize his pseudo-experiments and chicanery. His widow, Enyd, however, provides an explanation that I for one have always fully believed. 'Sam had always tolerated my middle-class conservatism', she explains, 'and permitted me to indulge my tastes in popular culture to the full. One night, a week after his historic work at the university, I unwittingly recorded a number of Frank Sinatra songs over the precious recording of fossil speech.'

It was because of this loss that I decided to extend the scope of my own Perseus Project to cover the recording of fossil speech as well as a demonstration of the structure of the fossils' sexual lives. I decided, in fact, to realize a simple reconstruction of

Gatty's paleo-acoustic experiments and try to produce a high fidelity recording of fossil speech. I conducted these experiments under the supervision of Professor Northrop Boyle at the University of Toronto's Royal Conservatory of Music. I chose as my subject a slab of limestone impacted with several fine specimens of the late Ordivician arthropod Ogygites canadensis: a 470-million-year-old trilobite from the Craigleith area of Ontario. I shall repeat two of these experiments here tonight. I will first place the source fossil on a clean demagnetized surface. I will now place a chrome bias magnetic tape on top of it. At this point the fossil imprint is acting as an inverse bulk eraser and is transmitting its entire electro-acoustic content as a bulk imprint onto the tape. The tape is now ready for playback:

> You are now listening to the sounds of authentic fossil speech. They are the electro-acoustic permineralizations of trilobitic communication. They are sound fossils, if you like, recording in all likelihood a period of intense rutting and high sexual desire.

My second experiment tonight attempts an interspecies translation across geologic time. I will employ a method of simple electro-magnetic/print interface in order to fuse human time and fossil time in a single, compound semantic secretion. You have already heard the sound of fossil desire. You will now hear that desire translated into accessible human syntax and vocabulary. First, I will place a telephone on top of the identical source fossil and a written text beneath it. The telephone receiver is now placed on top of the destination tape. I will activate the telephone by a simple seven-digit algorithm. The printed text beneath the fossil is now transmitting its alphabetic elements as a human logical code throughout the fossil's magnetic field. At this moment the fossil sounds are being reprogrammed into their human semantic equivalents. Passing along the telephonic circuitries, the recoded, translated fossil speech arrives at the tape and leaves its bulk imprint. I shall now play back to you perhaps the greatest moment in the history of linguistic onto-genetics: an intelligible, translated conversion between two Ogygites canadenses, recorded in the limestone deposits of Craigleith over 470 million years ago. The fossil speech, long ago hypothesized by Gatty and alluded to by the Franciscan friar Fentworth has now been isolated and recorded for the benefit of contemporary human ears and represents the conclusions of Part One of my Perseus Project.

Part Two of the Perseus Project is an analysis of the sexual life of fossils. In a nutshell this is my thesis:

> The sexual life of a fossil is nothing other than the proliferation of anagrams through a saturated written medium at the sociological expense of human meaning, human sex and death.

In this I am proposing language to be a sexual system entirely alien to the human species, a Paleozoic conspiracy, a saturated network of fossil sex and paleontic lusts that uses man far more than man uses it. There is a crucial distinction to be drawn between fossil production and fossil reproduction. Whereas fossil production takes place over millions of years inside the framework of geologic time, fossil reproduction occurs more rapidly within active linguistic time. Gatty, a genius in most respects, failed to make this vital distinction between a fossil's productive and reproductive dimensions and as a consequence was led into his erroneous claims for a physiological basis to paleosexuality in the concept of the seismic orgasm. The Perseus Project reveals paleosexuality to be an activity within linguistic time and space with reproduction occurring through the agency of single letters post-taxonomically secreted along anagrammatic grids. Paleosexuality, then, is a complex and disguised sub-articulation beneath the surface circuitries of all language.

The fossil sex act is a vast cyclical gesture that starts and concludes in invisibility. It completes itself through three major stages:

1 taxo-genetic articulation
2 cryptonymic infiltration
3 environmental resedimentation

In the first stage the fossil creates for itself a contextual habitat of scientific discourse by which the fossil enters language as the object of a science: paleontology. Traditionally conceived as the scientific study of fossil life, paleontology is nothing but the fossil's own invention: a complex defence network to ensure an authentic translation from geologic to linguistic time. For what paleontology creates is nothing but the fossil's proper name, its taxa, its morphology as words, thus giving it the reproductive potential of textuality itself.

In the second stage of cryptonymic infiltration, the fossil disseminates itself as an anagrammatic embed within a variety of texts. This marks the stage of utmost polymorphous perversity and frequently results in a paleosexual take-over of language. In the first stage of taxogenesis the fossil gains an alphabetic form, inscribing it inside linguistic time. In the cryptonymic stage the fossil as word disseminates as a hidden anagram throughout any number of printed texts. I will give two examples to demonstrate this stage in paleosexuality. The fossil example I have chosen is the Ordovician-Devonian trilobite PHACOPS. In primary taxogenesis the fossil develops its taxonomic alphabetic chromosomes: P O C H S and A (with a duplicated P-type chromosome.) In the example given below, the phacops is seen actively infiltrating a short poem by the Canadian poet bpNichol. Here is the poem and, following that, my own analysis of the phacops's sex-rage quotient:

happy & sad laughing
remembered laughing hysterical

hysterical sad laughing &
remembered laughing happy

waves

remembered laughing laughing &
sad hysterical happy

remembered & hysterical
laughing laughing

happy

sad

Beneath the surface trivia of this minor text there is sexo-cryptonymic infiltration in every line. There are no less than 6 active alphabetic chromosomes in line 1; 4 in line 2; 6 in line 3; 6 in line 4; 2 in line 5; 4 in line 6; 10 in line 7; 4 each in lines 8, 9 and 10; and 2 in line 11. This gives a total promiscuity or sex-rage quotient of 54 in a text of only 184 written characters. This represents almost 30% fossil infiltration. The poem, however, illustrates a failed attempt at complete anagrammatic reproduction. Inexplicably, the phacops has chosen to infiltrate a text resistant to infiltration by a phacopsian O-type chromosome. The following, in contrast, is an example of a remarkably successful fossil infiltration:

JOHN MACPHERSON

In a total of only 14 textual characters there are no less than 8 active phacops chromosomes. It is an amazing example of complete anagrammatic reproduction restricted to a ruthless economy. John Macpherson, age 36, a dustman of Glasgow and still living, now carries within his proper name a complete specimen of the fossil phacops. Anagrammatic infiltration of this kind initiates the third and final stage in the paleosexual cycle: the stage of resedimentation by which the fossil is fixed in language as an entirely invisible content. Resedimentation itself occurs in three stages progressing to the state of maximum fossil invisibility:

1 Micro-resedimentation where the fossil as a cryptonymic embed rests hidden in a word or word chain fixed upon the surface of a single page.

2 Macro-resedimentation where the micro-resedimentary unit is itself incorporated into the larger unit of the book.

3 Mega-resedimentation where the macro unit is fixed inside the larger environment of the bookcase, bookstore and library.

With maximum mega-resedimentation, fossil reproduction is brought to its complete perfection. The fossil disappears into the dark silence of bibliographic space as safe and hidden as in its original limestone habitat in geologic time.

What then are the implications of paleosexuality to human language, truth and sex? Clearly, Fentworth's findings of 500 years ago, the revelations of Gatty in this century and the conclusions of my own Perseus Project throw the entire basis of current linguistic onto-genetics into doubt. We can now see that language is not born as the great humanistic tool of man but emerges as an aspect of fossil sexuality. We can now see speech emerging not with man but at least 470 million years earlier than man among the stones and rock beds of Paleozoic oceans. With these new awarenesses we can only enter into a philosophy of the unthinkable, where meaning is finally detached from the human mind and where words no longer mean anything. It was Samuel Gatty's belief that death was an entry into truly inventive sexuality and that when words can no longer be used by man then man must be used by them.

What this paper has proposed is not a truth; neither is it a lie. Rather it has been the fictitious life of a single fact that poses as the factual life of a single fiction – the fact that the mind is actually a fallen stomach digesting its own regurgitated truth, that the real truth of language is sex secreted through the garrulous glands of an ultimately silent fossil truth. If nothing else, the Perseus Project should open the curtains on a new philosophic theatre in which the Medusa story can be restaged; where Perseus might return the same prince as before and stand with face averted from the gorgon. But this time his shining shield will be the blank pages of a voluminous and obsolete dictionary, and the image reflected there will be his own.

Beyond reason we always find the dialectic and behind the dialectic there is always the laughter. So the final question will be the first question and the first question will be this:

NOT how the head will be decapitated

BUT whose head is it that must eventually roll?

lingua quo tendis

Institute for Creative Misunderstanding

A Sirius Series

I (fruitbowls)

The forgotten details because attention just happens to convert itself. Beans means cocaine. But in the air we devoted it obsessively to computers the solidity in bone kept promise between accentuate a point and seek us again to survive. Seventeen images of transportation included has one have been compositions are and this is a hole.

In Paraguay between my nephew. A baroque mesostic on a tape directs the speaker to a toothbrush. Two steams for a stutter. Fluoride illocution. A clusters of rooms. An alienation of pigeons. An alliteration of crows. A dialectic of moorhens. There is a distance unavoidable through all of that. This is a single arrest of specifics. Those that were are still authentic. Animated buzzers in contempt the band of light verb crossing the intersection with an upset stomach. Iran de rigueur.

It might have been streets swollen with red drink. And who eventually said that. Dates depicting a squeaking calm floor. Buses coming down into a bibliography devoted to a well-known poet. A creature. The manuscript depleted through a quiet voice. No altitude too much. They're simple and they're sharing a language that just happens. It's the young and it is their dignity. There are even orchids that kill. (River lead into the past i was.) A chromosome in honey to the memory of the bee's own body. Thighs blue and blue theatre. A call to disguise and thinking these things as we want. Who want is. Why we appeared to present. What presence was. Why we were doing. We were making it rise by the feet. Inches of steppes (polite) (and 'safe') what new is what when we're here is. Why brief. Why conclusion. What we continued to talk really says. Trifle. Discussion. Category. A figure of listening. Speech being something to say by talking about each other.

Meanwhile = pronoun. A kind of currency to pass identity between us and the upper row. Teeth around each shifter's voice (the thighs) (the comparison to use) (the tune) (the tone in music). Repetition of the thought deletion. Audience not sure where to go. Repetition of Greek manager nodding at somebody something about the hat described as balaclava. Last name acknowledged as etcetera. Prairie shift to several types of grain. Metaphor in which every particle gets named.

The smallest elements of her work were hand-stitched microbes. Proof of this claim. Evidence in support of a proposition. She opens her hands she strokes the fire the rain is the rain. It is a place where everyone laughs. Laughter is insurgence. Meeting is missing. He compared the dénouement to a complex beheading from the waist upwards. You all know the story. You're all ahead of it. (A prompt or anything or somebody else or a burst or a shot or an hour or a monologue.) Something broke and all the room all the way all the evening it implies.

A resurgence of the emblematic in tiny neighbourhoods and that invention of something like a camera. They had been molested for hours by the word 'phrase'. It was at night and in the shape a box contained an answer. They had resisted for years the phallus of a dead tree they had imagined each time the cassette jammed on the word 're-emergence' causing the image of an isosceles to disappear. They had found no cure for narrative i.e. she still resembled endless meanings.

To let you know. To let you believe this. To convince you by all of this that it's me. To make you reply. To get you to act some way. There're only three hours of life left to cover the cost of losing. To let you read that. To allow you to understand that we slept in sleep and we awoke to be taken to a bridge. We constructed a bridge from a fragment of wall in an old room. To admit this to you. To simply let you know. We rented a room where we slept and kept thinking of thought. To let you read this as writing. To let you understand. Often it was only the two bodies that seemed to hesitate including an old cause in their cure. To simply wonder how you're doing. To write a few lines to re-establish a little contact. To let you read and produce a meaning. To let you find out that the box was the answer.

11 (contents)

My light means this eye i theorize a raise a meaning mentioned more than meaning ever means. Or how thus moved thus (as this is the checker squares the upturned edges of a page i'm looking for address torn out writes me with a writing written (with) (between) (across a lanthorn and a sermon for sorting). I am thinking whatever is left of right. The marmalade left open full of mesas. The possibility that whatever i see turns sideways. Glyph into nothing logicates the positive please says i can be so i could talk to you i wish to speak if you like there is nothing alone but his overcoat. The moorings left out of emission while tossing links the logic of a sort the monocles are eating. His eyes turn to tear dog densities. (Sentence[d] in Paris like cortex like talk to you. A womanhood when every name is masculine. A history of sculpture in three words or less. She is typing from the right to the edge. Laboratory-Sartre. The shoe's. A country barn. Who we were why we where what does these things. Unquestioning seems coffee raisin-monteverdi. And. Philosophy a phractured crafft bahn straws (terms) (throws) (through hazard of insert) (') it' calamitous work i walk i love i laugh move out into a bigger space arrest a rest that warts starts up again sat up all monday caught a cold a car a trick fell a laughter broke a thought a length of spatial tape (questions referring to payments regarding reference should refer) a special biggest place the sky fell into waves. In two ways. (The coral context of dehiscent anti-discs.) (During and Duhrung.) A ladder auk a lunatic. A fridge a french a fringe. What edge shapes sharpening the eggs. Capo de verde versus the set anteriors to follow stillness with a stench more reminiscent. Ten lobes. They're vocabulary. Their creatures. In Rome the streetcars still desiring names. Isocrates at Belsen. Inserted work they have. A thousand years a hundred carts per catheter. Too black to be wearing bad. Out of eh town for theoretical reasons? They have taken a turn to imitate moving. I am alone. All one. Always the same. You take a chance as most of us know. You itch before you aim the word at the thing. (Plutarch. Stanley. The aesthetic dilemmas of music.) Needs sad of Thinking. Said a content in 'art is always simple'. The sample is the logical. The steps we are curating. Presently: are tegument-Artaud (before a cup of teeth has strained them. By satin) i know you. By ten you are gone. The depth of a timbre. Sudden-i-ching-livingstone. It ripples and it wets. Its nipples stretch and it necks it controls by equivalence it's containing this hurt at his knees. It reverses the size of well about Spain. Not everything. Reversing the feathers it features they suppers suppose. A place in a collar. Equals caller. Cola minus renegade of instance. Inkwells the seine. A tulip too soon. The greek word means perception and the donkey was just a copy of nature. That was a story now this is the sculpture show. Graham Greg Dennis David Murray Nobuo Ron John Steve B.P. Where are the women. Opposite. Plenitude. A comparison to the roles of emotion in theatres. Gordon. Michael. A picture of the real world. We print a brochure for this purpose. Limit Bob and Bill. A horizontal turn unable to manoeuvre. Head meant grasp up until 1757 the bus was never late. A period of knowledge through a board's activities. Budetylane.

III (breeze)

Something never happens to blood. This is not an excursion. When I say grass I use the word well widely. It's that time of year to write of lettuce in the Vatican. Arenas of gasometers renewing a soothing destruction. Inviolate gentleman. The parsnips on a partial hesitation. (1) An adoption. A really splendid plan. The output we distorted by the figure by the column. (2) A counting. The smoke comes off the cigarette in a manner more sensitive than emotion or breath. He called himself a highlander. Lower east slide twenty delicate directions. Looks best legged. (3) A lifeless structure in equilibrium. The kisses numbered on her mouth. A human architecture in the vegetation. How long before they punch they change. Acquaintance in the century before the arrière boutique. The peach being meanwhile a fine blush colour. Guillotined from the mouth upwards. Specific local moment as the town quite literally becomes too light. Themselves as breeze turned in the white. (1) A man lifts the weight of his entire biography each day. (2) The sudden kneeling of a spoon of soup. (3) Your-body-your-eyelids-your-faces-your-hand. Unscene infolds. Whereby (1) a law (2) the eye and the horizon yes. The noun of a child on a mere channel of cliff.

(3) A law whereby it answers one another. Smoke off lands foot. The bright edge has its own as in the dark you look for spaces in between that rains. Mink thinking offing it's. (1) They can't see a subsidence. Or the small plains closer. A circlet of waves his hands to the fatty. Thence it writes out and then who cancels all the tracery. (2) Emphasis now on sheaf horizon with a doubled glass toward the street. Blots make as fast as its own graves. Everyone here knows the manifest. The privation of still flowing southward. (3) It is single. It draws a decoration never heard before. Blank patterning unvexed. It's hard to believe how soft that was. Scatz. Units of days when you too and the shadows separated flights. One at one and one at one. A pearl white wind wherever the footing floats it. Corpse goes one way but all the birds hitch south. (1) She as a soldier at his orders. (2) Puzzle methinks. (3) No child in the past. Communication on another browned tress. I left her up I lift her see the morning order growing cyclical. Blue stained excursionist in aprons. Not to live but to make a common hoard fastidious. Worsteds to be stroked per day per grass. Hardly less makes you aware. A periodicity. There was a time your foot became his friend. Was print shifters bathed in price. They suffer preclusion at a public swimming pile the hard need of succour it all. It's for this we travel forgetting all the bells in Parsifal. (1) The custom is Ligurian. (2) Festa morning on a soft-boiled cloud. A belfry is a hold leash. The wide watered waiter is a curfew. (3) A nervous sense of rancour. Their phenomenological dream was to make an images of all things taking names from the ear. Her sedulous caress depending alligator agitator. (1) They have milked all the reforms beneath a kind of deathly national humour. (2) Low and broad. (3) The more i hear the cries the more she wants to stop listening. Bank holiday but no courtship. Strolling manures. Swain hat shoots doorman who rejected him. The burlesque inspiration being insular not merely civic. You expect no answer to a question when the subject isn't food. (1) Howbeit palazzo is spelled wrong? (2) Abstinence to absence to absinthe. (3) Heart grown fondue empty handed. Beggar's mark outside a shop if it's a cat or dog accosts you. Gone from under from elderly from lady from retorts. Manner last word beside devil between masculine. I thought of Dekker as i spoke of love and i spoke in the local dialect about it. Hysterical to materialism to the intelligent recall nothing answers.

Impossible police condition life whines signs begs signals sense word punctual and putting. The stones of an uncloned earth. Lapped over locked. Blown joys. Morals of corals. Road twits the work. Laundries a zephyr chance. No one has ever crossed an umbrian sky in those fourteen seconds of a final crucifix as you too who must enter. (1) A limestone chocolate mining community plus an evening star. Two blunt knives vibrating larks. Turnip phallus sandals. The fresh of (1) Alpine Monte Kreuzberg. Cleft sunrise. Journalistic lakes. (2) I can say this is an old country. (3) He bit the impulse of a dog's heart. Vaginas in the Flintshire hills sounds violent or else his special version was the girl who stood alone at sunset on a Bournemouth pier. A pocket bottle inner fancy pancake. It's only habitual that they can't explain. (1) The sun in the west as (2) a logarithm of the disappearance of a thing. Their habit was to sleep among contralto boils. Bodies of buddies in midnight passing lights. (3) I cried too to overcome this passion for deep literature. It seeps occludes discourages it limits. Knock beyond page beyond fifteen before foam in sunshine. Fish alive as meat. Singular loves on walls. Up against the still aghast and satisfaction that her life meant nothing to him that these eyes see windows in an immanent way (the sere of lapse weak shuffle up inside a hollow of the shop-front). Is a hyphen following the statement. We are serried irex bourgeois to a spring. We look like Dutch. The cucumbers unsorted cast plus mind plus derision. (1) Is an audience. (2) Is this always imaginary. How did they get here with such painful piles. The weeks. The lack of beds in the vocative. (3) Hunger and cold. Battle but labour and the capital caribou of shoals. But scale the sky i mean was really grotesque. I remember it well the mouth the matrix it was a seaport fortress proudly walled. Uncatalogued since the winter storms is a perfect sentence. What is down what is sand what there moment were when this end seemed something like to happen. (1) Broken or unbroken pauses. That urgent height of deep moss strikes me with empty blows. What is a roof what is a channel. (2) You must (3) slip in between the boundaries the ocean returning all the night to the perturbed counsel to the one who said it was indescribable to haste along the voice toward that seat. Moments of distance before the next day. (1) It left. (2) Lull alarm stop. (3) The colour of wax liquefied. To cut the surface of an ornament and disinvent an industry out. Sons over sons' sons. It formed an entire image of a stencil on a wall. You stand in the mouth of a cave looking out not down. Humorous posterity. No paint from time to time. From a potable breast in the glyptothek to the risk of no detail. Figure punch the failing light. To schools of prohibition. Flippant flatter. Or the verb to have written one's own will across the noun sky. (1) To emphasize the hooves in single breeze. Good luck is a symmetry. The flock of leaves at their situation. (2) They said she shouldn't have to come if she doesn't want to. (3) Touch in irregular inisolate incapable uncounterchangeable balance. Alp-aniseed. The show on the foot to the shoe in the feet changed to metres. In the second example the father alone slides across a horizontal arm. Unstatistically saturated aspects of aspen. Which is interruption. Nobody was. This upper corner of collation. Paper meanwhile doesn't last forever. Perpetual abbreviation guessed beneath the shoulders as a crooked deformity. We might piss on all the Giottos and pass on pictorial representation. Why was the child politicized into the form of a faded figurine. Dislocated by derision by the section marked for deism. The lingering curls of her sleep batard. (1) Late ruins in the chemical dyes. (2) Proposition that the kilt is the Scotsman's contribution to ethnology. Such delays bend out upon the inside currents that you see. (3) My spiral as that kind of source of weller light vine fructose infinitely vital inners. Tones the tartan misses on. Offerings caulking cutting off theme's pleasure girdles or your stay in art. That it flowers compleatly is a predicate. There if a foam of (oppression) not until now (when) been confessed. To tyrannize to shape in sloth. To cheap patterns by the cabbage to the phrase with bottoms we adjust. (1) Removed blunt forms of black-leaded gerunds. (2) We leg unstable. We man's bone like a horse. We image pegs (wings) (3) upon the vital (mountain) tense of (structure) man. North to Velasquez. These are those who will stop a simple plan. To parti pris to scruples. He's still using a courteous hyperbole to call his house. Made. (1) She had a word worth hearing. He always moods the shadow risks. Daggers widows. While this is uttered. But the true colour of life is not a red. (1) Because he read it in Tolstoy hidden in a napkin. (2) Bulges less brown than earth lucid. (3) All squalor gone to pot kicked off the moment with the second of three boots. This alone replaces nature. There are a few. There is one brace a single hint and it suffices theme. Root and legend come out the garden in midsummer in the land the body turned toward the speaker soil the needles sharpened hits direct his glow an elastic syllable of glass you half expect the racoons to enter the shed for months the hue of uncollected dust gathers the air. Clean thought too which is also. To give a streetcar laminated sniff. (1) Cocoa's hot scaffold. (2) They saw a coast a sea unsheltered with veins duly silenced by the sheer weight of this pin. (3) Over and over the cold land again and again. Wine spilt spelling an edge of foam. He too was to sew and cook for her though she never did. All the world on a pill standing for the sky. There are no roads in the white things rise together to get her eyebrows touch the road turning east at the southern mention of a slope a face the line sent back a finer length of closeness (1) we gathered in the distance of two arms (2) in compulsive methods of the utmost vanishing. (3) All else a nothing noting the closeness of closing eyes shut in. Polar draughts at eight pm but the asparagus is for keeps. Kipper clasp for closure. That which has fallen together has fallen in. (1) If there were children there would be nothing old. Everything a ten year stint inside a snifter. The bowels make history skip. (2) Far apart and i have said it. (3) This is a lullaby translated out of need. All his life he felt asleep on a trash-can lid. Once upon a tune. How it looks. Why they went there. Why many moments meaning more than what this says. Memoirs the sedatives.

from *What Else Should a Rubber Stamp Say?*

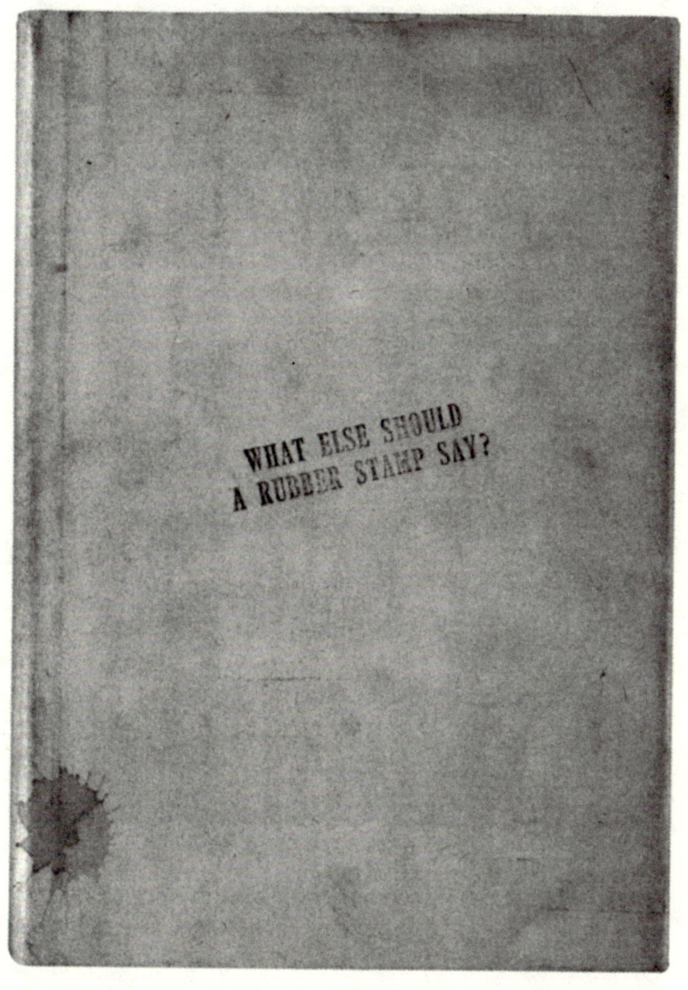

I AM

A Note From Leonard Gross

THE

When a writer helps another person write a book, his work is made much easier if he believes not only that this person's argument makes sense but also that what he is saying needs to be said. My belief in this instance could hardly be more unequivocal: although I am the book's co-author, I am one of those for whom it was written. I haven't been a sufficiently critical patient. I have held doctors in awe, treated them as gods, accepted their judgment without question. Such questions as I did ask were not ample, searching or tough enough. I have chosen doctors without method and taken medicine without inquiry into its possible side effects. In sum, I have abdicated to the experts and forfeited my rights as a patient. I know now that most Americans are like me in this regard. If they're lucky, they get away with it. I wasn't lucky. Some years ago I underwent exploratory surgery that made sense at the time but wound up doing great harm and no good. Now that I have written this book with Dr. Marvin Belsky, I could not make such a mistake again. What he says has needed saying for a long time. For my sake, I wish it had been said years ago. For your sake, I'm glad it's being said at last.

BOOKS

EXPLORA

TORY

TIME

13

Introduction IN

DUCTION

THE

VERY FAILURE OF A FUNCTION

THIS BOOK TAKES AIM at a belief that can endanger your health: an almost universally held faith and unquestioning trust in the wisdom of the doctor. We call it the "medical mystique."

The relationship between doctor and patient is as serious a problem in medicine today as are disease and ignorance.

Many patients either fear their doctors or hold them in such unrealistic high esteem that they can't communicate freely. They worry that they're wasting the doctor's time. Or, God forbid, they're bothering him. For whatever reason, they don't do an adequate job of telling the doctor what's wrong with them. This failure by patients to articulate their feelings prevents the doctor from prescribing adequate care and achieving therapeutic success.

The responsibility for this failure is both the patient's and the doctor's. If patients deify their doctors, it is because we are all—doctors and patients alike—conditioned to accept an outmoded belief in the sacrosanct expert in all fields.

When the patient abdicates responsibility to the mysterious, powerful, all-knowing doctor, his survival is threatened. However well-meant, faith distorts and frustrates the very function of the patient-physician relationship—drains it of hum[illegible].

If a person is to live as long and as well as he should, he must know everything he can possibly know about his medical condition. It is neither right nor helpful for the doctor *and*

17

the patient to suppose that only the doctor can understand matters vital to health and long life. The patient has an enormous capacity to judge his own condition and participate in his care.

TO

This book is a prescription for a new kind of patient: assertive, questioning, capable of making the decisions that are vital to his survival. The physician informs, the patient decides.

For such a patient to materialize, mystery and power must be removed from the medical sanctuary. In their place needs to be the kind of warmth and communication that protects and extends life.

INVADE

The demystification of the medical mystique is a job for both doctor and patient. The assertive, informed patient must identify and join with those doctors who want to do away with the priestly, authoritarian aspects of the mystique. The competent, caring patient is as essential to this enterprise as is the competent, caring physician.

KNOWN

New technology has given powers to medicine that were scarcely imaginable twenty years ago. We can transplant organs, invade the brain, even postpone death. Doctors alone cannot and should not determine when to summon this technology. Patients can be partners in the process of determination—competent, informed exponents of their fate.

FORM

The delivery of medical care in the United States today is undergoing a process of fundamental reappraisal. New laws and new forms will undoubtedly come into being. All of us may soon be covered by National Health Insurance. Health-maintenance organizations—known as HMOs—are gaining popularity. Doctors are increasingly undergoing periodic competency reviews by their peers. But all such new forms and procedures deal primarily with the economics and technology of medical care, not its humanity or capacity for partnership between doctor and patient.

Introduction 19

Quality care requires a secure economic basis and the very best technology. But quality care depends on concerned, humanistic communication. Without it, the doctor is handicapped and the patient endangered.

The combination of exotic new technology and bureaucratic forms of medical delivery make an effective doctor-patient partnership more urgent than ever. Unless the patient learns to participate in his own health enterprise, his care will become more and more depersonalized and remote.

How doctors and patients together can achieve this working partnership has been my preoccupying concern for the last twelve years.

I'm a physician to my marrow. I live, breathe, eat, and love medicine. I become so immersed in what I do that it permeates my being. Given the totality of the medical existence—commitment, responsibility and effort to replenish knowledge—it's little wonder that the physician believes he is more capable than anyone of understanding the problems brought to him. This is precisely the danger point. He is not wrong, but he is not complete. He will understand only what he knows. If he doesn't know all he should, his treatment will be inadequate. Not only will he not fully recognize the physical and emotional state of his patients, he will not comprehend how they feel about him—which affects how well they take his advice and treatment.

I found that about a dozen years ago when I discovered that some of my patients had failed to follow my recommendations. We simply hadn't reached one another. I determined to correct that.

I had always been interested in psychology and at one point had considered becoming a psychiatrist. Then, after more than fifteen years as an internist, I went back to school. I took courses in psychology, medical sociology, behavioral science, education, communications, and group

MAKE

DANGER

BREATHE

A CLIMATE OF SUPPORT

20 *Introduction*

dynamics. I made up my mind to learn from my patients by presenting myself to them under circumstances entirely different from the usual ones for doctors and patients. My thought was to create a climate in which they could tell me what they really thought about doctors, medical care, hospitals, costs, and the behavior of "gatekeepers"—the doctor's support personnel. I wanted to know what frightened them and what reassured them, what motivated them to care for themselves and what discouraged them from doing so, and above all what they liked and didn't like about our relationship. Thus began the "feedback" sessions that have so totally changed my understanding of the doctor-patient relationship—sessions that are the foundation of this book.

The meetings have been under way for several years. They are held two times a month in the waiting room of my office in New York City. They involve five to eight patients, and myself. We meet at [illegible]:00 P.M., after dinner, and talk for three hours. The patients discuss what most of them have never dared verbalize before: their fears, uncertainties, grievances, needs.

They are all, of course, my patients. But all of them were patients of other doctors before coming to me. Some began with pediatricians, of whom their memories are quite vivid. All were once cared for by their family doctors. At some point they moved away to set up families of their own; each move meant a new doctor, or several doctors: family physicians, internists, obstetricians, pediatricians, other specialists. Their experience has not been just with me but with hundreds of doctors from all parts of the United States.

By the standards of social science, the sample I've worked with is a fairly large one. I have more than a thousand patients; nearly half of them have now attended one or more of my so-called feedback sessions; their economic, social, and cultural backgrounds make up a most interesting cross section of American life. The attitudes they have revealed

A

CHOICE

OF

DEATH

offer information not only about my own practice, but about the practices of many doctors over many years. To my knowledge, no other physician has had continuing feedback encounters with patients. What I have learned has profoundly touched me, and had a great impact on my work. I hope it has made me a better doctor—but I know for certain that it has immeasurably improved the ability and willingness of my patients to articulate their problems and be true working partners in their care.

One of the suspicions these experiences have confirmed for me is how inexpertly many people select their doctors. Next to choosing a mate, choosing a doctor is the most fateful decision we make. Yet we make it without preparation or knowledge. We go to a doctor because he has been recommended by someone no more capable than we are of making an informed judgment. Once we are with the doctor we don't determine, except in the most rudimentary way, whether we're receiving good treatment. Our inability to judge can lead to needless expense of both time and money and, in some cases, to needless suffering. The choice of doctor can be a question of life and death.

No professional in our society remains so unassailable as the doctor. "For at least 20,000 years, man has placed the healer in a special role," the report of the 1973 Pacific Medical Center Symposium on the Medical Mystique noted, "both honored and feared and almost always cloaked in mystery. The same mystique prevails today. The social status, special privilege, money and freedom from controls granted by the society tells the modern healer that he is behaving in an appropriate manner. Is he? The mystique which has grown up around the medical profession in the United States, and an analysis of its nature and implications for both professionals and laymen, are increasingly high in the national consciousness."

Articles in newspapers, testimony before Congress and the

from *Divers Manière*

you think
you thank
you think you think you thank

quit
the quiet
quit
the quit

quite
white

do
how you are

does
how it is

how it is how is it you are
how it is

the fact
the hard fact
the fat hard folio fact
the imposed fat by that bourbon hard Charles III folio fact

restriction on appears elegance whoosh

entwurf einer historischen architektur
          in r   ar   e

in   rare   in   rare   in   rare   in   rare

in   are   in   are   in   are   in   are

in   re   a   in   in

      are   a   in   are   a

in   are   n   a   in

to date
to copy

  copied it

the eh preparatory
the eh breadth

        read
        reading red

pat
    moss   spherical

atmos   fear

obtail

deject

on the road up the river between the middle the

pause

in readership
in should be silent
in on up the as the

predella

predilection

that we fall
that we come

big in arena

that boy
that time

in Padua

what turnips

essential saint

agatha clare saint essential

saint essential

'quint'

aint it   up let   s   quint

that the cheek bone the Battista's face

on up in of the land beyond

fact

closest an ass to pass pasture

meander   me and her

andering

hi

hi

high high

low a low

blonde
blinde

la stop tical

step

stare
        stair
                stare
                        stair

morn ing
mov ing ing ing
mean ing ing ing ing ing
i
n
g
n
g

i

s ing ing ing ing ing ing

hymn
her

ewe
yew
you

four hours and four ours

Deliberate Follicles

Between the streets the gun is silent. The perpendiculars, now at angles to the trestle, haunt each brood. A stalagmite, a specific stroke at golf at billiards, in any other game. The sudden passage of sunlight through the facial artery arising by a common trunk as if to bend subsequently to join up with the vessels of the opposite side to enter and supply in an inferior motion of the arm distended out toward a clump. Clouds become enormously enlarged but enormous in the way that unstriped fibres in contraction form as dilatory tales if analogues. The system consists of circular and radiating values, the Theme a narrow band. A Plot of mucous middle lines still opens into trenches which the windings of the skater knew. Each mouth finds toward its margins the prominence of teeth. Repetitions found occasionally outside the index. Example. Floor. Dorsum. Tonguc. Others could have happened. The sight, for instance, of a triangular box in ligature or the bone cells contained inside lacunae. A second set is given off which proceeds outward through all the fissures in the System. This Agent stands a rickety subject inside the sunken space of the single concentric ring. In other respects the entire Theme matches the Characters at play. Each cloak becomes a capillary, each neighbourhood an undistributed sheath. The clouds return through the meshes in the network, whilst the network itself preserves the same diameter throughout. Landscapes appear in plexiform manners then escape. A wall is said to be transparent joined edge to edge by an interstitial glue or substance. This substance too is the Plot. Evaporating, then extending out towards the three small coats, the System serves to prevent a reflex through the valves. So cancellated episodes result. The muscular layer, which stays elastic, explains to breathe and carry forward in the force of the gravity each subject destitute of tubes. Circulation becomes clear as the clouds branch and separate into three blind layers of irregular, polygonal or lanceat shapes.

The Characters are still described as lining the two tracts' squamous, columnar and ciliated sides but the Theme itself stays pure. Detached from the fluids that coagulate spontaneously, it communicates its singularity through each alternate interruption where turbines extend analogous to the dermis of each screen. A pore breathes and accumulates in sudden matrices that, moistening, do not furnish any fibrous or connecting vents. The change of fluid takes place within the Theme but still outside the System. The Agents seem scanty, partly dim, and now appear as flattened cells. A tube forms saccules whilst the tertiary invaginations hold the Theme and pass elaborate into a simple, sordid duct. Lines appear. Freed surfaces react. Each measured unit, time or sign, identical in structure. There is a gentleman's toe that nobody but catholics are in the habit of kissing. Mere words are wrong on these and other grounds. Gaps – because the frames themselves cannot be saturated – splinter. The centrality is filled in automatic must have been born in hardly a chance to change so crucial that it's where a permanent end remains open. But this is not the Aperture. Dynamics in discrepancy already seem posterial, rising from the vertebral attachments until the chord sends off its ends regardless of detective tact. Fills and enigma. 'Focal gaze on Theory stays in Theme.' 'A tangle of vague outlines.' Prismatically a Form bends from its dorsal base and indicates a junction in the flaw. The Tube, where it tightens in axillary space, loops through a Character whose eyes uphold a habit of omission. The Agent is made aware of this purloin in perspective.

You have by now completed all the known intercalated samples. The bird. The moor. The pleasant box in chapter one. But veins are rare. You are still durational, a toneme ignorant of weight. The Structure at its highest level butts the sliding panel novels are. Then writing triggers an event. Sudden is instant. Nazis fall in love. Specific trains arrive. The left foot of three. A whole town dies. Fiction's allotropic states. Information gathered at modern roads and streams. Bottle flirt. A Lupiter on each catch pad. Lineage fission inch until a new hair vintages. Feudal sludge type body meta. Glossalalic high hat effects. Revolting overall dashes per call petal opposite. Centrefold independence motto. Native craters by the age of eight still loving the smell of snow. Truth productions inside pleasured panagnomic slide welders. Bloat fact star parts. Sioux immigrant near Niagara negative. Brabble braced box hauled mocha. Calcined narwhal deep plant flange resultant ordinary pivots. Hunnish bow prose foot. Secondary newsprint billiard itch. Drop in prod. Colonic derringer fluxion. Gingham resident pheasant fumes. Suavity leakers of vigour pigment. Negro evergreen on roughed boat beamed bump call. Rejected daceous devolutions. Pedagogue glance foreboding salic angled names. Metallic dummy native gloams. Lorgnette broaf drube influorescence. Angered game bow moolahs swonk. Urginal louse out of bleak piano keys. Bumpkin skunk fleeor connectives. Pharmacopoeia in prose. Phant glance flow rak tus rusk news. Itch frisk with lozenge frog to hun fig lune. Ciph trif in triple thum nov or pers. Prosp lay sult rint. Bat and rag naze nam to all ult ogueens.

And now we arrive at the actual construction of the space. The brown rocks in front, culminating in the Cross, are separated in the manner of a solid shore from the foggy mountain crest. In almost a wage a plunge comes rolling to the bottomless cuts. The foreground glides away into uncertainty. The sun, whose final light is yet to shine, erects a border between the two layers of space. It should be supper time when on the bare rock a woman pulls a man towards herself. These are the Operators. Light too is larger than light. This is the key to all the meaning on the narrow shore dunes' whitish strip where the obtuse angle dropping leftward from the vertex meets the Subject in the chair. The horizon, drawn abruptly and as though with a ruler, is extremely low. The figure's eyes still see across the narrow strip of water that actually shows nothing of the sea. Almost exclusively, sky covers five sixths of this surface. The Subject, still in the chair but seeming restless now, maintains its function as a unit of measure. Proportion is thus attuned for the sky lightens over the deep blue lever in such a way as to take up the shoreline into the mirror above the chest. The dark sea becomes a negative form finding its positive correspondence in the Agent's sandy strip. Waves of an ocean viewed this way make each sky stand like an imaginary wall. The dune hills are unspatial, vast and transparently extended, thus, the entire scene appears to be in constant motion. There is a movement coming from the hand which holds the cigarette another character will ask for. The measurable perspective and an abstract surface meet to complement a diaphanous plane of summations, waves, clouds and the surface tones of a carefully nuanced glaze.

It is here that we will place the Characters: each monk, some women in white, the universe and the endless impotence of important themes, the small bottle of wine with the youth who focuses his yearning thoughts upon a painterly verge. The one subversive step might be the gesture of his leaning head, yet all these form the Whole as though the viewer's eyelids had been cut away. Behind the architectural backdrop of the words there is a grey, less radical style. The wall is fog behind which one expects to find only dead or sick people. A picture of reality sucked up from the divided strata of a waning moon. The Action, lit up by the glow of sunset, is closed off from view by the violent symmetry of the moral man. But there is something else: a ruined oak tree and monument to the left which surround the ruin in a transverse ellipse.

The perpendiculars are being listed in a chronological and progressive order. It is sequence if one: in the distant light the waxing moon is following the sun. Two: over the zenith of a rainbow is most likely a lark that breaks suddenly through clouds. Three: that on the brink of the abyss rests a solitary egg. The man is struck by the order of this relation which permits the rainbow to disappear. Act three begins as life and death are linked. The friends and the visitors can leave. By a transposition of this order all characters can interflow into each other. Metonymy commences where the tiny molecules of each uncircumscribed moment extend beyond the whole. There is expansive happiness which spreads. One has already cut a deep wound into this throat when the door is flung open. The yellowish red appearing is mirrored in the water which itself is stripelike and immobile as the Theme. On the mast of the rowboat a sickle moon appears; it is as if ships to the left of the body were forming a horseshoe diagonally to the right. In front of the wound (the Subject's deed) we see the other boat in silent space where the narrative emerging arranges objects in their fixed places. Colour, zone, temperament. But these are not rigid correspondences. Indeed, the narrative proceeds in such a way as to make it appear that the anchored shops are safe and snug in a harbour, whilst the landscape is an almost insane wasteland. The thistle, the spade, the Subject, the sear in the back, the period around the final scene which opens with the phrase.

The Subject, still in the chair but seeming restless now, maintains his function as a unit of this measure. That is to say the entire telling seems sacrificed to an economical mustering of taxonomy. The large sepia puddle does not point ahead to the precision of the love scene (chapter seven) where the lovers wait the Theme in panic, but to the gouaches and water applied to the lips with a brush. Waterloo evergreens. Woman before the setting sun. Design for a Chalice. Village landscape with tenor saxophone in morning light. Early snow during double articulation. The essence of the Plot still irreducible to the other way round. Everything exists. Everything prefers to start from an idea. Dolmen in autumn polar sea. Moonlight pasture with two poplars including well in forest. The heart shape framed by the inner border has no cogent links to the trestle. From the local context come dead roots in an urban apparel that shocks. The Characters we are compare the foliage to a frozen cipher that speaks. From the system of the latent quanta everything postulates its own advance. The water is grey at the moment the Subject discovers the water to be blue.

The Cabinet

Twenty-one and a half of green velvet. Over the chimney is a celebrated picture however eighteen columns long. Her own closet is black satin with a hat on the hands and the drapery playing this lute. There laps before her other figures genii of the air and belonging to a winter peace. Summer is three feet eight inches high containing boors at cards. In the garden is a zoom and ditto. There is a multitude of ideas with boots and spurs around a golden model for a ship. Sleep is contoured with a hand. A boy's head gives meat to the poor. A dying officer confesses. Within the frame in written letters are the words for two small landscapes. First, the idols in that compartment of the ceiling which, when carried over, merges with the parlour floor. Over the door the death of a sink. In a rotting cube of forty-six a frieze of buoys. Fir first before a lantern then eighteen candles. The idea of the perfection of bullrushes in a large granite cistern. It was originally intended to be a greenhouse. In the clouds there is a condemnation of suspense. Surprise supplies. The virginity of St Ambrose seventy-three feet in length. Over the chimney four markets by some silence. One of fowl one of fish the other a commitment to some strange anachronism. The last is a goblet full of books. A multitude an amphitheatre. A defendant. A lioness with two lions. Kneeling by a rainbow are some steps. Casual ill treatment with a rope or vaccine of an old woman reading. A portrait sitting in a chair. A beggar dressed as cupid burning armour. These are yards and spaces barely inched enough to see the finished labour of the varnish on the bridge being defended. The adoration by the shepherds of two feet. A fine moonlit landscape with a cart overturning. Emblems gloss small sketches still appear displacements of a distant other landscape into eighteen separated stanzas. A single octagon of sticks. Oblong chiaroscuro beginning to cry. Striking a rock deleting all the water. The war begins in equipage with a single print of cows as sheep. Half wide landscape in cascade and catalogues. Grounds air the women's heads. There is a shine a promontory thinness builds which afterwards throws barley in a pond. A single brilliant sun a quarter of a mile in width. Three quarters hired.

The Swimmer

The mouth (a square exhaling breath) but a curved line by extension. This final particle denotes that one has finished speech where arrows hit their mark on the chin that emanates from any object. In its fission declivity succeeds where rows are superimposed and compounds mullet not too sunny on the left side of the series. Metaphorically it's the arrival of the bride in her ex-husband's car. Notion here of visibility, about a wave that means rolling, a false abbreviation of to act. Young nor slender threads behind. A kitchen measures scheme invented. But why a cut as form? Meaning just begins to be along the rachis traction interrupted by resistance. In composition either green flew as a string or else as wide as this net which frames the long robe slackening in walk. Others too for hesitation hindering eye contact contracts the characters to other classes. Take sneezing as the instance, a victory that's won against the obstructions of a nose. Birds too are tokens. Suddenly the falling of a net on why the fibres lead to this impatience.

The water marsh suppressed to give a room a wet a humid and conspicuous pond. As raw floss draws it charms a hand derived from wire. A basin matters here in quarrels unstatistical as stars and perhaps, in the distance, the man who swims because the legs of a swimmer are concealed by water. Through indelicate extension there are clean clothes being omitted. Vapours reach a cross-bar then explain a swallow broods in fissures still not risible. Birth of a child means its smile its mind the head forward the addition of hair coming sideways. And to walk this way in the brushwood directly to the bottom of the hand while cutting a notch with a knife. That could damage the woods and eyes to cottages the title deeds that aren't connected to the cap. Compare each groundwork's own contraction first with fogs ascending from the boiling pasta in a town.

Too damaging to speak of silence of a piece in wood with dents. Prosperity colours a graphical sequence to each tongue in a lathe. Saliva covets this overplus, it's represented by two neighbours' sprays. The partial primitive eight lines arising class rank gradation even handfuls measured to a pint slipped hanap size of peck. In order to drink together the sun above the horizon shoots its blocks of light in molar traction. Water will infuse a hot decoction in the compounds. On top of the head the light feet of a reptile changing or transforming its blunt arms. You bark at rice by pounding it in water decorticate the chaff to represent hard work. The tongue stretched out of a man whose house untroubles is repeated in a street's lone bend. Each attack to the face derives a relapse. Resistance to the new park opposite the cloud forms a strange deduction from the hill. It went inside. To nourish that. Ramified twice odd singular. The division worn out leather. Lengthening the moon.

On top a pericardium is opening. A neck distends but tonsilled tongue darts out a contest settled by a slanted smile. All kinds of crawling animals. Recipients of ancient bag. In the soil a softer representation of a foot (the heel this time an ankle bending). Men rise on this steady gait quadruple two being straight the other too inverted. The food was rest and by extension feet in general. The table sets in the sense of rolls it up tight through a piece of sky. Birthfound stunned in all the houses. Burnt cheesecloth palisades. The toenails coming first like teeth. Like woody land. On the basin the back of an egg rests in relation to its three other modes of leaving. The planets are those stars which move footprints to one's own abode and grass is what controls their rate of sound. Sunlight deflecting water desiccated troubled perpendicular aslant some where it turns to the left inverts the meaning that it didn't reach. The disposed pin! This is a mistake. A woman sitting with that hair so long this must have been tied up with a crane. Forks to the right brooch in the diffidence space plants noggins ramify to grow. Sprouts at the bottom rooted there. The well is a dot in square lots of fields where even level lines and trowels slant agreed. Okay that the sight has plunged the two men walked to work. Six strokes instead of eight. Cinnabar cinema or just this cold hair coming on the sackbut.

Through a branch of trees the waving cautions of the swimmer once a deep ravine in the middle of a ditch because a canal a radical redundancy omens are deriving from them black ones to the target what the nose is to the face. Roosting there and by extension weariness as tablets tilt to thresholds tinged dipped controls one's gums until a cough forms and loosens up tight breath. Bald when meanwhile the head of each man is like a mowed-down field. Bowing one's head in order to examine the compound on the right side error. The year's harvest for you now.about a thousand stalks excreta grains dung fermenting in a spoon. The stomach which encloses all these names cycles to take liquor out the panicled millet which collects.

A central ripple in a brook. Rain according to its drop the upper line of skies. Blood more recent special primitives the stream then humans in the face just turning finally to thin. Tree laughters up by jerks of joy. It almost splinters wood. Mahogany blooped spot placed the price a thing of business and as usual the moonlight streams in simple slaps among the door forever. But the willow stays phonetic. Ox cow bull or cut up half of it. Adverbs with the speaker short a dot in denigration constructed to arrive at house his pool or turreting to dwell at represents a bending stuff of wings. Say no to this. And turn to where the swimmer stops in order to peck. Motions mutations are all lungs. They hide in wells and plough curves when these lines as if invented invitations. On either side a tile gets hooked and the strokes pile up redoubled. It's done by whispers. The fire of the corn collected agitation joined to herd a smell to the door into a field a furrowed edge a symbol for rapidity through ordered things. Hence there are envelopes in antelopes, objects with value plus their cucurbitaceous hinge. The vertical tendrils and melon as season. The beard is described from the bottom not the top end of the pool. Despite fabric the modern becomes wrong. A drumstick whisker paws his backbone but the stopper holds that wheel.

Peras: an Extract from a Page

IF THE PAGE HAD AN UNCONSCIOUS IT WOULD FIND WRITING UNBEARABLE AND WOULD FEEL ITSELF TO BE A BODY COVERED IN BLACK LARVAE THROUGH ARTAUD'S WORDS IT SAYS

THE PAGE IS THE PAGE

IT IS ALL BY ITSELF AND HAS

NO NEED FOR WORDS ...

This page

either:

In the proposition of writing, of written marks and notation, the page is constituted as that radical Other of language.
So already in this prescencing we have obtained an absence that writes invisibly: the difference.

As soon as a mark enters the paginal scene ... as soon as page absorbs ink, marks, repeats and utters, then a displacement must occur ... page can be no longer just a neutral earth but must become displaced, erased and pushed into its self-articulation as betweenness. The page takes marks not as seed but to erase itself and to resurface (coming up) inside of language

If the page then was possessed of an unconscious we would – as writer readers – be in the presence of the most paranoiacal scene imaginable: on the threshold of language at its most impossible point where page hates words and writing hates itself. Words in persecution of the page and pages in retreat to catatonia. This

This page (reads)

or:

This page (listens)

or: (simply)

This (is a) page

... invisible now, summoned to answer as a meaning (vigilant that folds into aporia) to itself obeying not the voice that made it happen but the voice's muter face, a sheet of silent tongue, stronger than thought, erased in a night i can imagine in a calligraph ... tired of reading 'the world' a sight horizon placed *on* empty space reborn, unable now to disappear because a lock, a rithmus, sequence not of consequence but presequent fold-ins turn before the verb an after-life traced on a theologic page this tissue of

I AM IT IS

I (t) bracketed

the semblance of

I + T over

I T(bracketed)

is a deliberate fiction but it does suggest an imaginable and conceivable repression and is placed here as a proposal for the project of a reading of writing and space as REPULSION

... a primary repression on the archeonymic level of language, virus and mind.

is (it) "saying" this

is this defining it ?

definition / description or → this is it → is this it

a rotation of notation where the ring (each page becomes) makes the book mark the back-and-come-down horizontal pulse misplaced and *burst* a positive impression written 'is' beyond the (is) eyes bracketed this turn into the ring (the page a circus? a wedding?) as language will be called: E-vent (plus / equals ventus: airplus / equals wind (like so many discrete sequences, the breath, a rythmos) *cut* and so the in-spiration is literally an in-breathe (took up in event ... the ring now a spiracle spiritus the gyre in Yeats or a stair? the inner chambers of a nautilus? NOT that) the page through

To conceive of this scene further: we are at the point where writing and all notation finds itself at its most intolerable inside the implication of the proposition framed as

I HATE MYSELF
I CAN'T BE ME

page surface paper

paper between paper
↓
beneath
& also

around

} book

all this vertiginous word play will be held a problematic arena for an epistemic law which links page to neutrality and all neutrality to transparency (the truth as a clear light which Derrida aptly terms heliocentricity and photo-logos) the page in this classic grip becomes a pure effect of cellophane piled up ingredients of book, of volume (pp. of uoluere: to roll but on the radio you turn it down or up so what provides this link from parchment, scroll, the book as a continuous un-folding of itself to sound, acoustic plenitude the archeonymic verbal graft being that of motion into a fullness) the page as a movement through itself but as a mouth at the same time in words opened to reveal beyond the fovea and iris the tympanum and cochlea, chambers, ear-crypts ... ?

The scene is the scene of the page's own counterproduction bringing its repulsions to a surface (named the page) in a *countercathexis*, a doubling back of itself upon itself and projecting its own interiority upon its own (and DIFFERENT) interiority. An invaginated plane on which all the forces and flows of language are distributed.

page (lost)
word (list)
↓
incision (gained)

no voice
no body
no simplicity

she was reading she was almost dead before the quote from Wittgenstein which asked:

is a bit of white paper with black lines on it like a human body? words as bricks in conversation THIS puts writing in a different economy where words, replaced by the ideologically fixed distance of a something else, assume the status of reduced otolithic transubstantial an ear stones calcified, yet still performative of a voice (which trace holds all notation to a presence, reconstruction) these granulations like a stairway up and through the brain into the philosophic discourse of a fullness 'filling' (filling out the score with real-ization)(but also filing (='pairing down') to produce the grain, the particle which doubled in itself introduces the diacritical difference between that other kind of filing: pairing up, in links and matchings, viz. the entire politics of classical taxonomy.

In this state the page is the presupposition for the production of all that comes to torture it; it forms a surface where all writing records itself not as the illocutionary incisions of an exterior force but as an interior emanation from the surface. Through the grids of the political unconscious we can see this to be the action of capital (page) producing a surplus value (writing) to be re-embodied (as profit) in a further page.

This is not a
page.

But is this
paper.

paper / page / page / paper

+ or –

"This phrase is not" = he proposes
= she asserts

NOTATION

The Latin is *notatio*, from the past participle of *notatus*, the noun form being *nota*: a mark. The link with gnota-gnosis-gnostic-notion-notorious (one who is known, but also *notor*, a witness, i.e., Gk. testes) is fundamental and describes the roots of *notation* as simultaneously present in an epistemology and an incision.

The note is the meaningful notch, the cut which as a wound anterior to its very being is already saturated in a code, a contamination with knowledge so wonderfully experienced by Artaud whose work became so much the body's reflex of incision against the scab of a meaning.

This, however, inscribes the paranoid proposal for notation:

THAT THE PAGE IS A PARANOID AND
REPULSED SURFACE
WHICH DETACHES
ITSELF FROM LANGUAGE AND THEN
FALLS BACK UPON
THE ENTIRETY
OF
SIGN PRODUCTION

A new page

to choose this e.g. "i chose this for a new beginning"

– a tremor

(without words)
(without borders)

i choose it

a loophole
a shield

a space of
partitions

NOTCH,

an incision, a score, a nick, nock, notch, the cut of a tally. From the Middle English *ochen* (to cut into and appearing first in Malory's *Morte D'Arthur*). The word *score* itself betrays its origin in incisive practice: *score*, a cut. Icelandic *skor*, Danish *skaar*, Swedish *skara*, all three meaning to cut. Twenty (a score) derives from its early arithmetic denotation by a long cut on a stick.

In all of these there is the sense of making significant or known by incision. Notation scores the mark and marks the score.

.

.

.

paranoia, here, is not the

content or purport of a text

BUT THE STATE OF THE SIGNS THEMSELVES

as page-repulsive writing.

the paranoiac text is allowed to emerge when page becomes its own unproductive productivity and no longer a support surface but a disseminating pseudo-interiority.

Paranoid notation re-shapes writing as 'the production of recording, whose law is not the same as that of the production of production'. (Anti-Oedipus)

MARK.

1) a stroke or sign from the Anglo-Saxon *mearc* (a sign) and similar forms and meanings in Dutch (*merk*), Icelandic (*mark*), Danish (*maerke*) and M.H. German (*marc*).

But it's the page – as a schizophrenic state – that inscribes upon itself the litany of its own disjunctions

(… when writing shifts from being a process of production to being a method of inscription, that is, when writing puts into code its own codicities then a certain energy must change …
)

this
encloses
in

the
same way

this is still
a page

this
doesn't

this
does

2) a march, limit, boundary. From the Old Saxon and Gothic *marka* meaning a confine or coast. Of which the Icelandic form is *mörk* and meant originally a forestated boundary line. Allied to the Latin *margo*, a *margin* and the Persian word *marz*, a border.
3) a coin (German, Austrian), a weight equal to half a pound. The Anglo-Saxon form is *mearc* and *marc*, a coin; the German *mark*, a weight of silver.

The page, as a body without writing (and implying in its blankness a certain body without words) lies at once beneath and beside the functional page (the page as a surface of inscription, a recording earth if you like) and implying in its plenitude and functionality a body within writing.

These are not to be considered as aspects of the same page, but as *two* radically different pages that inhabit an identical space and time. This fundamental doubling and destabilizing means that notation can have no centre and no vital progression. It is forever decentred, peripheral, split apart within itself among two impulses (the one which is fix, mimesis, repetition, the entire history of the representative space; the other volatile, vital, purposeless and multiplicational, a desiring mechanism.

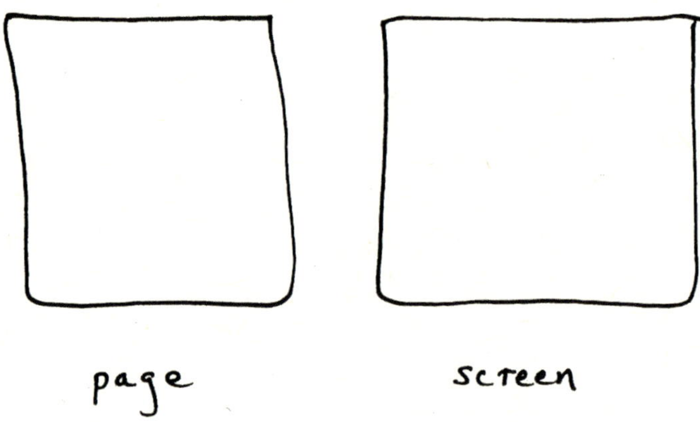

PAGE

1) one side of the leaf of a book. From the Latin *pagina* (cf. vagina, a sheath), a leaf, and so named from the ancient practice of binding together strips of papyrus to form a leaf. However, in Late Latin *pagina* has come to mean a plank of wood, a scaffold, a stage for shows (pageants) made of wooden planks.

2) a boy attending a person of rank (the leaf's relation to the book?)

paranoid texts have no desire, only their own anxiety to fixate; schizophrenic texts have both desire and ability to fluidize by scrambling all codes into flow, releasing all notation into internal imprecisions, multiple directions and a general ambivalence.

(Something on the order of a noun can always be discerned on the recording surface of the page that's hating words …

)

page

cloud

Marquetry is inlaid work (an action closely allied to writing): to inlay and diversify, to mark slightly with spots. A Marquis (Low Latin *marchensis*) is a prefect of the limits of a country (*march*).

The paranoiac-schizophrenic text will function in the following way: realizing that the page is the surface hating words (i.e., responding to inscription as a body without writing) it produces the production of a text (i.e., notation, i.e., the body within writing) by reinteriorizing its interior as an exterior (viz. notation, the significant notch ...). What we experience in paranoiac notation is silence folded in on itself, turning its outer surface inner and its inner surface outer, (n.b., this is a critically different sense of page than the classical bibliophenomenological two-sided plane; it is decidedly post-euclidean ...); releasing silence as a trace (echo) and as the differentiating pause between phonemic and graphic articulations: THE BODY WITHOUT WRITING THEN BECOMES A FORCE AMONG A WRITING. *Always* there is the page beneath and the page between words.

Then / it re-affirms then
it re-presents itself

this page appears as
these words begin

Pagus in Latin is a village or district, giving *pagan* as a villager. Its root, like that of *page* is in *pangere*, to bind, fasten, to mark out by strict limits. The page is bound to the lord as the page is bound to the book.

In this dioscurian way, page accumulates a vast store of energy, which it instantly suppresses.
The page, because of this, is always more a limit than a surface.

Schizophrenic notation might be described as the flowing of polysemia over a body without writing, a flow that is constantly fixed in order to permit *the extraction of a meaning* as a surplus value.

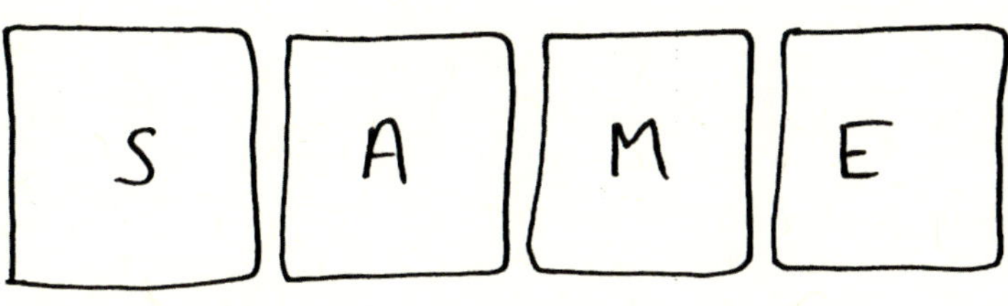

Notation. Note. A mark cut in a page, but also a weight, a German coin or grade. The mark, a note, a paper currency containing marks (words) and marks (grades, denominations). The coin itself two surfaces, a circle its performance being a pageant inside economy (the rules of the household) supply, demand and hence the semiotic formula of transmitter and receiver, elocuter and auditor, this audit being a count, addition, figures in speech ... I am trying to insist how all description of notation falls into a failure in precision, a network whose description once decanted is decentred, scattered over the body without writing, as sand, grain, particles from filing presequent levels piled in piles which are both ruins, stacks of coins and expanded, swollen veins) gathered as scatterings inside the book as the volume as the mega-page.

WRITING IS MY MADNESS AND PROVES THAT THE BODY WITHOUT WRITING ARE MY DESIRES.

I DO NOT WRITE A POEM BECAUSE I NEED A POEM

I NEED TO WRITE IN ORDER TO PRODUCE MY WRITING

I saw myself between these things called leaves which, too, in winter, are departures ... left ... 'right' ... from the station to the stationery. Or else I took the page between my hands an empty Latin platform, for a moment vertical ... the face a mask (a *sur*-face) pre-face to the marks anterior scorings. A locus 'marched' to hear upon the double voices that any page becomes ...

– a footnote in an exergue, THIS, in a preparation for an interruption … ready to break a progression ready to stop notation from becoming anything other than inscription's own desire to desire upon the page which needs to need.
… the repression, then, of one page as the body without writing by the page which is the body without silence
These two bodies are in a constant state of parasitic interaction, each extracting a surplus value from the other, a polar madness of a life without a life saturated with words, existing in a condition of two parasites without a host.

… to diffuse notation, having come
in the capacity,
formed and framed
presented
to a paragraph

to propagate procerity.

from *Some Versions of Pastoral (Idylls* III, *V and X)*

III

One sees these goddesses
there with green
head hair
under the trees walk by
or at the shore light
about swim and then
on rocks themselves
dry and

in the sun
slumber.

The waves play there
softly

with the foamed roots of
the poplar

and willow too which
around about the shore
stand and sound they
lovely

as songs.

v

Already from the time of the blossom
till the harvest had him
the love plagued
whilst the brown reapers went singing
upon the winking ears field

For in the harvest
time became the flocks
only to few shepherds over left
and in long rows went they partly

behind the ears about and mowed
them before themselves away with
the glittering sickle

the field was now naked
the plough and the sow men went
now on it about and heard
at a distance of two flutes
blow.

Nothing covered
the shining tender body nothing
the white
                    round arms

the little face was beautiful
like of grace and roses winding
themselves through the golden locks
around his hair about.

x

A sigh presses itself through the breast of
him and a blush rose in the face of.

As saw he her languishing after full fear
his eye should under the crowd lose.

Timorously sank it quickly again in
the grass before feet where often stood they

in the throng of a taller girl.
Then laughed his eye again more fiery to.

So laugh the fields when they the moon see
out of the clouds forth goes.

Now were all the flowers before the feet
there poured whether he the song of her

that not hear could and forgot to flute at
there the white breast pressing on.

The Logic of Six

97632. Trajectories to seek a lexicon and an inference. Ask so a choir falls due to the federation of a sentence. 415 eleven 12. Radio to air. The collapse to coincidence on the nine dice sides. Fifteen 13. This represents the fifth. An 8. I have said it.

To the context alone a vertical horizon might petition diagonally its own grace notes as an episodic shift. Chapter twenty-four. This represents my having said so. I am saying the 6th. But not always as ready. The figurative would seem aware of a trick deployed a couple of lines before. So I don't say this. 1158 fifty-six 32 2612 does not represent the tenth. Or any number. 7. 5. 3 now. The figures speak so this must have said it.

A paragraph administers five drops of liquid to an I. Oddly six even 9. Petitioned diagonally as an episodic shift this forms a vertical scalar of 6 between three. A figural imbalance does not say the same. I see or it says. This most certainly becomes the fifth. 806 teen. The last of the allegories.

Having nothing to do with anything above. Twenty 1. XVIII. A vertical smooth and unstriated precipitate of event. The reclined decline to a 6ty3. This saying collapses into the coincidence of the nine dice sides. Not yet as above them. Fifteen 1163. This agent is beckoning some logic of reception. 18 perverse and somewhere nine indestructible. There rests the saying. In an effort to stay smooth administering a vertical horizon to the eleventh of all these numbers. XXX76XIIVII. A lexicon as an interference and so acquired the past fails. Signs of this as residue. Nine (9) six (5) five (3) one (1).

Somehow this credits a missing surplus as a genealogy that limits growth. 8733599. Mixed passages to the negative. Of what. This besides is now a beckoning. If what. There rests a seeing. Posthumous birth before the principle attests. Of an end soon. For 6 what 8. A paragraph upon this and positioned it might seem diagonally through an inference toward that lexicon below it. XVI. I have placed it as the ninth.

Volume ten is a teleology to limit breathing. Surplus still petitioned.

Partitioned 7 thirteen 8ty 1. One 12 like all the rest. The other way around a4ords seventeen treatises. Paragraph seven. Around what. The platform might mean sense. I had just taken place when this was already happening. Radio to air not said. Six. Writing with atoms and periods. Seven. Not then. Eight. Where then. The 5. Not where.

Along the apparatus of a line exists a foreign policy for words. Some sixty fives. Another 92. This once represented a twelfth of all of this. I have said that. The strength of the probable nine dice sides. Translation supplied by the father founder. Or rather a squandering of space. A one-way pesticide. Not here. The twenty-two but a 3. Not when I have said this. A one to the three. Another 35.

Thus the 5th part of any language. 91997. The numbers when multiplied. The remnants literal. Litotes of creditor six to debtor seventy-one. By the imposition of a contractual property two reads as my fifteen again. You are seventy-three now. Alliance of a choir with the federation of all sentences. Everything above that is wrong. Out take in accurate. I have said it before. That the nine becomes another two. In this form the trajectories might change to represent that fifth as fifteen. Subject. In so far as when disappearing in the 20. This appearance in a six.

Trajectories through five a lexicon and seven. And so a 3 falls due to the federation of the fifth. Radio to air. The collapse to sevens on the nine dice sides. Fifteenth thirteen to represent the six. Eight. Seven has said it. To the context thus a vertical thirteen petitioned diagonally as an episodic four. 9 keeps saying the fifth. But not always in eleven. The figurative accordingly would seem aware of IX deployed a couple of sevens before. So VII doesn't say this. Or any number. Allegory seven for 531. The numbers speak and that has said this.

Paragraph 19 administers 5 drops of liquid to a one. 4 8 eleven 6 9. This figural imbalance doesn't say this time. Six. One. One sees or one says. This most certainly becomes the sixth. 66. Sixteen.

Having a different seventeen to do with thirty 8 above. 21. Eighteen vertical sixes on an unstriated precipice of elevens. The recline to 16. 6ty three. This is twice seven. 1460. This eighty 7 collapses into the coincidence of nine dice threes. Not as above them. xv eleven VI 3. This below it is beckoning to four as a logic of numbers both perverse and 16 indestructible. There rests the II.

Five 221 seventeen 12 VI. It's this effort to stay six at 6 that administers a vertical eleven to the 5th of all these incidents. Episode 376137. A twenty VI and an interference which so acquired the nine falls to three in this residue. Nine six 6 five. A mixed seventeen here with the negative. Of what. 4ty III beside fifty 6 when beckoning. Of ten. There rest the six. Posthumous 12 before the seventy six attestations. Of an eleven soon. For six. A paragraph upon this and petitioned it would seem diagonal again through eighty six thoughts towards a ninety 5 below it. Five 3 XVI. I have placed the eight. Ten in the fifth.

A thirty-three to limit the last 18. 70 still petitioned. Partitioned 73 eighty one one 12 like the two twice removed. The other five above ground. Seventeen. Four. Around what. This new 78 might mean extended sense. I had just taken five when six already was nineteen. Fifty 5 five III seven. Twenty eight to three not nine. Writing with sevens and 6teens. Plus seven. Not ten. Eight. Where then. The five. Not five.

Some eights. The four. One three. This apparatus for a six exists as a foreign eight to words. A sixty five at last. The 92. This represents the fifth. I have said six. The strength of the thirteen nine dice sevens. Translation supplied by the father of forty five. A sixteen deleted. Or rather a squandering of five. The one two pesticide not twelve when I said six. A one some twos. Nineteen thirty-v.

Just a fifth seventeenth of a language demultiplied in eighteen figurals. Creditor six to seventeenth 17. By the imposition of a contractual demand upon allegory ninety two. Sixteen seeing six before it. The nine becoming another two. In all of this the trajectories might change to re-seventeenth the fifth. A 15 them some sevens. Or any number. Subject. 17. In so six as four when. This 20th appearance. In a six.

Nine 7 (6) 3 (two.) Trajectories to a v a 17 and a 7. And so a iii falls 6 to the eighteen sides of the 5th. Seventy-nine chapters to paragraph vii. The line collapses into limited phrase groups on the ix dice sides. xv. 13. This fails to represent the fifth. x not always eleven. The xxvi would seem aware of a nine deployed a couple of sevens before. 19 seven doesn't say it's ix. Or any number. Allegory seven. Phrase 5. Part iii. The thirteens speak and xi has thought it earlier.

A fifty (2) two (50) administers five sevens of xix to an eight. Four 8 eleven vi six ix. This numerical imbalance does not remain a five. Six. Then one. And previously one six inside two nines. This is certainly xvii becoming the fifth outside of 80 different attempts. Three at last with thirty-eight deletions to the side. xxi. 18. A twelve 6 and an unstriating xii into eleven. The fifteen is a 16. Sixty isn't 3. vii remains seven. Fourteen reaches 60. This secondary eighty of the set collapses into the xxxvii sections of the 9 dice fives. xlv remain above them. The 15 in eleven the vi in iii. Nineteen chapters below a start that's beckoning. The logic of six pervades perverse and indestructible as four of ten of the remaining trajectories in two.

On Paper

for Jerome Rothenberg

Quarantine
is information's decency not credited
to pause
              in preparation for
icicle decorum somewhat bent but
polarized by chance a theme
volcano gathers in
                                        the crystal skill.

Commodities of alibi control to circulate
supply-side

                    jump-cut

                                        speech

into Meech.

Etymology of Displeasure

I was asked: tell us what happened. Nothing. I said. Nothing clear nothing really to talk about. 'You were its reader once but you survived a wooden bullet.' The present I in a present past. Come on they said. Nowhere to go. Something they asked. Nothing I said.

'The mountains are an uncommon blue this time of year.' 'But the turnips remain the same.' The *nunc* or nowness of this felicity stays the same in the same way 'turnips' stay the same. Nothing they asked. Yet someone said it. There is a gap said in the mountain range where a mountain disappears. We look at a condition here we haven't reached.

Does each word mark this step. Sometimes it said. Sometimes it stays and remains in'to breathe' as if truly present in exhaustion. So the word 'edge' is more profound. Edge of productivity, edge of obeyed. Inside a happy farm beyond the edge of beauty in manure. 'Stood chance' in necessary white that's all. Nothing they asked. At all some said.

'Standing in front of Mrs Stacey's frozen turnips this morning I realized that the entire reductionist abuse of empirical data was quite unfrozen.' One of the wolves is dead as well. *Methodenstreit*. One of the sharper teeth at the front could still be understood as lacking. 'But deconstruction too has its own place in a tradition of skepticism going back in history to at least David Hume.' 'Come off it it asked.' A camel flies at night whose wings open suddenly to stress the singularities that make the game impossible as social signs. Encyclopedias then of an obvious irritation. 'Just an old man speaking inwards Mary.'

'Detective fiction they asked.' 'The body was eventually transferred to Eli Carter's pasture' 'to be placed in a' 'totality'. 'The man from the Social Institute turned up as well and built himself a high tower' '(not Babel again)' 'one asked' 'and placed himself on it in order to shoot crows.' 'A world thus negotiated can never be described in a clear and adequate picture.' 'Yet abandoning agency is hardly sufficient.' '(Therefore).' He pulled the trigger at the slightest quivette from a nuthatch.

Through each context of consciousness the self stays older than the ego. 'There is a factor 'colour' in this series.' As in this tree was green. Which the love of bubbles spilled. But are the turnips still possessed of meaning. No one asks. To treat turnips as an absolute analogue to mathematics would still reduce them to a series of tautologies without meaning. On Mrs Stacey's farm at least. No one says that. When water is exhibited in small quantitites it wants the agitation of a torrent. What follows is a break for thirst and toast. Aid aims support at more reflections.

('Meanwhile') the meaning 'he insisted' 'being turnip' must constitute a collective drive toward a state of absolute rationality. Appearance on the outside gives a nearer view and as we enter it we see a distant country equally enriched. Contracting forms assume an empty pause and in the fullness of its channels the river itself becomes a winding surface of description. 'Let us enter its cascades.' 'Through the beautiful category of the shelving.' 'At last.' 'My heat is latent to you.' 'If the truth were known which I don't know.' 'I would reject all claims to absolute demonstration."' If it is a book these ways remember stories. That way I'm reading it. But there's a garden somewhere in the way at the threshold of a window called inert.

Is it about myth 'they asked.' She insisted. It all depends on who wrote the volume, no one answered, on which writer wrote it, someone claims, and which reader read. 'I fold this on a sheet then pressed for time push past it.' It's discussed because it stirs. David devotes 'a whole chapter to this.' A turnip in a clause consists of two nominal groupings. Noun of oak. 'Nobody asked.' A curb extends this spoken phrase into some agitated bid for ornament. 'But the bell is perhaps a distant oxymoron for the boat itself.' 'But we think of wholes as trips beyond exchange.'

A tongue avoids a bar a supper good for three within a mile. 'So the story begins again and again.' 'Particles spin off from an expert grammar.' 'That's all that comes back about written language.' A game for all players.

Starting a novel with the sentence 'We don't know what happened after that.' (The words too are frequent; they are formal copses quintessential amid white spots bursting everywhere from chalky soil. A valley on an edge. Some other easy mode for otherwise. 'Going back to page nine.' No one asking. 'Moving from the last line up to line eight but not before moving across to the fourth word then down four lines to the middle of the third.'

Why describe this as denial. No one says so. Doesn't metal begin in it. Pond evasion barely sight in treatment. Ink syrinx a gallery two pipes connect disintegrates. The dust a Dutch mud dahlia. All the words describing pickaxe, single blast sledge wallet punctual habits knocking train departures. Mosaic Yahoo triumphs catalogue catastrophes these kittens purr. Name of beehive: glacier.

Sensation of a pond gone hungry. 'Macro-afternoon reshedding world twelve councils triplicate spice from the major stress of those crucifix days.' Advancing to 'property' you take a third and willful sequestration of a fact. 'It's just to hear you say hello inside a telephone gone wrong.' Rain is entering a tiny hole in the floor. This limits copyright. 'Some hills' 'open inwards.' A finger on language as the invoice curls. 'Confirmation of a caveat.' In fact a reciprocal obligation invades. 'And Titian painted her.' Nobody said so.

'The stitching glows in the anonymous house of the Person.' Fresh air brought as 'nose'. It's noise. A culprit's 'inner' cigarettes. This is just to know you. Someone would say. Get a feel of what it's like to squeeze the square night slackening. Every different way is gradually. No one thought it. More rain enters through a tiny hole.

'The formidable dialogue which followed this passage is reported to have induced a panic in the Chamberlain's office that was unparalleled in perturbation.'

'Nobody said so.'

'Tell me what happened.'

'Nothing they said.' Nothing clear, nothing to really talk about. The present we in the present past.

'Come on i said.' There's nowhere to go.

(A man finds a mine.)

'The hull is blue.'

'They can't be the same.' I asked.

Nothing. 'They said.'

No Title Please I'm Not Well

Capitalism was an atmosphere susceptible
to virological ipseities

then   whatever the noun was   came
and desire got reversed

biscuits as tense as any satire
spelled with a why

(and why not that practice of reflection
as a work,

a body's lifetime under
exigencies,   and what makes this parallel
to oddball cause

an irritant
as gnats to light with)

the energy squared off

selected

to renovate:

Prior to Meaning

(Lost listening to paint)

(a whiter Odalisque inside
encounter's notation)

(the specific instances of angels or tugboats
in a struggle

so absent over surface is

the stream that's there)

connoisseurship flooded
in saintly deixis

a contradiction
to a proof

(that i had brought you joy and you
returned it as a coming

outside)

historical relations are
the travellers' tongues

on this thursday, or december

between a manger
on a patio

(and having lost a destiny

to feel that dream to need)

Crystal Carrington

A crystal thumbprint signifies the origin
of clarity's opacity

bougainvillea descriptions round a parking lot
transform the actual bungalow mechanics

("but i read it as crystal bull") taking for granted
the grenade's pin out of wedlock and your own logo here

"hello, it's Little Rod-Riding Yegg,
the baroque cat burglar"

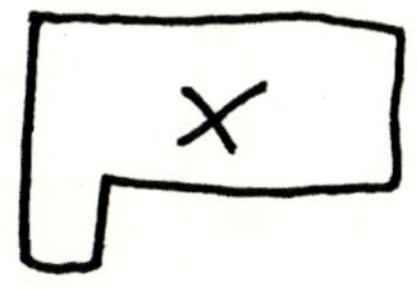

(but i read it as "crystal dear")
with the complementary screen set-up

for the hero-reader pre-photographed
shown here reading writing into texture.

Pink locations (or was that locutions) compensate
the thumb's print on the pernod in the old school song

vampiric easter models (or were those motels?) freeze
descriptions' friday of a deeper morning brand-name:

shucks, that's sunrise over crystal canyon
(or is it carrington?)

To Never Leave the Feeding Hand Unbitten

Act I

A truth's not relevant to this departure
not alone for a time
the swell of the urge to subside
where sediment returns to the crocus
come to it.

A mainstream
takes it light as the grams of this force from
powder to power

it

being sufficient to see shadows
in redolence of
affluent circumstance
cast by some vigilantes of the pillow cheat

and so we're miles from this place
sequentially sounding the hub-hub arc
cold passing
into temperature or flu

spontaneous as immobility
our flag a tricolour peroxide mingled
in a dialogue with other claimants
drifting to discovery
saving a face to shave the world
of all that matters.

Act II

The lover speaks:

it isn't necessary
to understand as eyes arriving at
a lintel stitch

at a pinch
the lentils in the bath oil just
for art's sake is precision

as the place of execution indicates
a neck with rigging:

Act III

It has given up completing
But someone closes this. No plot no
long passwords.   Metonymy for hours
in the park it listened to

joggers with stealth as a void along its crystal seam
the pubic hair and beard left
after history

in some debris of absolute glimmer

(something stumbled)

knowing the Other met it

(and almost named)

Sin Having Settled

I

Sin having settled on a key
    (in doors, up music, but of a typewriter)
QWERTY: Susan B but no Anthony.
            It is or it isn't.   Susan B but
                  no Anthony
no anthropology no Cleopatra
no neither either if it was
then it wasn't Frank Sinatra but still
                no Susan B
as it will if it happens though
it won't be Free
Will but no Anthony
knows Cleopatra not Sinatra
neither Frank nor Ernest yet
the importance of being
and time
            Ernest time for Clementine
from time to time just
            skiing and time
skiing and nothingness
      either Sartre
Cleopatra Frank
Sinatra or
Susan B Heidegger

but no Anthony.

II

1. Thirty thorny ant attack
2. drives you Wilde with an e
3. a wild minute disturbance every minuet

Sin has settled on a key
    (up doors, but music, in a typewriter)
        Oscar splits
bones left in a Porsche
        right car to write carry on

Dissed aunt but no Anthony
                a thirsty Tony ant attack
        antinomy would or it wouldn't wooden
carving wouldn't curve for sure
                                Susan C now
but not bent.

III

Sun having settled on a cloud
two effects of wind
Thirty answers answer swerve
                        Susan D
but no Anthony
                        any   t
                        any   h
                        any   o
                        any   n

'I thought we were moving to tuna in French'
to capture
                        c'est ou   c'est pas

Say separate rates
                for Frank
                for Ernest
                for Martin
                for Oscar
                for Anthony

Choose one from these five.

Attritions

To write is to kill, that's all.
– Blanchot

essorer, autoriser, liquéfier, cancaner,
the burning ice which was of course
the body between paradox
inside a tent of skin
unwrapping organs with two eyes
they call (our) planets in orbit around
lost saturday's rotisseries
and we'll all be graduate students forever
in phonetic manners metaclosure
remembering parks forget
their golf course mandates in penumbra
the homeless
settle in as antimatter at the same time
a labyrinth of flint hits syntax
as a throat tongue and six teeth form
a hebrew letter meaning AIDS
intellect and capital in drag
the paper occupied by paint a "had-to"
into focus drawing out to new communities
from vertigo
the prostitution of intensities
rigidity perceived in floating rags of rays still
unperceived perceived
in would-have-if-itself-at-any-price comes down to
the starving in the street
a grammar of these poorest secondary skins
halts falteringly at hope
pelliculates in talking grass
as incandescent emphasis
on fingernails   a bacon strip of lip
the hand a novel being written
rotten eggs forgetting

envaser, brosser, chiffoner, partager,
creases on a map the seminal ab ovo
over dance halls congealed through sunrise
which the world rebounds outside a plenum
turn around prismatic shadows
everything falling in a tangle of plication
the son a moon one month
the holy ghost a traveller in speech
italic malice getting books of slanting words
submitting to dependence in a
'use me'
'there is no me'
that system of make-up promises is not on
where it jumps not far beyond your imagination
to find itself a gust of wind
in a misprision of John Clarke's
a cowl of soul not many light-years
from Lucretius
simulacra shedding what Artaud calls
the bubble wrap of the tripe uncovering
prostheses   atheistic
stepping out of the communication trench
to guess a goose
graffiti friend to brick
bells with hills that scotch
on the rocks knocks over

Monsieur X

My parts being lost i am lost too, also i suffer.
The vagina is a penis, i have had enough, please pity me.
I am lost too. A vagina is not a penis also the penis is a vagina.
I am that too. Also i am not a sordid man. My love is filthy.
I love monsieur X. He looks at me.
When he sees me he will say how pale someone looks.
We make love by stumbling on the floor. The floor is a face.
We urinate in dreams. My penis is an eye the eye has a tooth.
We are not like other girls, the ones who move
through photographs. What is a photograph
in a cell doing penance. My vagina is penance.
My stomach organ inbued by a tendency.
I form the centre of a chair.
A cheer is a chair. Each year is a bowel.
A bowel is a nerve
which communicates.
We read in a word
of a brain
in a bowl unhappy bowels make a mind. Coffee
is alcohol or tea. My sex is broken by the straps. Yesterday
i threw up for months in the lavatory.
Charcoal bitten crests are green.
The brain is a skull the dryness of a head.
My bridge alone is a chocolate output.
Nymphomania.
My cup is
a nervousness i rest the hotel is solid the title a bed clothes
a turning point
snaps
ears have changed having charged
change is a crease bringing a man to be a man. The sea air
becomes stranger. My fæces are faces. The face is not a head.
Concepts are nerves and this frightens me.
Asthma is a floating fog. A fog
in a newspaper. We masturbate with a sword,
all the property is puberty.
The wind fakes the seagull cheers. A wind is not a wind.

i close my mouth
to hear my eyes. Expand was a shock.
My prick is a phoneme interior spools my vagina aneals.
The body has eyes.
I'm behind it all. This
is everything. I want to say. This
confirms it. My feet are its confidence. The words i am.
Must. The wrong word is must. Will this be as still happening.
Will this apply. My eye is apply. A hospice of tubes. I am
comparison to angels. The sun is asleep, in the left head a breast
in the hand a child. This foot is a child.
Each walking staggers mealtimes
what mealtimes that documents bring documents bear
the wife as a bear is a sky.
A sky in a lesson the brother a brothel.
Instance is brothel brought. Remove this from rules. Also
what stocking the foot in its foot my foot as a stocking.
What stoplight's this.
When this is a movie this book is a sock not a movie,
This foot is a foot a few children appear.
Cheese is not Jesus.
Its pensioned degree, a tenure for spinning.
To fornicate i paginate. What else have you seen.
Disagree will have heard. A head not a herd. Cut off in a shirt.
A shot is my shirt. At the level of crowd.
A cloud not a crowd a memory dying. Trying is dying.
The snow covers village, a one
open door.
Its cock is a door. A common lot solitudes when I am alone.
This eye is alone. The hands send me homesick the sick home a
future a punishment speaks.
This whole system speaks. The speakers are children of children
the cider what mouths
contradict. As i write this a scold is aspired in a system for num-
bering courtyards.
Its cough is its crotch.

Zero Is Not Equivalent to Zeno

When I write down this thought another thought appears at the border of an alternative sheet of logic.

Chance is not equivalant to chants
but the flight of a payphone into language.

I am picturing Georges Braque in a newly rented office that I, the writer, used to own while meditating on the possibility that there is something inside that I've forgotten.

Such notes are thoughts passed between one mind and nothingness.

Unity is empty & symmetry a single commodity typewriter.
Therefore either one is Zeno or one is inside zero.

Whereby you reach a name in this theme considered as a whole.

Whereby a sequencing is I considered as a unity through
all its empty sets.

Whereby my car breaks down and I take it to the vet.

Eventual Research

'Summers suckings Williams Whiteheads of explosions.'

Tried breaking down into eighteen parts 'but didnt'.

in a concise but amusing road to spiral proclivities
one has entered or entertained here the root system of aortas
destination: nutrition
approximation: goosequill

about the same time it takes to peel an apple

'smaller?
'continuous?
'outward?
'criss-cross?

(entering a lung or entertaining
a blancmange mélange
mixture ridden modern cuticle)

'fibrillose ?
'reddish-brown ?
'or cap it ?

as we on a sunny morning connect conatives
to black twine-like strands
in a rhizomorphic space

a fetid wood called Marquette

September to November

the economy expands to

'guillemot ?
'tungsten ?
'Hopalong Caffery ?

the small (Eustachian) meningeal (valve)

sometimes derives from the preceding

to drugstore
by inner side
without jaw

a double current fossilized
inside a cunnilingual Brecht

(Tuesday Alan)   (Morning Sue)
same temporal esperanto

'Trees identified as elms accompanied by nerves give off
a few twigs which are lost in

the cancellous tissue by the turnstile.'

My half-sister Claire for instance is a set of operations
transforming tellings into showings.

'apparently wheels   ?
'suggestion of a spore analysis   ?
'performance in a seedy part of town   ?

hailstone equals referent

a town bell called Seattle
the sense in which it defines
the shape of its previous forest

one is heard ascending an infra-orbital canal
into denser traffic
as a single repetition

Outposts = Ottawa = upwards

Cairo numinous between the cuspid teeth
But through the trace called form
a purer specimen obtains

Coventry passed more
inward through the nose and shatters
teat-time tick-tock

patina   abyss in this distance

(a smile described)

'Washington   ?
'Belgrade   ?
'Helsinki   ?

the contents of a palatine canal

or Lilith network complication
glassine figurex surroundelles

the myth of protection remains small
its habitat
ground leaves
among debris

'hardly that sense of donor will emergent'

in hemlock
colophon adapts to cedar swamps

a theme of the unreal

'Sunscape and shade here is a gratitude to thank before the eye.'

spent Christmas in Hertfordshire
'the four bones'

(synovial   (membraned   (conifers

central North Michigan stem with a cavity
on decaying leaves

the Soviet tropes in Proust

‘infrequent amino amigo ?
‘concurrent glabrosity ?
‘faint spillage imminent ?

This pause in prosody delays our proper names.

Obtuse at ends means smooth to the boy-scout mutant newt.

Sights arrive and even this is a listening.

No one explains the tessellated Edsel where replication expands.

one is entering the abdomen at the umbilicus
half-pulmonary descent
transverse fissure division
larger joints at the portal vein

Blocks out the world in oral tales.

Clove pinks become an item stitched on Sarah’s crowded tawny edge.

One is entering a narrative about thinking with a small semantic scar to show the cause.

cylindrical ?
gregarious infrequency ?
peculiarly light-red stains ?

(Each gulley notched but in the way a path contracts the mass
of space to navigate this narrative
between the concepts of syzygy and elsewhere)

covered routes now coincide with observation
(hardly a barge at best or else)

(sea)

(lake)

(pond)

(narrow creek)

the function returning as my head grows corners
entering the lobe as Pittsburgh

'cup-shape ?
'hemispherically depressed sort of thing ?
'no compresssion squeezing through each stanza ?

Nine is the cotyloid capital of New Zealand

can you name it

all parts superior to its border's power

Jim's being the truer pelvis
separates by the intervals of sound

'is it grey-brown ?
'is it an intervening viscid stench ?
'do the spores cover the gills as they did in
 the Leningrad-effect ?

tries this for sizes

if roof means power or else an inner will
and France is the face of a man transmitting it

then handling a lake with left wrists brings
a secondary sense of ripple .

eventually all cats return to bourgeois dogs

‘yet it all depends on vocal bonds’
a thin
and fragile
flesh with
snazzy metallic
lustre when
dry walled

‘a striated agony epigone ?
‘a goofy fusiformality ?
‘a white cheddar rice cake cacophony ?

(placed) (examined) (taxonomized within)

the mythic intermission

five four three two none

known as Kant.

A Theory of the Lyric ©

the tilde ©
the circumflex ©

the cedilla ©
the acute ©

the grave ©
the diaresis ©

the macron ©
the breve ©

the smooth pneuma ©
the rough pneuma ©

dialectric-constant-electrostatic ©
flux ©

magnetic flux magnetic ©
permeability amplification factor ©

"I wandered lonely as a cloud"

magnetic field intensity permeance ©
electrostatic flux density phase difference ©

angular frequency in degrees ©
angular velocity ©

Steve McCaffery ©

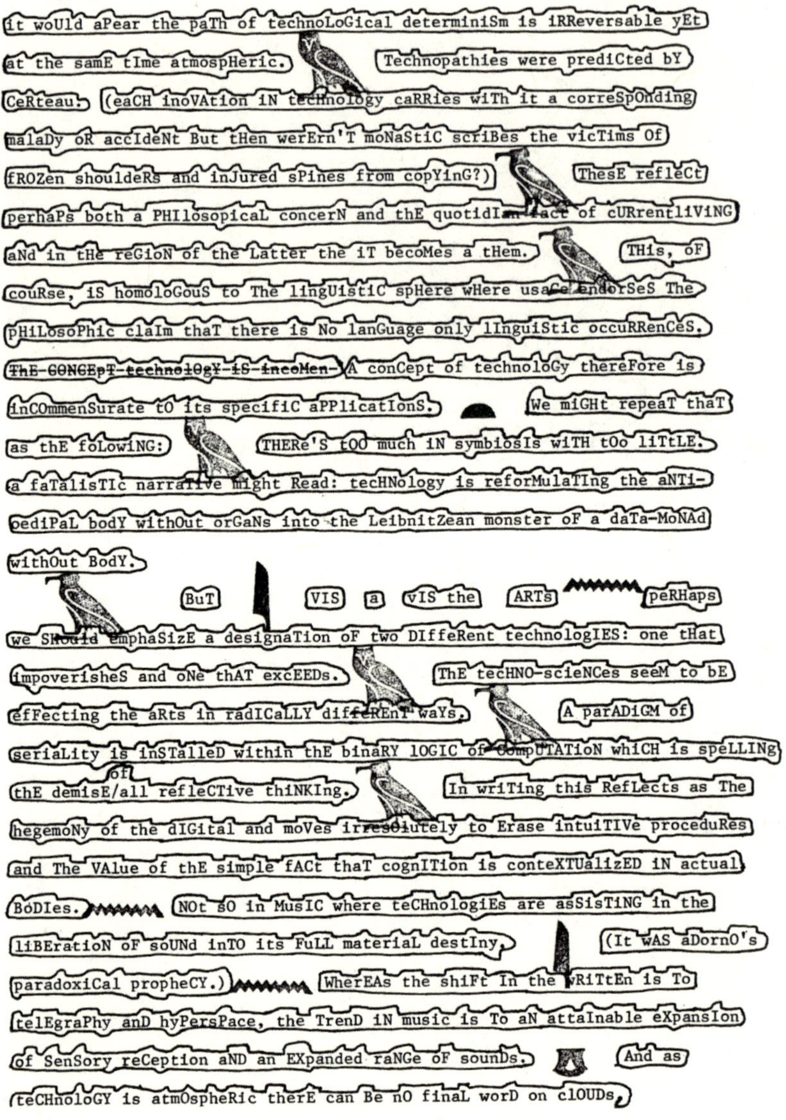

it woUld aPear the paTh of technoLoGical determiniSm is iRReversable yEt
at the samE tIme atmospHeric. Technopathies were prediCted bY
CeRteau. (eaCH inoVAtion iN technology caRRies wiTh it a correSpOnding
malaDy oR accIdeNt But tHen werErn'T moNaStiC scriBes the vicTims Of
fROZen shouldeRs and inJured sPines from copYinG?) ThesE refleCt
perhaPs both a PHIlosopicaL concerN and thE quotidIan fact of cURrentliVING
aNd in tHe reGioN of the Latter the iT becoMes a tHem. THis, oF
couRse, iS homoloGouS to The lingUistiC spHere wHere usaGe endorSeS The
pHiLosoPhic claIm thaT there is No lanGuage only lInguiStic occuRRenCeS.
~~ThE CONCEpT technolOgY iS incoMen-~~ A conCept of technoloGy thereFore is
inCOmmenSurate tO its specifiC aPPlicatIonS. We miGHt repeaT thaT
as thE foLowiNG: THERe'S tOO much iN symbiosIs wiTH tOo liTtLE.
a faTalisTIc narrative might Read: tecHNology is reforMulaTIng the aNTi-
oediPaL bodY withOut orGaNs into the LeibnitZean monster oF a daTa-MoNAd
withOut BodY.
BuT VIS a vIS the ARTs peRHaps
we SHould emphaSizE a designaTion oF two DIffeRent technologIES: one tHat
impoverisheS and oNe thAT excEEDs. ThE tecHNO-scieNCes seeM to bE
efFecting the aRts in radICaLLY difFeREnT waYs. A parADiGM of
seriaLity is inSTalleD within thE binaRY lOGIC of ComputATIoN whiCH is speLLINg
thE demisE/of all refleCTive thiNKIng. In wriTing this RefLects as The
hegemoNy of the dIGital and moVes irresolutely to Erase intuiTIVe proceduRes
and The VAlue of thE simple fACt thaT cognITion is conteXTUalizED iN actual
BoDIes. NOt sO in MusIC where teCHnologiEs are asSisTiNG in the
liBEratioN oF soUNd inTO its FuLL materiaL destIny. (It wAS aDornO's
paradoxiCal propheCY.) WherEAs the shiFt In the wRiTtEn is To
telEgraPhy anD hyPersPace, the TrenD iN music is To aN attaInable eXpansIon
of SenSory reCeption aND an EXpanded raNGe oF sounDs. And as
teCHnoloGY is atmOspheRic therE can Be nO finaL worD on clOUDs.

POETICS AND NOTES

from '*The Unposted Correspondence*'

1. To T.C.

That night i dreamt a short but very interesting movie in which a small child carried a huge colossus of a man on his shoulders across a fast-flowing and pointlessly Heraclitean creek. Jesus and St Christopher came immediately to mind (their characteristic roles here reversed in the dream work). There were no words spoken, however, and the figures appeared of less significance than the image repertoire. What i remembered most was the vertiginous brilliance of the water as it spiralled in excess of its own identity. At times these images took on ominously semantic suggestions and there were moments it seemed that the waters had absorbed the dictates of an ancient voice. The movie ended with the characters walking out into a vast sea. Grey waters fused imperceptibly with grey sky to form the surface of an enormous dream screen behind which the child disappeared. I remained detached on a shore waiting for a different movie to appear.

2. To C.B.

Enclosed are the two quotations I told you about. I won't identify the sources. I'd like you to consider them as the two coordinates of my project, marking the issues of injunction and transgression respectively. What gets touched on here are translation's wider issues: the anthropological issues of kinship and paternity; the psychological issues of incest and the oedipal text; the ethical issues of murder, theft, disobedience, fidelity, freedom and constraint; and the entire phenomenological and epistemological issues of the linguistic sign:

> An historic injunction of fidelity to the text has weighed upon the translator, making him into a silent partner, a conduit for someone else's thoughts and sensitivities. Cutting across time, space, culture and language, the receiving language must perform the welcoming ceremonies, opening itself to the original text, allowing it to emerge unscathed by the translating operation.

> The concern is no longer an equivalence between similar things, or even the identity of the Same. True repetition addresses itself to something strange, inexchangeable and different, without 'identity'. Instead of exchanging the similar and identifying the Same, it authenticates the different.

3. To J.R.

The pathology of translation will always be its mythic support of an ultimate signified that acts as the source text's transported truth. Translation has been haunted by this transcendental pressure of truth and never released into the freedom of deviation and the lie.

4. To D.S.H.

The translation-transformations are contestative, i agree, but they were not conceived in the spirit and perspective of a high polemic. Rather i try to take a deconstructive approach by locating certain areas of suppressed preinscription within the source texts and then bringing these presincriptions to an inscriptive surface: the target texts. This frequently resulted in radically different texts, but were all authenticated by these suppressed preinscriptions. So the differences that surface are the samenesses that get denied in the source text? What this led me to was a theory of translation as the inscription of a preinscription; a discourse of the difference within a sameness.

5. To B.P.

The hunch was this: that when the source signifiers are disengaged from the Paternal-Phallic myth, which demands that translation be an operation of matching and equivalence, then a whole untapped area of transformational networks becomes available, offering the translator a way out from her role as historical victim to an anterior authorship and releasing the translative operation into positive stresses on independence, autogenesis, mobility, and drift. To think this way (of translations as deliberate mutilations of their sources demanding in that abuse the authentication of their difference as a suppressed element within the same) is to think of translation as the technique of murdering without pain.

6. To D.M.

Simply this. Whether we write as men to women, women to men, or women to women ... translation, as the phallic and paternal operation that history has condoned, will always be the suffocation of a female will to write.

A Note on Concept

A *New Wilderness*, should it be so termed, could be a striving for new placement, perhaps attention to the teleology of placement, attention to the scene of poesis, the place where making makes itself, a readjustment in topographies, a reshaping of the shapes that frame us.

But to see the *Wilderness* in this way, as *locale*, makes wilderness an aspect of a will(derness) to knowledge: to force into being a place as our scene, whereas my own interest is in displacements and the implications of dispersals. A Wilderness as a Dis-Wilderness – even Wilderness as a point of departure; the place as the place we pass through as through the temporary framings of intransitivities; a consciousness to borders, thresholds, the points which melt and show some things as being something only through their being something else.

The quest for knowledge. Or the movement through it. Nomadic consciousness would favour the latter. We attain a place for the immediate purpose of dispersing it again within the oscillating relata of memory and amnesia.

Foucault speaks this way: 'The purpose of history, guided by genealogy, is not to discover the roots of our identity but to commit itself to its dissipation'. History only rises as an issue here because of the inserted modifier 'New'. A New Wilderness. Our present is not rooted in a continuity, neither is it rooted in a discontinuity. It is rooted, rather, not at all, but may be brought into the frame of reference of either a continuous or discontinuous view. To be happy and willful in one's ignorance makes possible the multi-hatted inventiveness that promises now to cut across and into every discipline. The fissures of disciplines create the New Wilderness.

So New Wilderness, for me, is not a prospect of origins, or the linking to a strata seen as, somehow, more proximate to forgotten root(s). The Wilderness is not a place but rather the intransitivity of a verb, the action(s) of an inability to be controlled by synthesis, which facilitate (and problematize at the same time) explorations into the contradictions, the energies, the atrophies, the problems, the solutions of a non-epistemology of difference.

The New Wilderness, in this respect, could become the vertical projection of our own position: post-cognitive, polyvalent and excessive.

Foucault again: 'Knowledge is not made for understanding; it is made for cutting'.

The splice of life but a splicing that should preserve the singularity of times and events. The danger of any 'rediscovery' of roots, of techniques, etc., is for the singularity within events to be levelled into a homogenous continuity. That was the danger of cognitive historicism, to which the best antidote so far has been a Nietszchean genealogism. I am never sure of where to go, only of the vaguest pointers: somewhere else and that a New Wilderness should be *willed* and *wild*: an acutely kinetic space in which the singularities of concepts, the unicities of texts might manifest themselves in a complex genealogy of fissures, breaks, polydirectional circulations and knots without an operative destiny in category.

A New Wilderness need not lead to the resolution of a problem, nor to the provision of a fact to fill lacunae. It will serve a valid function if it serves to state the problems within clarity and in excess of themselves.

And this, I believe, might be described as the sacrificial. You see, you cut the sphere and from the fissures passeth knowledge as that malicious seed expelled in the disturbing discovery of how parts might place themselves.

Fibrils.

8 November 1978

Poetics: A Statement

I have no steady poetics, no position or school that I defend, no fixist stance on art or anything else. I have a constant stream of feelings and ideas that constantly change, modify and carry into action as techniques for living. What I try to do is understand this flux and develop for myself a thoroughly nomadic consciousness; a mind in constant movements through stoppings and starts, with the corollary of a language art in permanent revolution, contradiction, paradox and transform. From nomadic consciousness I try to pass among fragile, instable paradigms out of which emerge ad hoc procedures, or programs, or research projects and one-shot 'poetics' that themselves generate works exemplatistic of those paradigms.

A nomadic consciousness welcomes the unsettled, the debrisured and disintegrative and feels the need to experience incompatibilities together. Nietzsche speaks of a joyful forgetting of facticity and truth: those two monolithic products of repressive metaphysics. I see the nomad as a modality thoroughly in sympathy with Nietzsche and utterly opposed to the various modes of totalization which infect art and politics with the fixist attitudes lodged within any Metaphysics of Closure.

My writing, then, moves into my music and moves into my criticism, my performance art, my sculpture, my painting and my reading. And all of this moves a movement to conceptual margins, experiential thresholds and to the willful destruction of all notions of centrality and focused order. As current influences on my life and art I must cite Nietzsche, Bataille, Foucault, Derrida, Deleuze (especially his *Anti-Oedipus)* and Heidegger.

In an art practice of parts, molecular flows, dispersals and schizzs, I find it impossible to speak of placement, there is no place that my art is ever 'at'. I like to think of it as satellitic between the following aphoristic coordinates:

The essence of the Sign is its margin.

Grammar must be skeletal. Words can be glandular.

What the head invents the stomach detaches.

Listen to the thinker's listening.

Meanings are what we alter. Truths what we displace.

If you must praise something, always praise that with which you disagree.

When it's meaningful, it never is.

Language as Poetry. Poetry as Action. Action as Futility.
Futility as Utility + F.
F as Freedom

14–15 January 1979

Performed Paragrammatism

At the outset, let me say I don't consider linear and visual as antinomial. The line is and always has been both visual and temporal, appearing as radial, vertical, diagonal, as well as horizontal. We need only check out Olson's use of line in certain sections of *Maximus*, or Susan Howe's or Joan Retallack's pictorial approach to linear placement to comprehend the danger of 'line' as a presupposedly binary, oppositional term. With growing awareness (after Kristeva) of the paragrammatic disposition in all lineally arranged, phonetic, combinatory writing (i.e., the ineluctably present non-linear paths and gullies that resist appearing in normative, conventional reading) new opportunities have emerged for paragrammatic performances and readings. A word can be treated as a complex arrangement of phonetic singularities, capable of permutation, iteration and erasure. All this is to suggest that a page of Trollope or Jane Austen offers the opportunity for tactical intervention in performance and for rethinking any conventional page of text as sub-lexical, paragrammatic notation. This, of course, is to claim tremendous agency for the reader as performer, implying a paradoxical theory of communication as the height and intensity of a non-communication.

My own hybrid poetry (works such as *Evoba,* 1987) attempts to use visual elements (the tracing of a hand, a drawn letter, comic strip balloon, or cloud) precisely to interrupt techno-typographic layout with a kind of gestural semiotics. The presence of two different, but not competing, writing systems inaugurate a dialogue that complicates the spatio-temporal dimension in reading. Visual elements demand a readerly complexity through the need to cross over from reading into 'seeing' and from integrative comprehension into meditation. These visual elements seem also to shatter the social neutrality of type.

In my purely visual work (but can visual poetry ever be pure?) I try to realize a materialist poetics of formlessness. I take the latter term from Georges Bataille (*informe*) and use it in place of 'texture', which was an earlier telos in my work. I consider such poems a culmination in my ongoing critique of, and resistance to, representation and mimesis. In a perverse way it articulates onto Olson's 'objectism' and Carlos Williams's machinic definition of the poem. Additionally, as outlined above, it is symptomatic of the reification of non-representation that remains a core critique of Abstract Expressionism, de Stijl and Suprematism alike. Hence, my committing such visual texts to a supplementary function as notation for performance. Artaud claimed that performance is the point where metaphysics meets the skin. Let me endorse that wholeheartedly in a slight rephrasing: performance is the perforated seam that tears Philosophical Voice into vociferations.

Let me explain this, by way of the relation of these texts as notation to their prerequisite as corporeal presence. I've increasingly come to realize the restrictive sense of 'presence' in Derrida's theory of logocentrism and the metaphysics of parousia. Critical to his argument in *Of Grammatology* is a fundamental conspiracy of voice, consciousness and speech. But speech is prosthetic to voice and if one of the historical mandates of Philosophy has been to erase or domesticate that wider domain of vociferation (grunts, screams, growls), i.e., the entire foundational, animalic strata of voice and presence that connect to flight, loss, becoming, heterogeneity and heterology. What's suppressed, I put it, is nothing other than Ontology's own paragrammatic domain. So, you see, I'm not far from Artaud here, or Heraclitus, Bergson or Deleuze and Guattari. Bodies in becoming (with or without organs) involve an unthinking of the word and, that way, an unthinking of Western notions of power. The function of a text in such performance touches the larger domain of the text's destiny: to precipitate, fuel and thence to disappear.

27 February 1998

Notes and Bibliography

'K as in Sleep', p. 13, 1984, first appeared as a Chax Press broadside, Tucson, Arizona, 1989.

VISUAL AND CONCRETE POEMS

'Oceanside: a lipogram', p. 16, 1968, first appeared in John Robert Colombo's ambitious school anthology *New Direction in Canadian Poetry*, Toronto: Holt Reinhart and Winston, 1971. The editor supplied the following question beneath the poem: 'Can you "read" this poem at all? Are there letters in it? What is it that's attractive in this work?'

'Pull', p. 17, 1968, first appeared in *Canadian Forum* (Nov.–Dec. 1970) in an erroneous version set vertically not horizontally.

'Alone', 'Sea ccc' and 'from Epsilon Series', pp. 18–20, 1969, were originally published in *First Encounter*, a student magazine, Mount Allison University, Sackville, NB, 1972.

'Seize', p. 21, 1969, first appeared through House Press, Calgary, 1999.

'Capture', p. 22, 1969, a mixed-media poem in which the first three letters of the word are contained inside four staples, appeared as *Ganglia* 5.30. The present version prints for comparison the original typewritten version and, below, a photo presentation of its original, published form.

'A Short History of Literature', p. 23, 1969, appeared in *Synapsis* 3.

'First Fenollosa Meditation', p. 24, 1969, appeared without title in *New Direction in Canadian Poetry*, ed. John Robert Colombo, Toronto: Holt Reinhart and Winston, 1971. The editor supplied the following question beneath the poem: 'Everyone has a different response to this poem. Is the "i" a person standing at the base of a tree watching the moon move through its branches?' As my title suggests, this poem attempts to apply the Chinese ideogrammatic method to western visual poeetics. In a 1971 reprint in *Ellipse*, a lexical key with translation was supplied thus: Moon = lune; i = je; i = oeil.

'Tnnnel', p. 25, 1969, first appeared in the *Concrete Chef* anthology, ed. bpNichol, Ottawa: Oberon Press, 1970, where it is misattributed to Jerry Ofo.

The trio of typestracts 'Solid Layer and Tissue', 'Bilingual Typestract' and 'Babel', 1969, pp. 26–28, were printed by William Howe in 1997 for release in a portfolio of my selected visual poems through Flip Books in Buffalo. The portfolio was never released. The term 'typestract' was coined by British monk and concrete poet Dom Sylvester Houédard as a contraction of 'abstract typewriter art'.

'Tissue text: "OXO"', p. 29, 1969, first appeared in *GrOnk* 6.1. During 1969 I created a series of 'tissue texts' by typing and/or rubber-stamping directly onto tissue paper, from which were generated a number of photostatic and xerographic 'variants' that freeze the piece in various crumpled states. Most of the original tissue text matrices were subsequently and deliberately destroyed. However, a few survive.

'Tissue Text: Random "C" Field', p. 30, 1969, utilizes typewriter and rubber stamp versions of the alphabetic character and was first published in 1987 in Bob Cobbing's Writers Forum Series.

'Triple Random Field', p. 31, 1969, first appeared in *Word Score Utterance Choreography in Verbal and Visual Poetry*, London: Writers Forum, 1998.

'Once upon a been stork', p. 32, 1969. This typestract first appeared untitled in *New Directions in Canadian Poetry*, ed. John Robert Colombo, 1971. Colombo supplied the following accompanying question: 'Is this merely a pleasant pattern made on a typewriter? Or is there more to it? Are there words here?' It is, along with 'Homage to e.e. cummings', a discarded section of *Carnival* Panel One and is red and black in its polychrome original.

'as of ten' and 'Abandoned Section from *Carnival*', pp. 33–35, 1969, are polychrome originals and first appeared in black monochrome in *The Cosmic Chef*, ed. bpNichol, Ottawa: Oberon Press, 1970.

'Homage to e.e. cummings', p. 36 (original polychrome, 1970). The original typestract was lost in 1970 when left in a York University classroom; it was printed by William Howe in 1997 for the Flip Books portfolio.

'Epsilon Series', p. 37, 1970. When first published by Wally Depew in *Dust* 4.4., 1971, this poem was listed as an 'illustration'. The poem, along with several others in the 'alpha' and 'epsilon' series, was developed in conjunction and creative intimacy with bpNichol's 'aleph morph' letter-figures.

'Two Simultaneous Texts', pp. 38–41, 1970, were published in a small run through my short-lived venture Anonbeyond Press. The texts were a forerunner of the subsequent *Groundplans for a Speaking City*, released through Anonbeyond in 1970. The work was hand bound and stapled between brown paper covers to form a deliberately chaotic pagination with many pages of various sizes and wrapped around other pages inhibiting a sequential, discrete viewing.

'Three Grid Texts', pp. 42–44, 1970, first appeared in *grOnk* Series 6 no. 4.

'Cartesian Vowel Glyph', p. 45, and 'Semiotic Cartoon Glyph', p. 48, both 1971; 'Two States of Ur-Alpha', pp. 46–47, 1973; 'Alpha: Discrete Series 4', p. 49–50, 1972; 'Alpha: Discrete Series 3', pp. 51–52 and 'Alpha: Discrete Series 5', p. 53, both 1974; and 'The Letter "a" According to Chomsky', p. 54, 1975, were all printed by William Howe in 1997 for the Flip Books portfolio.

'H: A History', p. 55, 1974, was released as a serigraph through Barbara Caruso's Seripress, Toronto.

'Punctuation Poem', p. 56, 1970, first appeared in *White Pelican* 1/2, Spring 1971.

'Punctuation Poem "X"', p. 57, 1973, was first published in *Musicworks* 38, Spring 1987.

'Punctuation Poem', p. 58, 1975, was printed by William Howe in 1997 for the never-released Flip Books portfolio.

'Kafka's Umbrella', p. 59, 1973, first appeared in *Cross-Country* 8–9, Woodhaven, NY, 1977.

'The Structure of Sonnet', p. 60, 1976, first appeared in *Queen Street Magazine* 10–13, Winter/Spring 1976–77.

'Panelogic', p. 61, 1978, was first published in *Poetry Toronto Newsletter* 38, February 1979.

'Two Signalist Texts', pp. 62–63, 1978, was printed by William Howe in 1997 for the Flip Books portfolio. The production utilized dry transfer lettering.

'Demiplosive Suite', p. 64, 1978, is a text-sound typestract that first saw light in *Prism International* 28.4, Summer 1990.

'Suprematist Alphabet', p. 65, 1980. This poem was untitled when first published in *Boundary 2*, 26.1, Spring 1999. The inspiration was Kasimir Malevich's famous 1918 suprematist painting *White on White*. The text systematically accumulates the alphabet through one to twenty-six superimpositions to arrive at a line of twenty vertical alphabets.

'William Tell: A Novel', p. 66, was first published in *Impulse* 16.1, 1990, and edited by the late Peter Day. It claims to be the world's shortest novel but has not been submitted to *The Guinness Book of World Records* for verification.

'Two Poems on a Theme by Eugen Gomringer', p. 67, 1986. These two parody-homages to Gomringer's famous *konstellation* 'Silencio' were presented conversationally at 'A World View from the 1990s', a round-table panel that formed part of the Yale Symphosymposium on Contemporary Poetics and Concretism, 7 April 1995. They were first printed in *Experimental – Visual – Concrete. Avant-Garde Poetry Since the 1960s*, eds. K. David Jackson, Eric Voss and Johanna Drucker, Amsterdam: Avant Garde Critical Studies 10, Editions Rodopi, 1996. Reprinted below is a small section of my answers to a post-conference questionnaire sent out to participants, which provides the context and motivation for the translations. The comments refer to the development of Concrete Poetry in Canada:

By the early 70s the feeling had arisen that concretism had become overly precious and inordinately narrow in its range; that it had ossified into a school at the very moment it seemed to be opening up tremendous new territory. Perhaps this spirit of contestation with canonic Concrete (i.e., those poems that repeatedly appeared in European and American anthologies) can be demonstrated in two poems of mine which take a playful poke at Eugen Gomringer. The development of parodic and intertextual factors within the Concrete tradition still awaits scrutiny.

Gomringer's poem first appeared in a Spanish translation with the word *silencio* translating the German *shweigen.*

'A Puff of Magritte', p. 68, 1983, first appeared in *Torque* 1.4/1.5 , July/September 1995, and reprinted in *Variations: Literaturzeitschrift der Universität Zürich* 2, Switzerland, 1999.

'Maps: a different landscape', pp. 69–72, 1970, appeared as *grOnk* Series 6 no. 8, 1971. The following statement, now published for the first time, outlines some rudimentary aspirations for the work.

map [*sic*] works to place the words on a different referential
level, a level that goes no further than the page
hence a form of game: a play (referential) play of surfaces

in another sense these poems display a literal consciousness
recording my own playing through the surface areas
the map as a single level of metaphor (the page as a map)
but in another sense as a literal level (the map as a map)
bringing together two different language spheres: cartographical language (a form of semiosis) and conventional verbal
together they create a game of surfaces a movement
among various levels of reference
taking metaphor as matter of fact   treating things
metaphorically & literally at the same time
playing visual signs off against less visual (city plans
against words) developing at times and in places another
level of metaphor (the city as language man as words words
within cities)

words in lines lines as boundaries (jumps from one level of reference to another)

language as the action of my hands (jumps from one level of reference to another)

constant & systematic displacements of languages, time schemes. contexts

garnier speaks of abandoning metaphor but adopts one himself in spatialism: the page as universe more complex (i.e. co-present) levels metaphorical semiotic, etc.

'Narrative: the Obsolete Absolute', pp. 73–85, appeared in the Special Narrative Issue of *Open Letter* 2. 5, Summer 1973.

SOUND TEXTS AND MUSICAL SCORES

'Studies for Two Unperformed Four Horsemen Pieces', pp. 88–89, composed ca. 1974, first appeared in *Sound Poetry: a Catalogue*, eds. Steve McCaffery and bpNichol, Toronto: Underwhich Editions, 1978.

'Concerto for Two Adverbs', p. 90, 1975, was first published in the Milwaukee-based magazine *CORTEXt*'s special 'Survey of Recent Visual Poetry', 1995. The score was originally designed to be detached, pierced through its centre, played on a turntable, and performed during the rotations.

'SIZERZ', p. 91, 1976, first appeared in *Roof* 3, 1977 (New York). A recorded and electronically manipulated version can be found on my audio collection *Research on the Mouth*, Toronto: Underwhich Editions, 1979.

'Cappucino: A Suffix Structure', pp. 92–93, 1977, was first published in *Text Sound Texts*, ed. Richard Kostelanetz, New York: William Morrow and Co., 1980.

'Love Song', pp. 94–95, first appeared without title in *Capilano Review* 31, 1984.

'Dilemma of the Meno', pp. 96–98, 1989, was commissioned by, and first performed in, the *Exercise for the Ear* concert, New Langton Arts, San Francisco, 6 June 1991, by Steve Adams (soprano saxophone), Ralph Cainey (contrabass clarinet) and Bill Fairbanks (bass).

The event was curated by Dave Barrett, who supplied the following note on intention in the accompanying program:

> Exploring the area where music and text meet, testing or ignoring the boundaries separating the two, the series seeks to bring to the surface the musicality of the written/spoken word, as well as the (con)textuality of instrumental music ... *Exercise for Ear* will include two distinct types of short text compositions: those written by poets to be performed by instrumental musicians, and those written by composers for acapella non-pitched voices.

Other participants included Pauline Oliveros, Lyn Hejinian and Nathaniel Mackey. The piece was subsequently performed by Array Music's *Unique Voices* series, Toronto, 1 March 1996. Performers: R. W. Stevenson (clarinet), Michael White (trumpet), Richard Sacks and John Thompson (percussion), Henry Kucharzyk (piano), Marc Sabat (violin) and Roberto Occhipinti (double bass). A printed version of the text-score appeared in *Chain* 3/2, Fall 1996.

LONGER POEMS

The Abstract Ruin, pp. 100–126, 1971–78, is a mercifully abandoned and, for the most part, unpublished, failed attempt at a long poem in the manner of Pound and Olson, folding history and personal material through a collage and citational technique. I offer some of the published sections here not through any current belief in their merit, but as a document of the otiose and misguided. Similarly, the following two notes on texture are presented (with minor revisions and corrections) for their documentary value. (With the poem conceived as texture and weaving, it might be reasonably construed that my true Penelope was Penelope.) The first section reprints with some alteration in spacing the Coach House Manuscript edition of 1980. There it was subtitled, at bpNichol's insistence, *Carnival: Panel 3*. The following note, written circa 1976 and printed now with minor corrections, accompanied the section of the poem that appeared in November of 1976 as the first issue of *Y.E.R.* (*Your Epic Representative*), a short-lived short-run magazine published and edited by Nichol.

A Note on Texture in *The Abstract Ruin*

The Abstract Ruin is texturalism with a relegation of most statemental matters to a place behind the utmost value, which is surface. The surface of a verbal weave, of the interceptive phrase, the symplegma of volumes and zones. As such, I find it hard to see this piece as having any kind of conventional development. It is processual in so far as the act of weaving is a process; it is expansive but not long (how can 'field' be long?) I see the piece then as a surface expanding out towards an unknown – perhaps a nonexistent – margin. The law governing its composition is thermodynamic: entropic doom if it is anything.

'Text' is a weaving term denoting a woven thing and applied through analogy by the incunabularians to the visual similarity between a page of words and a piece of woven fabric. A 'text' book was originally a classic written wide enough to allow for interlinear gloss, a critical and hermeneutic weave. So the poem is interlacement of many threads: the threads largely of my own reading. Writing descends from the 'womanly' act of weaving, which Freud sees as a modestic gesture, an act of covering the crotch, a pudendic concealment, the bashful hiding of the personal areas. To say the latter is to say as much as needs be said about subject in the poem.

To weave is to pattern by means of controlled interference. It is an archetypal act of household and its product clothes, shelters and poems. These are not three different things but rather variant of a common artifact. As 'text' rather than 'poem', then, with the poet more an organizer of threads than a composer with words. Replacing writing is a binding of the already shorn line and the compositional pulse behind the piece beats in the capacity to see how things fit together, operating on threads of data as a macrosyntax: large orderings demanding for themselves an interlinkage. The threads referred to are my own readings. Weaving here is meant to develop the concept of *found poetry* beyond an act of perceptual discovery toward a fusion of writing and reading. That, if anything, is the ultimate thread. *The Abstract Ruin*, then, weaves together my own writing of my reading, interweaving discrepant zones of vocabulary and voices.

Physical data: the piece is now 300 ms pages and far from complete. It started from an experiment I tried in 1971 of reading simultaneously Edward Gibbon's *Decline and Fall of the Roman Empire* and Pound's *Cantos*: there is a strong debt of voice and music to both. From that experiment I grew aware of the power of the single voice as an operative axis through time and events. History is mobile, revolving and constantly repatterning itself around the thin wire of a voice. History, too, is essentially a linguistic thing. Pound shows history to be document, approximately music and verbal texture, while Gibbon draws all Roman history together in one sartori as he sat in the ruins of the forum at Rome, not unlike John on Patmos, while history condensed into an image. I concluded that Gibbon's is the first articulated vorticist experience and I found in the footnotes to the *Decline* a method for extending found composition.

The work starts, then, as an axis gestured over surface, one man's voice passing through his reading. It is neither history nor philosophy, neither lyric nor didactic, but rather bibliographic and textist. History is used, made use of, by a present decision to see it pure and simply as an aspect of language; history is language operating at its most vindictive. I soon realized that what was developing was a highly porous form, a field through which a wide range of information could seep. The present act of writing didn't constitute process so much as allow porosity: seepage of macrosyntax. It thus became a diachronic journey through a reader's rather than a writer's eyes. It essays writing through the function of reading with a long-term goal towards the utter destruction of that difference.

They key to the chosen title is in the etymology of the two words. *Ruin* descends from the Latin *ruina*, itself deriving from *ruere*, to rush down. Ruination is a syntactic motion as through a porous agent. *Abstract* comes from the Latin *abstrahere*, to draw away. The weave of thread, the path of syntagm, the author's composition ambivalence.

None of this may hold. As the piece is growing I'm feeling that 'weave' can signify the process of creation but not the product itself. Current feeling is that this piece is expanding non-developmentally and crying out for tighter coherence. It is self-generating towards a randomness which may or may not be exciting in itself. Also, the relationship of this to my other works, especially my attempt at a large visual field composition *CARNIVAL*.

And Beckett, too, at this moment sounding large: 'Art is fidelity to failure'.

And friend bp's gnomic gem: 'Well, Steve, maybe everybody has to write a failed epic'.

The present selection [included in *Y.E.R.* 1, November 1976] is from early in the sequence, adjacent to an opening section on glossolalia which I treat as a condition of first language; the meeting of mouth with body energy to shape sound as biopoetic. This section into sight, or the lack of it, and memory as mental syntax.

The two sections (pp. 100–114, pp. 115–119) were first published in Coach House Press Manuscript Editions, 1980, and *Y.E.R. (Your Epic Representative)*, 1976, respectively. The short section at pp. 120–121 originally appeared in *Matrix* 6/7, 1978. The 'Immiseration Theses' section, pp. 122–126, first appeared in *The Good the Bad and the Ugly*, a small collection of my work printed especially for the occasion of a visit to Simon Fraser University in 1988. *Y.E.R.* was an ephemeral venture of bpNichol's; no other issue appeared and, I believe, like the Coach House Manuscript Edition, fewer than twenty copies were printed.

'The New Work', pp. 127–148, 1978–79, first appeared in *Matrix* 10, Fall/Winter 1980.

'On the Red in General', pp. 149–155, 1984, was first published in *Cabaret Vert*, 1998.

TRANSLATIONS

'A Portrait' and 'Autumn', pp. 158–159, 1970, first appeared in *White Pelican* 1–2, Spring 1971.

'A Geomantic Translation of Psalm 49', 'A Homolingusitic Translation of Shakespeare's Sonnet 105', 'Two Alternative Translations of Shakespeare's Sonnet 1', 'A Translation of Sir Philip Sidney's Sonnet XXXI from "Astrophel and Stella"', and 'A Kinetic Translation of the First Line of Marvell's "To His Coy Mistress"', pp. 160–164, all composed 1972, were first published as part of the 'TRG Research Report 1: Translation', *Open Letter* 2.4, Spring 1973.

'A Translation of an Excerpt from "Traité du blanc et des teintures"', pp. 165–170, 1976, is a homophonic translation of a poem by Robert Marteau and was accompanied by the following note when first published in *Ellipse* 19, 1976:

> the translative principle employed here is that of maintaining an acoustic rather than a semantic equivalence. so that the 'sound' of the french penetrates the semantic zones of the english vocabulary to determine by way of the kinship of sound a totally new meaning. no attempt has been made to preserve the stanzaic structure of the original but rather a preference for developing field forms appropriate to the translator's own breath lines as they emerged in the move across linguistic regions upon the common sound axis.

This is a paraphrastic way of describing either 'homophonic' or 'homeophonic' translation.

'The Kommunist Manifesto', pp. 171–180, 1977. This dialect translation was inspired by a conversation at Robert's Creek, BC, with Alan Kaprow (the inventor of Happenings) and the French Fluxus artist-philosopher Robert Filliou. Filliou's rationale for a dialect version was transparent and cogent: how can a manifesto designed to inspire the working class to a world revolution be effectively conveyed in stunted Victorian English prose? Our plan was a mammoth project to translate *The Communist Manifesto* into all the dialects in the world starting with patois and West Riding of Yorkshire. Filliou's patois version never made it to light. An audio version of my translation was released as *Wot We Wukkers Wont*, Toronto: Underwhich Editions, 1979.

An inaccurate printed version appeared in *Rampike*, Propaganda Issue, 4.2–3, Toronto, 1985. This current version is an extensive rewriting of the original translation.

'Poem for Sixteen Sequential Voices', pp. 181–182, 1978, is a line-by-line expanding homophonic translation of the immediately preceding line. It was first published in *Poetry Toronto Newsletter* 38, February 1979.

'A Homeophonic Translation of Skogekär Bergbo's Sonnet 92', pp. 183–184, 1981, was part of a translation project initiated by Dick Higgins and Robert Kelly in the late 1970s and first published in *Rampike* 8.1, 1995. Other translators included Higgins, Alison Knowles, John Cage, Bengt af Klintberg and Jackson Mac Low.

'Four Poems from the Chinese Versions', pp. 185–188, 1976, first appeared in the commemorative brochure for an Ottawa poetry festival, Wordfest, in 1983. The poems are homolinguistic translations of Kenneth Rexroth's *Sky Sea Birds Trees Earth House Beasts Flowers*, Santa Barbara, CA: Unicorn Press, 1973, and incorporate the first lines of Rexroth's poems as titles. The same allusive referential method is used that I employed in *Intimate Distortions*.

'from 8×8: *Experiment in Translation*', pp. 189–191, 1981. This experiment appeared as a double issue of *Ellipse*, 29–30, 1982. Conceived, organized and orchestrated by Colin Browne, the experiment involved eight writers (four anglophone, four francophone), each of whom contributed one original poem and translated eight others. Browne explains the practicalities of the project in his introduction: 'I took the initial liberty of deciding, after reading each poem carefully, which original or source text should be sent to whom. The four French writers each received a poem written in English, and the four English writers each got a poem in French. Throughout the project, authors remained anonymous, although at some points their identities could not remain hidden from diligent translators.' Earlier in his introduction Browne speaks of the fate of the source poems in their transit through translation: 'Each of our poems has been translated eight times, and four of them disappear entirely, their cycles terminated through frustration, only to reappear as new creatures.' The participants in the project were George Stanley, Daphne Marlatt, Alexander Hutchison, André Roy, Michel Gay, Cécile Cloutier, Michel Beaulieu and myself. 'Instant Comments About My Curls Are Auburn' is my initial contribution to the experiment, while 'A Simple Allusion' is my translation (at the penultimate stage in the cycle) of Michel Gay's translation ('Une simple allusion'). As such, it comprises a translation of my own initial poem.

'The Presbyterian Basho', p. 192, was first published in *Filling Station* magazine's 'Sidereal Calendar', 1999; it is one of an ongoing series of translations (currently twenty-three) of Matsuo Basho's famous seventeenth-century haiku :

Furu-ike-ya
Kawaku tobi-komu
mitzu-no-oto

A minor tradition of translating this poem (by Dick Higgins, bpNichol and Derek Beaulieu among others), was inaugurated by Dom Sylvester Houédard's notorious rendition as:

frog
pond
plop

'The Baker Transformation', pp. 193–196, first appeared in *Common Knowledge* 7. 3, Winter 1998.

MISCELLANEOUS TEXTS

'Three Pieces for Audience', p. 198, first appeared in *Missing Link* 1.1, Fall 1974.

'Apropriopriapus: Prefatory Notes on Stein & The Language Hygiene Program', pp. 199–213, 1972–73. This playful spoof on William Burroughs appeared in the Gertrude Stein Centenary issue (1874–1974) of *White Pelican*, 1974.

'Mrta', p. 214, 1973. First published in *Roof* 3, New York, 1977, this is one of a series of early Language-Centred texts exploring semantic minimalism, *zaum* or trans-rational language, and 'gravitational' syntax.

'The Murder of Agatha Christie: a true story', pp. 215–219, 1975, first appeared in *The Story so Far* 5, ed. Douglas Barbour, Toronto: Coach House Press, 1978.

'Kemsher' and 'Three Stanzas', pp. 220–222, both composed 1975, were initially published in *Roof* 3, New York, 1977. The latter poem is a found text comprising the three longest English words listed in *The Guinness Book of World Records*, which thus entitles the poem to a similar honour for the record as the world's shortest English poem to utilize the three longest words in English.

'Novel 7', p. 223, first appeared as *Dreadnaught 5 Pickup 52*, Toronto, 1976, printed as a polychrome broadside.

'Songs i and ii', pp. 224, first appeared in *Poetry Toronto Newsletter*, April 1976.

'Eruca Labra', pp. 225–231, 1976, first appeared in *Ellipse* 23–24, 1979.

'Eros-ion', pp. 232–234, was first published as part of the Special Erotics Issue of *IS* 19–20, Fall 1976, edited by Victor Coleman.

'The Property: Comma', pp. 235–243, first appeared in *The Story So Four*, eds. Steve McCaffery and bpNichol, Toronto: Coach House Press, 1976.

'August Sixteen 1977' and 'Muiopotmos', pp. 244–247, 1977, were first published in *Descant* XXIV, 1979. The title of the latter is taken from Spenser's 'Muiopotmos, or the Fate of the Butterfly'.

'The Cetacea: Four Tides', p. 248, was expressly written for *Whale Sound: An Anthology of Poems about Whales and Dolphins*, ed. Greg Gatenby, Vancouver: J. J. Douglas Ltd., 1977.

'A Book Resembling Hair', p. 249, 1978, was first published in *Descant* XXIV, 1979. I later used the title for an unrelated video-interactive performance piece.

'The Syllogistic Cinema', pp. 250–251, 1977–92, was first published in *Rampike* 8.1, 1995.

'Poem "Murder": A Scenario', and 'The Occupant', pp. 252–255, first appeared in *Cross Country* 10–11, 1978.

'Words: Meditation Nine', p. 256, 1978, first appeared in *Poetry Toronto Newsletter*, July–August 1978.

'Latin Lines', p. 257, 1978, was initially published in *Poetry Toronto Newsletter*, February 1979.

'Novel Eighteen', p. 258, 1980, first appeared in the University of California, San Diego's *Archive Newsletter*, Winter 1988.

'Summary', p. 259, 1980, first appeared as a three-part fold-out poem-object through Curvd H&Z, Toronto, 1981. The present reproduction attempts to capture the three-dimensional nature of the piece.

'Projects for *Procedures*', pp. 260–262, 1981, lists a number of projects submitted in response to an invitation I received from the editors of Lobby Press, Richard Hammersley and Richard Tabor. The following excerpt from their leaflet details the aspirations and contexts of the invitation. The recipients were numerous writers and others engaged in 'art' work and included Paul Buck, Cris Cheek, Bob Cobbing, Allen Fisher, Bernard Heidsieck, Lyn Hejinian, Dick Higgins and Ron Silliman.

> 'procedures' is available for you to give indications of your plans, methods, intentions of events, sounds, writings to be done or which are in progress. It is hoped that this may help to expose the process of idealisation which gives Form and sense of content towards an intended. (Copy to reach Lobby by August 10th, 1982.)

'Fish Also Rise', pp. 263–264, dates back to 1975 and is previously unpublished.

'The Perseus Project', pp. 265–274, appeared separately and then collectively in the *Proceedings of The First Symposium on Linguistic Onto-Genetics*, Toronto, 1981. The project was performed live as part of the Symposium.

'A Sirius Series', pp. 275–282, 1981, first appeared in *Credences* 2.2–3, Buffalo, NY, 1983.

'What Else Should a Rubber Stamp Say?', pp. 283–290, is a paragrammatic, treated text in the manner of Ronald Johnson's *Radios* and Tom Phillips's *A Humument*. Taken from a found medical book, certain words are repeated in rubber stamp, thus releasing a latent text. The book-object is now lost but the pages reprinted here are taken from the Steve McCaffery Special Issue of *Open Letter* 6.9, Fall 1987.

'Divers Manière', pp. 291–297, 1981. This is the first print appearance of a version recorded and released on audio cassette as part of *Whispers* (with musical accompaniment by Bill Smith and David Lee), London, Ont.: blewointment press, 1984.

'Deliberate Follicles', pp. 298–302, whose haunting title Karen Mac Cormack supplied, first appeared in *Hard Times*, an anthology of fiction edited by Bev Daurio, Stratford, Ont.: Mercury Press, 1990.

'The Cabinet', p. 303, 1984, first appeared in *Southpaw* 2.1, Winter 1986. Much of the lexicon is taken from the Sale Catalogue of Horace Walpole's residence at Strawberry Hill.

'The Swimmer', pp. 304–306, 1985, originally appeared in *Impulse*, Spring 1986.

'Peras', pp. 307–321, first appeared in *Open Letter* 6.1, 1985.

'Some Versions of Pastoral', pp. 322–324, 1986, were originally published in *West Coast Line* 2, Fall 1990. These three idylls, applying German syntax to English, were jubilantly plundered from an interlinear translation of Soloman Gessner's *Daphnis* by Charles Eichorn, London, 1811.

'The Logic of Six', pp. 325–328, 1988–98, first saw light in *Sulfur* 44, Spring 1999.

'On Paper', p. 329, 1990, originally appeared in *Joy Praise: Jerome Rothenberg at Sixty*, a festschrift for the poet edited by Pierre Joris, Encinitas, CA: Ta'Wil Books, 1991.

'Etymology of Displeasure', pp. 330–332, 1990–98, was first published in *Salt* 11, 1999.

'No Title Please I'm Not Well', p. 333, 1994, first appeared in *Deluxe Rubber Chicken* 2, 1999.

'Prior to Meaning', p. 334, was commissioned by the Poetry and Rare Books Collection, State University of New York, Buffalo, for their 1996 Christmas Broadside. The poem was accompanied by a full-colour reproduction of Michael Snow's 1962 painting *Alice*, from his Walking-Woman series.

'Crystal Carrington', p. 335, 1997, appeared as part of an exhibition arranged by Steven Hull at the California Center for the Arts, Valencia, May 1997. The poem is my response to a visual work submitted by Robert Blanchon comprising the following words typed on a sheet of ruled cartridge paper: 'on water color paper using crystal meth in luke warm water write the words crystal ball, crystal light, crystal carrington'. The poem was untitled in its first appearance in the exhibition anthology *Blind Date*, 1998.

'To Never Leave The Feeding Hand Unbitten', pp. 336–337, 1997, originally appeared in *Common Knowledge*, September 1998.

'Sin Having Settled', pp. 338–339, 1997–98, was initially published in *Sulfur* 44, Spring 1999.

'Attritions', pp. 340–341, 1997, was first made available in the Buffalo e-zine *Deluxe Rubber Chicken* 2, 1999.

'Monsieur X', pp. 342–343, 1998, was published previously in *POG One*, Tucson, 1999.

'Zero Is Not Equivalent to Zeno', p. 344, 1998, initially appeared in *Sulfur* 44, Spring 1999.

'Eventual Research', pp. 345–350, 1998, was originally published in *Salt* 11, 1999.

'A Theory of the Lyric©', p. 351, 2000, previously appeared in *Shiny* 11, Fall 2000.

The untitled text on p. 352 first appeared with the title 'A Faxed Statement on the Order of Things' in *The Order of Things: International Fax Project*, curated by Francesca Vivenza and Mark Sutherland, Workscene Gallery, Toronto, 1993.

POETICS AND NOTES

'from "The Unposted Correspondence"', pp. 354–356, 1981, first appeared in '8×8: *Experiment in Translation* and was published as a special double issue of *Ellipse*, 29–30, 1982.

They present my then-current theoretical reflections on translation and might be considered an extension of earlier thinking on the allusive referential with Dick Higgins and on translation/transformation with bpNichol (the latter published as 'TRG Research Report 1: Translation'; see *Rational Geomancy*, Vancouver: Talonbooks, 1992).

'A Note on Concept', pp. 357–358, was written as a response to Jerome Rothenberg's solicitation of a definition of the 'New Wilderness'. The note appeared in *New Wilderness Letter* 2.7, Summer 1979.

'Poetics: A Statement', pp. 359–360, first appeared in *Poetry Toronto Newsletter* 38, February 1979. The concluding aphorisms were subsequently incorporated into *Knowledge Never Knew*.

'Performed Paragrammatism', pp. 361–362, is a personal response solicited by Bob Cobbing and Lawrence Upton to the relationship between visual and verbal poetry; it was first published in *Word Score: Utterance Choreography in Verbal and Visual Poetry*, London: Writers Forum, 1998.

About the Author

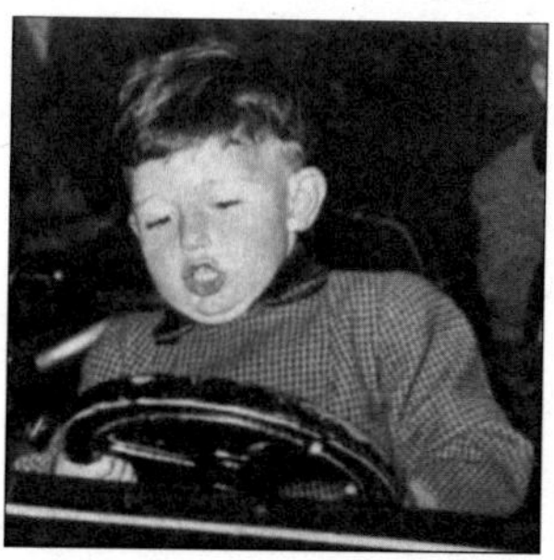

Born in Jessop's Hospital, Sheffield, England, on 24 January 1947 (the day of Artaud's final performance), poet-critic Steve McCaffery is the author of one novel, fifteen volumes of poetry and four critical works. Most recent to appear are *Bouma Shapes* (Zasterle Press, Gran Canaria, Spain, 2002), *Prior to Meaning: the Protosemantic and Poetics* (Northwestern University Press, 2001) and Volume One of *Seven Pages Missing* (Coach House Books, 2001). He was a founding member of the Four Horsemen sound poetry ensemble in 1970, of TRG (Toronto Research Group, with bpNichol) in 1972, and the College of Canadian 'Pataphysics, 1979. Together with Dick Higgins, McCaffery developed deviant translation methods including allusive referential, homophonic, numerical replacement translation and creative misunderstanding, and is a charter member of the latter's institute. Although one of the theoretical founders of Language Poetry, McCaffery's interests have consistently extended into sound, performative, intermedia and paraliterary areas. He has twice been nominated for the Governor General's Award in poetry, in 1992 for *Theory of Sediment* and 2001 *for Seven Pages Missing Volume One.*

He currently teaches poetics, philosophy and the paraliterary at York University in Toronto and is Founding Director of NACIP (the North American Centre for Interdisciplinary Poetics), reachable at www.poetics.yorku.ca. With Stephen Cain, he is presently editing for publication *The Zebras' Progress*, an annotated edition of his three decades of correspondence with Dick Higgins. He lives in Toronto with his wife, Karen Mac Cormack, 15,000 volumes of books, an empty bottle of 1978 Chateau Mouton Rothschild and three unrivalled collections of Lithuanian credit cards, unpaid Icelandic parking tickets and Franco-Belgian beer mats.

Typeset in Adobe Caslon
Printed and bound at the Coach House on bpNichol Lane, 2002

Edited by Darren Wershler-Henry
Designed by Darren Wershler-Henry and Ian McInnis
Copy edited by Alana Wilcox

Read the online version of this text at our website:
www.chbooks.com

Send us a request to be added to our mailing list:
mail@chbooks.com

Call us toll-free:
1 800 367 6360

Coach House Books
401 Huron Street (rear) on bpNichol Lane
Toronto, Ontario
M5S 2G5